Books of Merit

The Voice Gallery

The
Voice
Gallery

Travels with
a Glass Throat

Keath Fraser

Thomas Allen Publishers
Toronto

National Library of Canada Cataloguing in Publication Data

Fraser, Keath
     The voice gallery : travels with a glass throat

ISBN 0-88762-101-5

1. Fraser, Keath – Journeys.
2. Spastic dysphonia – Patients – Canada – Biography.
I. Title.

PS8561.R297Z53 2002   362.1'96855   C2001-904265-5
PR9199.3.F722Z477 2002

Jacket and text design: Gordon Robertson
Editor: Michael Holmes
Jacket photo (top): Tadashi Ono/Photonica
Jacket photo (bottom): Joe Madeira/Photonica
Author photograph: Innis Rozell

Published by Thomas Allen Publishers,
a division of Thomas Allen & Son Limited,
145 Front Street East, Suite 209,
Toronto, Ontario M5A 1E3 Canada

Printed and bound in Canada

To my mother and father

Acknowledgement is made to the following books and their authors for lines quoted in *The Voice Gallery*. Every attempt has been made to locate copyright holders in accordance with fair usage. In case of queries, please contact the author.

Cry, The Beloved Country, by Alan Paton. Reprinted with the permission of Scribner, a division of Simon & Schuster, Inc. Copyright © 1948 by Alan Paton; copyright renewed © 1976.

Invisible Man, by Ralph Ellison. Random House, 1995. Copyright © 1952 by Ralph Ellison. Reprinted with permission.

The Trumpet of the Swan, by E.B. White. HarperTrophy, 2000. HarperCollins Publishers. Copyright © 1970 by E.B. White.

Ford Madox Ford, by Alan Judd. Collins, 1990. Copyright © by Alan Judd.

The Right To Speak, by Patsy Rodenburg, with a foreword by Ian McKellen. Methuen Drama. Copyright © 1992 by Patsy Rodenburg. Foreword copyright © 1992 by Ian McKellen.

The Need For Words, by Patsy Rodenburg, with a foreword by Antony Sher. Methuen Drama. Copyright © 1993 by Patsy Rodenburg. Foreword copyright © 1993 by Antony Sher.

I know of nothing more difficult than knowing who you are, and then having the courage to share the reasons for the catastrophe of your character with the world.

— WILLIAM H. GASS, "The Art of Self"

The throat: how strange, that there is not more erotic emphasis upon it.

— JOHN UPDIKE, "Getting the Words Out"

CONTENTS

The Voice Gallery

I

Summer's End

I THINK MEMORY retains two kinds of summer: golden
ones of childhood and perhaps of early love, of sand-
castling or else canoodling by the kelp-slicked sea, and
the other kind, summers you are unable to let go, the black mon-
sters of mid-life an insomniac has got coming from hubris or just
bad luck. Recollections of this second kind are painful to recount.
They might open on a stifling August night, in an uninsulated attic
bedroom in Vancouver, where you are about to discover your wife
of twenty-three years has had a brain seizure in bed beside you
and died.

Wide awake, unable to sleep, I had been treading water amidst
the wreckage of a dream recently gone down. The large novel I
believed was finished, wasn't, and my agent in New York, instead
of shopping it around to publishers as I hoped she would, had
thought it needed reconstruction, if not, I supposed, a fire. So
I was clinging to the wing of this work, close to sinking inside
these humid nights, and doubting my ability to survive as an artist.
This summer had been a meditation on drowning, and now, near
summer's end, I heard someone else drowning alongside.

A gagging sound, a small splashing of limbs, then silence. In
the darkness I must have reached across to wake her. I sat up to
turn on the lamp, horrified to think she might not be asleep but
somehow . . . "You all *right*?" Moving in her direction I pulled her

to me—managing to pin myself, I didn't know how, under her dead weight at the foot of our bed.

She was drowning, we were drowning together in what seemed a disaster of my own hubris. I was bizarrely sure of this. Moving yet paralyzed, moving but going under, the pair of us inseparable in good times and now in bad. Having fashioned for myself this precarious life of an artist, I could no more escape the result than fallen Icarus could rise above the waves. No shoreline in view, no reassuring skyline in the pre-dawn. I tried opening my eyes and closing them. They refused to close. Her own eyes, in spite of my entreaties and fingers, would not open. Neither would her jaw. Her rigid limbs yielded nothing, though their flesh felt as soft as wax. Her life, our life, passing before my eyes, had slowed down so fast I now had time to commit the wanderings of my brain to memory.

It had gone downstairs to the kitchen, a domestic lifetime away. It seemed to think it had all the time in the world to scrounge through drawers. I can remember lying in our bed awaiting its return, watching the pair of us as if from the sloped ceiling, the woman below snagged in my limbs, and me deciding even in the face of her death that I lacked the courage of an impromptu surgeon. Performing a bloody tracheotomy with a sharp kitchen knife to dislodge what I thought might be an inhaled piece of plastic toothguard seemed more homicide than rescue. When could trying to save the thing you loved ever justify killing it? Was *this* how life ended—abruptly and without dignity, watching one's closest friend choke quietly to death, unable to act except in one's novelistic imagination?

My wife, long used to an undiagnosed, chronic cough, now seemed to have died mutely, in a sort of reversal of a cough, without any of the usual warning that her breathing was in temporary peril. No explosion from deep sleep, gasping for breath. That made it more unreal, her silence. She had passed away without voice.

Everything I seemed to know and fear came down to voice. My nightmarish voice was going to betray the guilt I felt. Up there on the ceiling, pressing against it for a better view of what I was in flight from, I remember the mortification of wondering in the face of her death: *Did husbands have to memorialize their wives in public?* If so, maybe grief would forgive the way I was sure to sound. I would plead grief. Yet grief, giving rise to catharsis, might perversely grant me the calm voice I sometimes spoke with on rare, traumatic occasions. But no. I could feel guilt ruining this grief, so that nothing would forgive the sudden *shame* of actually thinking of myself in the same predicament as she.

My self-obsession could not have lasted more than two or three seconds. I still hoped to wake up in a pile of duck feathers—the duvet having twisted round us and innocently exploded. I cried out to my son, in the adjoining bedroom, to rush downstairs and dial 911. Already awake, he stood beyond us as if watching something very strange. The last time the three of us were together in crisis was at his birth, him unbreathing, until the doctor performed a high-forceps delivery and saved him from smothering. How to breathe was something his parents still seemed to be learning, eight years later, in this close hour before dawn.

Switching on the stairway light, he disappeared in a heartbeat, and I remember next his limpid voice downstairs in the kitchen.

I had lifted my voice in a cry for help, and it had been my eight-year-old son who'd dialled Emergency. I could still hear him speaking clearly into the receiver, downstairs in the kitchen at 4 a.m. His capacity for speech already seemed beyond mine. Yet what effect would this death of his mother have on the way he might start speaking as an adolescent? How but in nightmare to explain to him my own participation in her drowning, unable to help, a man contemplating a kitchen knife and unable to swim?

I had managed to disentangle our bodies and to rock her still unconscious body, unwilling to let her sink further beneath the surface of the wine-dark sheets. I finally pried open her lips and was astonished to discover her toothguard still in place, a small horseshoe protecting enamel the way it was supposed to. How could she have *choked* to death? Unable to remove it, I then tried administering mouth-to-mouth resuscitation, blowing desperately.

A single, translucent bubble gurgled to her lips. I stared at it. Watched it inflate, in slow motion, then *pop*. What seemed infinitely fascinating in the space between inflation and explosion now vanished in the reality of her return to life. She groaned once, twice, I wouldn't remember. She did not wake up. Submerged beneath it for so long, she was drunk on seawater—alive but unconscious.

Life, mercifully, did not seem to be repeating fiction, where I had sometimes deployed the death of a wife, a mother, a son, in stories published in earlier books, as if the tragic and bereft could bring fiction nearer an understanding of grief. Of catharsis, I supposed. Possibly, in the end, of a fluent and fathomable voice. I wondered if this was what I was doing now. Trying to fictionalize the event in progress, thereby rationalizing my fear of it.

Killing the thing I loved, maybe, in order to savour it the more.

What followed next morning would slowly begin to change my life and allow me to revisit my shame with a deeper understanding of what had caused it. What had caused it, of course, was fear of my voice betraying me at an imagined funeral, should I be required to speak there. Fear of humiliation. But the shame went deeper. It arose from the realization of my inability to transcend such fear in the face of a loved one's suffering.

At University Hospital we waited together behind a curtain. The resident neurologist soon peeked through, a young man with a clipboard ready to conduct a few routine tests, he said, in preparation for Dr. Hurwitz. I did my best to explain what neither of us understood: how the inhalator crew and then medics had arrived at our house last night, been unable to rouse my wife from unconsciousness, yet declined to bring her to the hospital. They advised me to see her doctor in the morning, after she woke up. Uncertain she *would* wake up, I spent the rest of the night between her and a medical encyclopedia, trying to diagnose what I thought had happened. Near dawn I decided she'd had a grand mal seizure.

"What's the matter with your voice?" he interrupted. Maybe I sounded shakier than I thought. Occasionally asked this complex question, I had learned over the years to shrug it off with a facetious excuse. Or else, depending on the degree to which I had just made a spectacle of myself, no excuse at all.

This resident was in the middle of his examination and I thought nothing more of his inquiry. He then proceeded to ask Lorraine to do the things I could vaguely recall a neurologist once asking of me, many years before, during the worst period in my vocal life: sitting still while he banged her (my) knee with a rubber hammer, touching the end of her (my) nose with her (my) forefinger, repeating a sequence of numbers backwards, walking a straight line on the floor: all as if you were under suspicion of running your Rover under the influence of a low-grade highball like Canadian Club rye.

He meticulously and a little ponderously copied down each result. Proceeding as though from the textbook, and still utterly without a bedside manner, this young man could nevertheless appreciate the way she routinely knocked off his tests. Which didn't help to explain recent gaps in her memory, or the spells she'd been having.

He excused himself to consult with another doctor, dark-haired and good-looking, who now took over, bringing the resident back to my wife's cubicle. He introduced himself as Trevor Hurwitz and started all over, asking us what had happened, ignoring the resident's notes. I retold the story of waking up and finding her unconscious. Turning to me, he said, "How long have you had spastic dysphonia?"

His casual display of diagnostic brilliance shocked me. I had not heard this term spoken in twenty years. It was as if he'd just wanted to hear me talk. Maybe his resident had mentioned my funny voice.

His recognition of a rare vocal disorder most doctors had never heard of was impressive, but coming from a neurologist who spent his time wonking over brains, not voices, it seemed all the more impressive, in spite of what I later learned was this old-fashioned and inaccurate term for what I had. The man was clearly in possession of one of those med-school minds that responded like a vacuum cleaner to every lecture and allusion he'd ever heard in the course of an expensive education, which no doubt included recitative for the med-society's production of Gilbert and Sullivan on two continents, as well as an interest in the strange and recondite regions of neurotic expression.

I deflected his question with a mumbled dismissal: "Years."

He turned smoothly to Lorraine then, and asked her the resident's same drunk-driving questions, but with interesting variations, which he would then discuss with the younger neurologist, pleased to be making a lesson of it. The questions seemed fun for the patient too. Which earned her no leniency, because he booked her into hospital for blood and other tests that might, he said cheerfully, take a week. "Have you ever read *The Idiot*?" he asked. In fact, she had read most of Dostoyevsky's novels some years ago. "Then you'll remember his descriptions of epileptic fits," he said. "Just like your auras."

His confirming diagnosis of a grand mal seizure meant the following days were full of hospital visits for our son and me, where we heard about various tests and seizure medication. My wife arranged to miss her first week of teaching back at school.

She and I would talk by telephone every afternoon, as I awaited Robin's return from school, and, amused, she would say her neurologist seemed just as interested in my voice as in her brain.

"Incidentally," she told me, "he says to tell you that what you have isn't psychological in origin. It's physiological. It's connected to neurology."

This small piece of information emerged for me like a peak in Darien, slowly and with growing revelation for what seemed to lie beyond and behind it. Oceans, apparently, continents. It enlarged the sense of my own obscure role in this brain drama of my wife's. It even hinted at a brain drama of my own, possibly. "You should talk to him," she urged me later that week.

The CAT scan turned up nothing her neurologist from South Africa could find, no tumour, and he suggested that after her return home he would book her for a more detailed MRI scan. He had the easy ability to speak to her as though all of what had happened to her brain was a new adventure that fascinated him. Not that what he had to convey was very reassuring. She could expect to be on medication for two years, and after that, if she had any further auras or a seizure, she could expect to be on medication the rest of her life. Meanwhile, she might require another drug to counter any depressant affects of the seizure. She was fortunate hers hadn't been a *daytime* seizure, he said, or she would have lost her driver's licence. He told her interesting things about auras and managed to convey the story of her brain as an organ that remained as mysterious a frontier as deep space.

When I arrived on the last day to bring her home, I met him again. He wouldn't know until he saw the results of the magnetic resonance imaging whether the cause of Lorraine's seizure could be discovered or whether it would remain idiopathic. So far nothing had turned up.

We made our way down the corridor.

I said nothing of my voice until we were ready to part in the foyer. I then muttered something of what he had conveyed through my wife about a new treatment for "spastic dysphonia."

The last person I'd heard use this term had been a speech pathologist who had had to look it up in a textbook. After diagnosing it, she'd said there was really nothing more she could do for my strangulated voice. She had given me one or two vocal exercises to try out. She had recommended a psychologist. I never saw her again. So I had given up on medicine, apart from one laughable experience with Valium, and resigned myself to recovering a normal voice on my own. I never had.

Dr. Hurwitz was eager to tell me that the head of his department had helped pioneer a certain poison for treating dystonia. (I must have thought he said dysphonia.) The toxin—Hurwitz wasn't exactly sure how—was injected into the voice boxes of people with my "kind of voice," who then discovered they could speak again without sounding strangled. He urged me to look into this "dramatic breakthrough."

"The main thing is the disorder isn't psychological, like they thought it was for a century. It has to do with a malfunction in the brain."

It did seem distinctly absurd that in the same week my wife had discovered a disorder in her own brain, so apparently had I. Yet oddly, while her more common condition was to remain stubbornly idiopathic in origin, even after subsequent scans, mine at least would turn out to be from a recognized, if unexpected, family of disorders.

I managed not to succumb to the lure of a so-called cure for another year. I *was* interested and even hopeful. But I had a novel to rewrite. I found the trauma of explaining a nebulous condition to my own doctor, for the purpose of receiving a referral to a neurologist, daunting. I'd coped for two decades, and, besides, at times I sounded better than at other times. I was used to faking it, covering up spasms with effortful manoeuvres, avoiding stressful situations where possible, and usually escaping into silence at meetings—or, conversely, at parties, into sounding heartier than I felt in order not to have to say anything. In spite of the promise of another quackish-sounding cure, I wondered if the great *effort* of speaking would ever go away. Short, I thought, of my clamming up for good like a desk-chained hermit.

I envied Lorraine her job of giving to others, the daily satisfaction from work well done. I could remember the feeling of offering everything to a class, except for the year I was stricken with my vocal disorder, a new university teacher, when I agonized and only gradually learned in the four following years to control better whatever demon had apparently taken me over. Devoting oneself to the isolated business of writing, on the other hand, was a selfish act that came later, and its satisfactions were relatively infrequent and tenuous. The business of art was the business of perfection and it doomed the writer to chronic dissatisfaction. Teaching was more human, more forgiving.

I remember my wife reporting back to me a year later, after a checkup with her neurologist, who mentioned how the recent international conference of neurologists in Vancouver had evidently featured a session "on people like your husband," showing on videotape patients with awful dysphonia, and then remarkable vocal fluency, following surgical intervention with the poison he had mentioned to me. He was impressed by the results. It seemed too good to be true, I thought, chiding myself for not having made an effort to crash this conference, to see and hear for myself what wonders might be in store for the chronically strangled. On CBC radio, I had just heard another neurologist at this conference refer in passing to the benefits of botulinum toxin "for people who couldn't speak," the source of whose problem was "buried deep in the brain." Oliver Sacks, of course, had been in attendance. I needed an Oliver Sacks to tell my story, as I had little idea yet of what my story was.

Lorraine tried but was unable to drop her dependency on Tegretol, as she had hoped to. Two and a half years later, when I set out to travel around the world in pursuit of voices like mine, she took a leave from teaching and felt her auras coming back. It now seemed she would be on medication for the rest of her life.

My own dependency on poison became an equally addictive drug. Over a year after my summer of failure and shame, I would begin to change my life with botulinum toxin. I allowed myself to wonder if the struggle for a spoken voice, and the struggle for a writer's voice, might finally and equally be relieved.

Yet both voices were likely to remain only as telling as their last published book or druggish injection. Starting to receive regular syringes of poison in my voice box, I now hoped to speak with intermittent fluency into old age. I supposed when judged too frail to be injected any longer, I would revert back to my strangulated sounds, ignored at last as the arias of senility. My hope then was that some story I had written would remain to speak for me.

2

Coming Back to Voice

S A BOY, I had run fast. I came to believe that a quick athlete inclined naturally to excess and, had I chosen to pursue a career of criminal associations, I might have made not a bad drug addict or stock promoter. A teenager will acquire this crooked sense of self in trying to understand why something inside isn't right. With me you could even have said it became a moral matter, trying to account for the way my body didn't work in quite the way it should have.

Its fall from grace, *my* fall from grace, seemed to accompany thickening testosterone and twitching nerve ends that could be counted on to help me deke an opponent, fake a pass or jump high. But in the classroom it could also cause in me an unfathomable acceleration of pulse, and a heart that thrashed at my chest wall like a crazed crow, before the inevitable sound of someone deeply troubled, deeply *flawed*, emerged from my throat when I was asked to read aloud. If only this had had something to do with a breaking voice, things might have settled down. But my voice had already deepened, and except when I had to recite, sounded normal enough not to terrify and humiliate me.

It was as if the sound of my voice, after it began to go wrong in the classroom, came up from a guilty soul. A tempo in excess of rhythm, shaped in adolescence by a Catholic conscience, confirmed that my awkward body could also at times be a graceless body. If voice mirrored soul, I was an audible sinner. Knowing I sounded guilty only made the self-consciousness worse. The worse you sounded, the worse you probably were. This altered my sense of who I was. Such was my own inkling of what the Fall must have engendered, when Babylon and its confusion of voices ensued in Genesis and thereafter a fractured world. I felt increasingly split between a "real" self—and "me." Such knowledge said something grave and evidently ineradicable: that the portrait of the speaker did not lie. Thus it might be better, so far as possible, to keep such an unflattering portrait hidden until I outgrew it, or eventually managed to throw it from the attic window.

My reason for secrecy must have gone something like this: What was the good of trying to talk to anyone about a condition of shame that arose unavoidably from who you were? The way you spoke might be unfair, but so was acne. Talking about it would only draw more unwelcome attention to your condition. I felt orally scarred for no reason except that this was the way nature treated some teenagers, especially the ones in ties or tunics. I can remember feeling embarrassed for a shy, rust-coloured girl whose voice began to quiver and wobble like mine when she was asked to read aloud by our obese, home-room nun in the same class, an airless room of faint flatulence, growing less faint as the day wore on. It was as though this likeable girl had caught a somewhat milder dose of cacophony from listening to me. Apparently, I reasoned, a few sensitive teenagers like us were susceptible to disproportionately small amounts of dread, our unavoidable vocal flappings then giving rise to acute fear and shame.

I eavesdropped on my younger brother reading confidently aloud one day in his social studies class, where I had a study period, wondering why I couldn't sound like him, yet quietly proud he did not seem tormented by my vocal shakings, temporary though I hoped mine were. I began to feel an ironic ruefulness about this school which I remember wishing had been called Our Lady of Perpetual Health (not Help). There was no help here, especially for me, who never managed to get a grip on my jelly-like voice. I listened elsewhere for role models.

I listened to bus drivers effortlessly calling out stops along Broadway and up Tenth Avenue; to rock jocks chattering away on CKWX and CFUN. When I was sixteen a school friend and I drove downtown to the Cave Supper Club to hear the teen idol Jimmie Rodgers. We sat at a balcony table, feeling grown up in sports coats, drinking cherry cokes. *"Water!"* sang Jimmie, his ringing falsetto voice sometimes inflected with a catch. *". . . Wa   ater!"*

Almost four decades later I would remember our brush with greatness—talking shyly afterward to the singer backstage—when I learned that it was also a brush with my own future: I discovered that Jimmie Rodgers eventually lost his voice to the same rare disease I did. It was as though the occasional gaps in some of his famous sung words had been harbingers of his spasms to come.

My spasms to come.

Meanwhile, I determined to let nature take its course. I determined to become more self-confident, to free myself of my crow. I changed high schools. I felt more at ease in public-school classes and among new friends who'd never heard me flap. This just reinforced a resolution never to mention my voice which in social exchanges still sounded normal. Even in classes, where I was required to read aloud, it had settled down and this encouraged confidence. The tremulous sound seemed to retreat in this more expansive environment—or else I was able to finesse it better. I still knew I could never address the assembled student body, or, given the talent necessary, perform in the school operetta. But I was happier in a more anonymous place.

Over the ensuing years in university, I had reason to believe the dissonance and fear that had plagued me for a time in adolescence had abated. I was never as intrepid in public as I might have wished (as though moral cacophony, committed once, lurked in menacing abeyance), yet I came closer than I had been since childhood to trusting my voice again.

When this conviction began to erode, as a new and different dissonance emerged in my twenties, in a sort of exponential, grown-up leap from the old sound, I began a twenty-year retreat into my imagination, like a kind of aural Dorian Gray, hoping to preserve the illusion of an outwardly untrammelled voice. At times this was a difficult double life to lead. I was teaching at a university when my voice began—not to waver, but to fracture. I was speaking daily in public, yet having to curb my instinctive spontaneity for fear of the unaccountable gaps in speech. The *effort* of speaking became ungovernable. I was baffled. And ashamed I could not seem to help myself, not seem to outgrow the stain of my original younger voice.

Could mere voice have such power to define the wholesomeness of its owner? Evidently, it could. I seemed to have reverted to my teenage state of guilt and self-blame, but this reversion sounded far worse. The crow flapped, the voice croaked. At the same time, my sense of wonder at the natural voice grew, fed constantly by listening to how colleagues and students used theirs effortlessly and without dissonance. I began to hear how voices could sound beautiful. (As mine had done, for a while, when I started teaching and took pleasure in its amplitude after three years of quiet study abroad.) Once more I was convinced shame such as mine derived from that "real" self, an unwelcome stranger with tendencies to some unspeakable atavism. He was a character I was again keeping secret by necessity and inclination, when I wasn't unavoidably betraying him to the world. He was a character who would be hidden by me—in the years and complicity to follow—in the attic of fiction.

I had absolutely no idea what was the matter with my voice, except that it belonged to a character I believed was not only physically corrupt but mentally unstable. I began to think of him—of myself—as neurotic. I would avoid addressing departmental meetings for fear of being unable to sustain an unbroken voice in front of colleagues; in front of students, where I felt under less scrutiny, the strangulations did not seem as insurmountable. I developed athletic tics and laddering manoeuvres to cross lurking vocal crevasses. This seemed an apt metaphor, within eyeshot of the Rocky Mountains. Later on, after I became a published author elsewhere, I would sometimes turn down invitations to read from my fiction in public when I felt the effort required not to embarrass myself and others would outweigh whatever additional readers I might gain. I also knew from experience how subtle and enervating weeks of anxiety could be prior a to public performance. It is difficult for the vocally robust to comprehend so corrosive a dread.

There were times when I would cut my own throat just by opening my mouth. It could be funny, if also disheartening. "I can't hear you, sir. You sound all chopped up." I was calling long-distance to make a reservation halfway across the Pacific. Poor connections, head colds, hangovers—all might have become excuses for sounding chopped up on phones or platforms, had I chosen to use them. Mostly I didn't bother. I accepted the diagnosis, if any, of my listener. By then the innocence of voice, the unselfconscious *effortlessness* of speaking, existed as a kind of ideal beauty barely remembered from childhood. I accepted reticence as the better part of despondency, and this saved me the trouble of lying. The more I lied in fiction the less I wanted to in life. The irony in this, of course, was that I was telling the truth in my fiction and living a lie in my life.

Eccentric, but perhaps inversion had its compensations.

When I became a writer, my fictional metaphors gradually became *me*. To the extent that it mattered to anyone else, here was my abiding and debilitating secret living out its crow-coloured life in narratives set all over the figurative (and often literal) map. I wrote about voice by sublimating it, by taking on different voices, or by adopting some disease or other as a metaphor in order to write from a place deeper within myself.

As a writer at his desk, I could begin to live as if I *were* myself, speaking full out on the page to this veiled vocal obsession. I had no concern about being overheard until I was ready to be overheard without spasms. I might even deploy spasms in an arrangement of b   ro   ken w   ords, just to flush out the gaps in my "real" self's impaired cognition. Such a yearning for vocal suicide, if this is what it was, did seem to me an interesting way of creating fictional character. If I enjoyed any indemnity for a broken voice, it was in learning to listen to other voices as a way to see the world.

Back in Vancouver, after ten years away, within the apartment and later house where I set up as a writer, a calm life of unremarkable efficiency was punctuated by the happy satisfaction won from patching a roof or diapering a child. For many, a writer's imagination should seem quick, even hubristic, propelling the ideas he shapes. What a relief that my own, if kept in training, could still be prodded to run fast enough, and, in the scheme of things, stir in me a desire to keep venturing abroad, even to compose a thousand-page novel. To publish books of my own, eventually, however problematic it might be to promote them in public, which it did prove increasingly difficult to do.

Only after the unexpected stall of my first novel happened to coincide with that other crisis—the death, as I believed, of my wife—did I begin to learn of a "movement disorder" that might have been responsible for the way I'd begun to speak as far back as adolescence.

As someone *with* a movement disorder, but not knowing it, or even that specific muscle movements could be disorderly in an otherwise fit man, I had for much of my life sensed an urge to travel, to "move" in a way I could never explain except perhaps as the urge to escape a rooted, working-class childhood. It was as if the rare neurological disease creeping unsuspected down my brain stem since adolescence—and which would throttle my larynx in its full-blown state in my late twenties—required travel in order to exercise (*exorcise*) emotional cramps and moral flaws. I knew of no one else who suffered from this bizarre dysphonia. I'd given up mentioning it to doctors who had never heard of it. I'd given up mentioning it to quacks who not only *had* heard of it but knew all about curing the unwelcome symptoms.

I could remember visiting a therapist in Los Angeles who claimed to have a cure for my insidious habit. I was flying back to Vancouver from Peru, where I had been researching a part of my novel (to do with a quack, coincidentally), stopping over in California because of my interest in this man's published claim that changing my voice could change my life. I could not have agreed more with his premise. I *wanted* to change my voice. I had become a fiction writer partly to do just that. And I had been a model of artistic patience ever since. Except nothing was going to cure my habit, even if I worked at it a lifetime.

But for poverty and providence, I might still be sitting in his warren of tiny offices on Wilshire Boulevard, paying him US$150 an hour, reading from a page of stubby sentences into a machine with winking lights, while he is off next door tuning up a second customer, who is also suffering from bad vocal hygiene and a heavy wallet in need of slimming. His favourite analogy for my voice was a car. "When you drive a car and you put it in drive, do you leave the brake on? That's what you're doing. You're letting the brake hold you back." He told me to say *"Hm. Hm."* When I did, he said, "No. Put your hand on my stomach. Feel that? What happens when I count? . . . Feel that? Now, what happens to yours, when you count?"

I still wasn't breathing the way he wanted me to. He left the room. I was like a crow with indigestion: *"My mo   other closed the d   oor."* The lights on the machine winked feebly, near the very bottom of the scale. "No, you haven't got it," he said, returning to the room. "Your pitch is too low. Look. What's the light say? Get it up!" Exit. *"Two d   ogs ran after the c   ar."* Back in again, after more double-dipping. "You're like the guy in reverse, trying to go forward and wondering why people behind are shouting at you. Inside yourself, you feel like you're going forward, and here's these guys blaming you for something you don't feel." This one passed me by. "Keep working on it," he called from the doorway.

Apparently, I was a bass baritone, just like him. But mine was locked in the basement of my chest. Even my analogy of an attic, which I preferred, was under demolition.

The next morning, when I wondered aloud about the steepness of his fees, he was cryptic: "There are some interesting aspects to West Los Angeles." The pause sounded rehearsed. I felt my role was to keep the dialogue moving along. I said, "Expe   nsive, you mean." He nodded. "The rents are high around these parts." So must have been the cost of thin-soled, fine leather loafers. A decade later, when I re-encountered his preference in footwear at a voice conference in San Diego, he was still hustling business among the vocally misinformed to cover the high cost (I supposed) of doing business in West LA. I admired his latest pair of loafers with an uncharitable feeling of having some small claim on them.

Over the last twenty-five years, and for years before that, I was always impressed by how *easily* people spoke. For most of my life, I had felt a kind of wonder when I heard relaxed voices. How was it *done?* Not until Christmas of the year I turned fifteen could my parents afford a TV, after which we tuned in Kraft Music Hall Theatre every Wednesday night to hear Perry Como crooning to a rose with an ease that inspired me. I didn't appreciate opera singers, or for that matter Sinatra, until later. At college, I started going to debates and was delighted by the sheer bravado of competing students deploying their voices without notes, wobbles or hesitation. I began to review plays for the campus newspaper, just to hear actors speak their lines, but probably also to gain a public hearing without actually having to speak on stage myself.

Not that I couldn't do off-off-Broadway. By now I was teaching a class of freshman students, with some success, feeling my worst vocal fears were over.

BBC arts-talk shows in London, where I was a student after that, fascinated me. I remember listening to the heretical Aussie voice of Clive James, making its debut on *Late Night Lineup*, reviewing a new play from the Royal Court. Theatre continued to beguile me. Years later, when I was trying to write plays of my own back in Vancouver, I would turn on Dick Cavett's guests on PBS. My ears lurked like radar dishes, trying to detect the faintest of vocal quirks, especially after my own voice had gone haywire in my late twenties.

Listening, I must have hoped to catch some underlying spasm, some incipient impediment, of which my own spasm and impediment were merely an exaggerated case. Hearing someone else sound spazzy would somehow justify me in thinking I need not remain the freak in the attic—that possibly I was normal, and, given time and confidence to "get over" my insecurity, I too could emerge before the full glare of TV lights, or the black hole of a microphone, and acquit myself well. I actually believed I could surmount what continued to threaten my voice.

I little suspected my problem had nothing to do with confidence.

I went on writing. And was stumbling publicly on occasions when I agreed to read from my books, hoping to dodge the fault line of an unpredictable voice. Never quite knowing how my words would shake down, though usually able to cover up tremors and spasms in private conversation, I realized in meetings or in front of a microphone I could seldom count on my voice not to temporarily collapse. In a rare interview, say, because of the strain of listening to *how* I was speaking, instead of to what I was saying, this might lead to logorrhea.

After one humiliating debacle, at a large celebratory reading in Ontario for a fellow writer's fiftieth birthday, I happened to hear about beta blockers, sometimes taken by musicians for stage fright, and managed to persuade a physician to prescribe me some. I had lost my ability to imagine—let alone remember—that audiences did not actually frighten me at all. *I* did; or rather that "real" self who wasn't me did when he threatened, as he was always doing, to escape from the attic. I knew this because on those occasions when my voice worked half smoothly I could embrace an audience or a workshop with true pleasure.

That these and other drugs failed to make much difference led me to suspect the confidence they instilled was perhaps not what I was lacking after all. Even in relaxed conversations with my wife, when I wasn't trying to cover up, I still didn't sound the way I wanted to. I could barely *remember* the sound I wanted. By now I had grown increasingly despondent over the guerrilla skirmishing between two old selves, and my trying to guess which one of them might show up when I opened my mouth. It was all very well to think I had my "real" self shut up in the attic, but when I read my fiction to others I realized this monster was escaping the attic and mouthing off about me in public.

His betrayal shook me. My anxiety of course resided in the possible revelation of a self that wasn't "me"—when, paradoxically, all the evidence seemed to point unavoidably to the lamentable fact that it was. Even approaching middle age, I didn't appear to know myself, a profoundly sad matter, if only because I couldn't count on this voice to sound the way I felt, which was fortunate to be alive and (but for this contradictory despair) very capable of joy.

Eventually, I gave up accepting the few invitations that still came my way to read in public. I wondered how I was going to go on as a writer. I recall wishing for the nineteenth century, for an age before authors were expected to be interviewed, platformed, judged more on their public voices than on their private works. Even should I continue to publish well-received books (three had appeared, even winning awards), apparently no one was going to hear about them in the way they needed to be heard about, from the horse's mouth. My particular horse was out to pasture. I longed for readers—not listeners and watchers. I longed for anonymity.

I even longed for anonymity in my private life. Apart from meetings, where I was afraid to say more than a sentence or two, for fear of betraying my spasmodic self, or the telephone, by which it was often torture to make a call, there might be dinner parties from which I came away frustrated or despondent over a chronic inability to contribute much to conversations, for fear of betraying what I couldn't control. The odds against my sounding as if I was having a mental breakdown had become increasingly long. And this was especially true at functions that meant much to me, such as silver and golden anniversaries of my parents. The feeling of letting down those I was toasting was grim. Yet the longing for anonymity could be just as strong in shops, asking for a pound of coffee beans, or a baguette.

"B a guette" was a honey.

I refused to think of myself as "spastic," but this was how a speech therapist had once diagnosed my dysphonia, mentioning at the time how it was more or less hopeless to think of overcoming it. So why publicize the misfortune, I concluded, if it could be kept quiet? Besides, how did you talk about what you didn't understand, except as a mysterious weakness—not a *physical* weakness, moreover, like asthma or throat cancer, but a psychological weakness?

I could remember a time before this pathologist, when medical science was just beginning to talk about such things in the media, yearning for some sort of "chemical imbalance" to explain my dysphonia. I hoped to discover, say, the grim lack of papaya or pomegranate seeds in my diet, kiwi or kale, the excessive consumption of which would give me back a voice. But time taught me, with increasing certainty, there was neither cure nor treatment for the sort of voice barely mentioned in the literature on defective speech. And I had given up trying to understand its irregularity in terms of some physical trigger or vitamin deficiency. I had run fast as a boy. I was probably high-strung, and that was an end of it. I was back to psychological.

Then my wife "died," an event leading coincidentally and even absurdly to the knowledge—perhaps I should say the Knowledge—that I too was suffering from a neurological disorder, which had to do with nothing less than my huffing, mangled voice.

To learn after twenty years of believing there was something fundamentally the matter with your mind, because your voice stuck and seized up like a combustion engine missing half its pistons, that you had something *mechanical* and not *psychological* wrong, came as an inexpressible gift, even if this knowledge revealed that you were suffering from a rare, unfixable, neurological lemon.

It now seemed I no longer needed to feel quite so hopeless in my growing despair over an unpredictable voice, nor over the temptation, increasingly surrendered to, of retreating from the world. When my life had sunk so far down I was ready to drown, defeated by a condition as unpredictable as a quark, it began to rise again out of the dark matter surrounding a miswired brain.

I felt pretty good.

So began my meditation on coming back to voice—back to "myself." Five summers later, when I was corresponding with *The New Quarterly* for a feature about my work, I found myself replying to a suggestion that the metaphors I used were often related to the body. And though I'd come to understand my illness, and receive treatment for it, I was still reluctant to talk about voice except in a general way, in trying to account for the patterns in my fiction. I was *writing*, moreover, not speaking—à la Nabokov, I supposed, who hated to talk off the cuff ("off the Nabocuff," as he put it), preferring to answer questions with his pen.

My "coming-out" narrative was to have been the eponymous novella in a story collection following my novel. But even that was cloaked in metaphor, and would have done little to eulogize a creepy attic voice. It was the first-person narrative of a baritone opera singer, whose final lines about the imprisoned Oscar Wilde would go: "His true identity resided in the sincerity of his façade. Shame seems quaint now. A performer's curse . . . It just gets to the point where it is no longer possible, or desirable, to separate life from its stage." It would use homosexuality as a metaphor for a feeling of shame and yearning only gradually revealed. I supposed because of my own shame as a closet "spastic" (the shameful and faulty term I lived with secretly for decades), I had for a long time identified with closet "queers." I felt I understood, in part, how a close elderly friend of mine was for most of his long life a veiled homosexual. This was the author Sinclair Ross. I now confided in him how I was planning to set off around the world.

I had decided that travels with a voice might be at least as worthy a plot as Stevenson's travels with a donkey. "Except for business purposes, or to give each other the lie in a tavern brawl, they have laid aside even the civility of speech. 'Tis a mere mountain Poland. In the midst of this Babylon I found myself a rallying-point; every one was anxious to be kind and helpful to the stranger." Unlike RLS, I was hoping to discover another kind of Babylon, where voice might enjoy a singular, even exotic status, beyond whatever theatres and opera houses I hoped to visit. A pre-Babel state of oral harmony.

As a retired novelist, Ross assumed it was material for my fiction I wanted, and he was partly right. I had made no secret of my hope, on this journey, to visit as many glasshouses as possible. I'd always loved glasshouses, felt inspired by them, and he said he had too. He remembered Kew Gardens, from his war years in London with the Canadian army. He recalled reading Laurence Sterne's *A Sentimental Journey* at Kew. And so, with a wistful look, he would reassure me in his faint Parkinsonian voice, for which he refused to wear his voice amplifier, and to which I would incline forward to hear his whisperings over Met broadcasts of *The Magic Flute* and *Tales of Hoffmann*, that things would work out: "I'd go so far to say . . ." he would say—and—"I'd even venture to say . . ." And what he was slowly venturing and going so far to say was that I, almost forty years his junior, would eventually find what I was looking for. Distance, travel, *above all voice*, seemed to me bound up in these uncharacteristic idioms he chose in order to hint that the risk of my actually going out looking (i.e., listening) for what I needed would lead me to the narrative I desired.

Sadly, as it turned out, I would still be wandering through voices when he died, between travels to foreign countries he would never visit. Half a decade earlier, I had conceived and edited an anthology of worst journeys by fellow writers and famous travellers, to which my friend had wanted to contribute but never managed to complete his tale of transport across the North Atlantic, in a troop ship in 1942, before turning it into a nightmarish fiction that, for him, never ended.

I wanted this new book to be about good journeys. I had no intention of setting out to find more bad ones. And, although I might find myself listening to pilgrimages through one dark valley of soul or another, I also wished to hear of happiness and optimism. I recalled what Oliver Sacks had reportedly told his fellow neurologists in Vancouver: that he had always tried to live by his medical parents' maxim, speaking not only of the disease a person has, but also of the person the disease has. I would try to remember this.

My first trip was to seek out people like me, in a tiny diaspora of voices stretching around the world. I wanted to call up far-flung men and women with the same disorder and be invited over in distant cities to hear their stories. My search would be for those who, because of queer voices, had lost friends, careers and happiness, in vain sought elucidation, been admitted to mental institutions, tried surgery, seen quacks and bought spurious medicines.

I wanted to talk to priests, retired TV anchormen, pilots, erstwhile choir members, former nuns, graphics designers, wives of doctors, headmasters, ex-entertainment producers, fundraisers, textbook authors and ranch widows. I wanted to meet others who weren't vocally impaired: speech pathologists—some of them lonely, perhaps—oddballs, beautiful women, novelists, fellow travellers and old friends, composers, voice coaches, Third World doctors and museum attendants. I wanted to call them up; I wanted to run into them. I wanted to listen to each carefully, especially to how they used their voices. *What did it mean to have a voice?*

For one thing, it might mean having an authoritative enough voice to scare off muggers in Johannesburg. For another, it might mean being able to read from my books in Canada without sounding like I was being mugged in Johannesburg.

I also wanted to travel on behalf of Canada India Village Aid, on whose board of directors I sat, reflecting on voices in Third World countries. I kept wanting to get away in these years just to curry my aural, not to say oral, obsession. From the start, I wanted to listen to voices outside me instead of the ones inside. I wanted to sit in cafés and overhear the caffeinated and perfumed. I wanted to walk and immerse myself in the buzz of people, even people whose language I couldn't understand—whether Bengali or Xhosa, Mewar or Sinhalese. I wanted to sit in hotels over tropical harbours and hear the voices of dying men.

I needed to find a voice I had never used to tell the story of my emergence from silence and murk into light and air. What rules of genre might apply to a diaspora governed primarily by a sense of wonder for voice? (Could you make an art of vocal wonder?) The possibility of discovering such a place inspired me. I wanted to sit in glasshouses and listen to plants, to *talk* to the plants. I wanted a new understanding of free speech.

Past travels, whether to Cuba or Cambodia, India or Turkey, had seldom helped me listen to the human voice in the way I wished to, when the nature of my disorder had encouraged less contact than I might have enjoyed. I now wanted to listen to voices, by engaging as many as I could in conversation, and hear their curves and timbres.

It would be a year and a half before I left home. I still needed to learn more about the medical breakthrough for my voice. About the paradox of changing my life, in a strange and imperma-nent way: which was that the closer I came over time to gaining a smoother voice, the nearer I was to losing it again. It was this paradoxical cycle that afflicted anyone with laryngeal dystonia— anyone who chose to have botulinum toxin injected by needle through the neck and into the voice box every three or four months for the sole purpose of paralyzing nerve endings, over-energized by chemical transmitters in the basal ganglia, and so freeing one's voice from choking spasms caused by rogue vocal folds.

One began to appreciate the paradox of this movement disorder, made temporarily manageable by a deadly elixir brewed up during World War II for germ warfare, against unwelcome enemy movements. It seemed an astonishingly long way from there to coming back to voice, decades later, for those of us who welcomed this poison into our bodies. Yet who would not have felt a profound gratitude for even a poisonous paradox, if it delivered you a voice that sounded effortless?

Following the non-death of my wife, I had reached two conclusions about our vocal lives. Vocal identity comes surprisingly early—not until we cry are we truly born. And nothing rounds life off like a last word spoken on a deathbed. But there was something else perhaps, a toast or a eulogy, spoken by one's self for loved ones. Who was this self? I had to admit that at times I did not know any more.

3

The Stolen Trumpet

T HE NEW CURE was a surprise—unfortunately, for the wrong reason. "There is no cure," said Dr. Tsui, the neurologist examining me.

"Oh. B   ut I thought . . ."

Why I was wasting my time? After waiting a year to seek a referral, I thought a cure awaited to rid me of this voice that chronically buckled, clogged, did the splits. The only worry today had been that I might sound unaccountably *smooth*, a fickle occurrence, and so find myself dismissed as an impostor.

Not a problem. My stress level shot up nicely when I accidentally entered the wrong door at the back of University Hospital, thereby tripping an alarm, which infuriated a purple-nosed nurse in the extended-care wing who arrived to scold me like a child, miles from any doddering patient I could see. It was a rainy day in July, so things already seemed in reverse of what I expected—i.e., a day of strong ethereal light, leading straight to a door with pearly pillars and angelic nurses, who juggled harps in descending to deliver me from venial cacophony beyond my poor vocal control.

I really had no idea what to expect, only that I was expecting some variation on the elixir of life, shot into me with the polished velocity of a silver bullet.

Not this abrupt contradiction, from a smiling Joseph Tsui, sitting here in a crisp lab coat the colour of snow. He smiled wider.

"Let me finish. There is no cure, but we have treatment."

Botulin, explained Dr. Tsui, refined in the US in anticipation of germ warfare fifty years ago, and several million times more toxic than rattlesnake poison, was now used to treat dystonia. Dystonia? Packaged and sold under the trade name Botox, this spectacularly lethal poison was for a new generation of neurologists treating dystonia what the drug Sinemet had been for their predecessors dealing with Parkinson's.

I kept thinking, because English was Dr. Tsui's second language, he was saying *dysphonia*—as in "spastic dysphonia." I had never heard of dystonia. Dystonia I now learned was a brain disturbance, sometimes inherited, a muscle movement disorder characterized by severe, involuntary spasms twisting one or more areas of the body—in my case, the vocal cords—into strange and disabling, even painful postures.

He sounded quite cheerful about it. "Primary" or generalized dystonia afflicted several parts of the body at once, with spasms and contortions, and usually began in childhood. What I had was a "focal" dystonia known as laryngeal dystonia, or spasmodic dysphonia (SD), which assailed the vocal folds and thus speech.

"It's confusing, at first," he admitted. And often misdiagnosed, apparently, because of dystonia's physical complexities and because there was no definitive test for the disease. This, sadly, seemed why it was still relatively unknown. It relied on a clinical diagnosis. Focal dystonia, he told me, passing across his desk a pamphlet, was a condition six times more common than other neuromuscular disorders such as Huntington's disease, muscular dystrophy and Lou Gehrig's disease (ALS). But only a small fraction of these suffered from strangulated speech.

I was still trying to get straight the difference he'd articulated between "laryngeal dystonia" and "laryngeal dysphonia." They sounded the same—indeed both conditions produced deformed speech, although not all dysphonias were dystonic. (They could for example arise from stroke, nodules, tumours, trauma.) I was quietly glad to hear the old name "spastic dysphonia" had been unseated. The more accurate labels were somewhat softer tags than the one I was diagnosed with as a young man. "Vocal cord dystonia" was another term Dr. Tsui adopted, in accounting for what he was also calling my movement disorder.

He deployed his forefinger and middle finger to illustrate how vocal folds normally opened, but, in my case, how they closed involuntarily when I tried to speak, even without stress. He described how these clenching cords would probably respond to injections of botulinum toxin every three or four months, by paralyzing or blocking the nerve endings that misfired cells in my vocal muscles, so the cords no longer jammed and strangled speech. Thus far results had been good—seldom perfect, but most patients recovered their voices before the effect of the drug gradually wore off and another injection was needed.

Outside his window, skies were still overcast, but I thought I could now hear a harp. If a supernal *cure* was unavailable, maybe this temporary poison wasn't without the heavenly possibility of smooth speech.

I learned that the young biochemist who was asked to grow botulin for the American biological-warfare program had discovered any exposure to air seriously ruined the potency of his weapon. So his stockpile of poison was never used, until thirty years later, when he let a young physician inject a diluted dose of it into the hyperactive eye muscles of a patient with strabismus. Strategically paralyzed, the affected nerves weakened muscles enough to allow them to relax and the cross-eyes to straighten.

My congenial neurologist went on to say that by the late seventies, sharing this toxin, surgeons started experimenting on blepharospasm, the focal dystonia responsible for uncontrollable blinking. This disorder, previously considered psychosomatic, was relieved dramatically with an injection. Use of the original batch of botulin then spread into treatment of other dystonias, such as writer's cramp, Meige's syndrome, torticollis and SD. By the early nineties, the original bacterial brew had been bought by a pharmaceutical giant, diluted from its three-gallon jug, and renamed

Botox. Because of its potency, an effective treatment contained only about a millionth of a milligram. One ten-thousandth of a milligram could kill you.

Dr. Tsui asked if I had seen the film *Awakenings*? Well, this drug was doing for dystonia victims what the wonder drug L-dopa had done in the 1950s to restart the lives of those with sleeping sickness. Unfortunately, I learned he himself didn't minister to voice patients. He did limbs. Necks were someone else's speciality. I would now need to see an otolaryngologist. After seeing him, and a speech pathologist, I would then be eligible for a needle ("this long"—maybe six inches) in my voice box.

At least a pattern of consistency was developing, an apparently endless round in keeping with today's reversal of inflated expectations.

A month later I learned the first available appointment was not for another month and a half after that. I turned my expectations down another notch. Because of my novelist's interest in homoeopathy, I began to wonder whether the toxin used to treat my kind of vocal condition might have also somehow caused it. Botulism, I read, was "a form of food poisoning that is due to a toxin produced by the bacteria *Clostridium botulinum*. This toxin is one of the most potent poisons known. . . . Home-canned food that has not been properly processed may contain dangerous amounts of botulism toxin."

All those bottled jars of jam and fish, beloved of my mother and her mother ever since I could remember, hadn't they sometimes tasted mouldy? Yet any of a hundred other environmental poisons might have come into it. I was keen to account rationally for a condition I had suffered irrationally for years. What about genes? Had some genetic predisposition made me susceptible to those disturbances of viruses or chemicals in my brain's subcortical structures? Presumably, gene therapy would become the preferred treatment, once ongoing research into dystonia uncovered precisely which marker on thousands of genes, on any of the twenty-three pairs of chromosomes, was responsible for each focal dystonia. Botulinum toxin would then pass out of fashion, seen for what it was, an unpredictable drug of transient benefit. (Later, idling away a humid afternoon in an old hotel in Grahamstown, South Africa, I watched an Australian TV program narrated by the son of a vocally stricken ABC broadcaster whom I had interviewed in Fremantle; only then did I learn that wealthy women's cosmetic surgery in New York and California now included botulinum toxin—it was being used to "treat" wrinkles.)

Meanwhile, I awaited with resignation my own first injection—or what I hoped would be an injection. Again, what if I didn't sound spasmodic enough to convince a speech pathologist I needed anything more than the customary song and dance her unavailing therapy had to offer people like me? A stutterer would have understood that oases of fluency, though welcome, were few.

I was determined not to let this great opportunity slip away, by sounding unaccountably smooth. I needed to sound natural—which in my case was unnatural.

In September, I went along to Vancouver Hospital's Voice Clinic, in the old Willow Pavilion with its antiquated elevators and tiled, disused kitchens. There I met Murray Morrison and Anne Burgi, in a small room decorated with monitoring machines and an air of understated assessment. Fortunately, my pulse was being pecked at vigorously by the crow in my chest. I couldn't have sounded relaxed if I had wanted to. Dr. Morrison soon drifted out and left his speech pathologist, along with a visiting research fellow, to ask questions about my vocal history and then to examine my throat. They inserted an endoscope, connected to a video camera, down my throat to tape the vocal folds, asking me to repeat sounds as well as sing.

The crow squawked, satisfactorily I thought. I was relieved to think it was obvious to anyone who cared to look that I had insurgent vocal cords in need of pacification.

Dr. Morrison now returned and asked me to reiterate my vocal history. A tall, preoccupied man with fair hair and a twinkling eye, he listened, touching the rim of his glasses, periodically glancing at his clipboard. He asked me to return to the examining chair and read three or four paragraphs of suitably uplifting if depressingly weathered prose. He turned on his video camera. *The r   ainbow is a di   vision of wh   ite light into many b   eautiful colours. Th   ese take the sh   ape of a long round arch w   ith its path high ab   ove, and its ends apparently be   yond the hor   izon.*

I gathered he was taping me for one of those Before and After performances, as shown at the recent international neurology conference, illustrating botulin's beneficent effects on the vocally stricken. He then asked me to sing. I did a suitably miserable job of this too. I was in crow heaven, I thought. These assessors now understood exactly what the matter with me was, wouldn't be fooled by any intermittent smoothness, and they knew exactly how to help me overcome the overcomeable. Indeed, they *wanted* to help me overcome it.

This ENT said that before he injected my larynx, he would like me to have at least one appointment with Anne Burgi, to try speech therapy again. *Good n   ight*, I thought.

"Botox isn't a cure," he said carefully. "They're giving it to people south of the border who shouldn't be getting it."

A week or two later, Anne Burgi ran through some breathing and relaxation exercises I remembered from twenty years earlier. I then stumbled through two or three vocal workouts. She sympathized with my spasms. An attractive, soft-spoken woman from South Africa, she knew the history of people like me, misdiagnosed and passed from specialist to specialist, sometimes quack to quack, before referral to speech therapy—which, however useful in understanding good breathing and vocal techniques, turned out to be unhelpful in rehabilitating those whose problem was chronic. Unfortunately, there were still many speech pathologists who'd never heard of laryngeal dystonia.

My sense of trying to rehabilitate a spasmodic voice was like trying to correct a chronic golf slice: so much to remember that even if you happened to speak or swing smoothly every once in a while—body unfolding as it should—little felt natural and recidivism was inevitable. Even your most relaxed, natural swing sent the ball fading into the rough.

She recognized she wasn't making much progress with a duffer like me. After half an hour, she set aside her exercises and left it up to me whether I wished to go on with them after my first injection. She described two types of the disorder. Abductor, or AB, was the rarer form, in which the vocal folds "over-opened," producing an inaudible, breathy voice, for which there was no beneficial treatment. The more common AD, or adductor type, presented in the opposite manner: instead of freezing open, the vocal cords "over-closed" and produced a strangled guttural voice like mine.

She felt stuttering and spasmodic dysphonia were similar in what tended to bring each on: authority figures, having to speak in public, or before a group. What was less likely to bring on symptoms were also similar: speaking to underlings and children, to people you knew (rather than strangers), singing. She neglected to mention that spasms and stuttering could also occur any time, regardless of the situation and no matter how relaxed you felt. Unfortunately, the toxin had had no beneficial effect on stuttering. As for the broad similarities, she felt stuttering and SD were both caused by a combination of physiological and psychological factors.

This surprised me a little. Even Morrison, in wanting to cover three possible factors related to dysphonia, had mentioned "psychological" (along with "technical" and "reflux"). When I returned home that day, I was still not sure if by "psychological" my speech therapist intended to suggest anything more than stress. And yet her use of this term made me wonder about the medical profession in general and its traditionally loose application of the word— in particular as it concerned diseases of the nervous system and wonky brain stems. The history of ascribing neurotic causes to MS and Parkinson's, say, had not been an impressive one. And there remained this reluctance it seemed to exclude them from stuttering and spasmodic dysphonia, too. I supposed the *way* people spoke assumed that a "psychological factor" was somehow always at work, but why should we bother to mention it when we did not mention it in the way people undertook other activities such as eating Kentucky Fried Chicken, or walking their beagles? These pursuits each also involved certain proclivities of mind.

Preparing for my first Botox shot, I had time to meditate further on assumptions, including those that had helped undermine my life. One afternoon I travelled up to the Bloedel Conservatory, atop Little Mountain in Vancouver, to sit amidst the tropical foliage, humidity and blossoms. One of the parrots spoke to me, over the sound of running water. "Parrot," it said. "Parrot." Until I got close enough to distinguish between consonants, I thought it was saying *Bear it*. This only served to remind me of the circular and received thinking endemic to the medical profession.

There did seem to be an unexamined assumption that voice and mind were in some revealing relationship, such as eyes and soul were traditionally supposed to be. For some reason, a dystonically impaired voice was viewed differently than a dystonically impaired neck, even when the basal ganglia source of both movement disorders was acknowledged as the same. Certainly, no one would think to suggest someone with torticollis had a psychological predisposition exacerbating her crooked head. Yet assumptions of professionals, about one's voice, could still echo diagnoses originating in the nineteenth century—i.e., speech impediments as psychosomatic, within one's own control, *stress-related*. Naturally, they were stress-related: so was running the 100-metre dash, phoning to ask for a first date, applying to a mortgage company when your income was borderline. Your performance as a sprinter, lover, or house buyer in failing to win the race, girl, or cash was more likely to be judged in terms of speed, charm, and income than it was by a "psychological factor." No one thought to mention stress. It was simply assumed to be part of such athletic, social, and financial activities. Yet in the activity of *speaking* the voice was supposed to reveal something significant, even treatable, about a speaker's mind.

"*Bear it, partner. Bear it.*"

"T   rying to." I wondered instead if I ought to burst into Pinkerton's *Addio, fiorito asil*, if only to frighten the bird away.

I opened my notebook and leafed through it.

Listening to this parrot on its perch had reminded me of how the psyche, or soul, had entered medical diagnoses in the nineteenth century. Moral diagnoses had become implicit in nervous disorders attributed to the mind. Hysteria, previously diagnosed as a physical condition, yet with no particular points of reference, supposedly divulged a condition of soul or mind. Thus were "psychological" roots thought to explain what couldn't otherwise be understood—not least such "hysterical" sounding voices as mine.

In the same way that everything had begun to change for me with the knowledge that spasmodic dysphonia wasn't psychosomatic, so too, as I had been discovering, had everything in the small publishing world of this disease begun to change, in the 1980s, from one kind of assumption to another. Articles with titles like "Anatomy and Cell Biology of the Laryngeal Motor Neurons: Implications for the Treatment of Spasmodic Dysphonia," in journals such as *Advances in Neurology*, were unheard-of a few years earlier, and they swept away received wisdom and old presumptions about the disease.

Before this, in the long history of ascribing diseases of the brain and nervous system to the minds and mental states of patients, I'd found the titles of medical papers quite revealing: "Spastic dysphonia. A psychosomatic voice disorder" (1960), "Psychiatric observations on the personality structure of patients with habitual dysphonia" (1958), "The voice of neurosis" (1954), and so on back to the nineteenth century. The disease was initially described as an hysterical malady in 1871 by the German researcher L. Traube. Not until Herbert Dedo and associates pioneered their surgical nerve sections in the 1970s (an operation for SD since abandoned by laryngologists because of the high rate of recidivism), did an organic, neurological explanation for the once obscure, psychiatric disorder begin its ascendance.

A number of parrots had now started to squabble. The cacophony drove me from my bench, and eventually from the glasshouse itself, as if from Babel.

I was hoping my first injection in October would prove the watershed of my life. From here, all waters would run west. On the day of the needle, I sat nervously in the voice clinic awaiting my turn. Nervous because I still wasn't certain I would not be injected with a placebo of pineapple juice or Sprite, following on from Dr. Morrison's seeming reluctance to rush into anything at our meeting in September. Excited, too, as I was hearing for the first time in my life spasmodic dysphonic voices other than my own.

Choppy, hesitant voices in need of a fix.

A grey-haired man in a business suit was talking to a professional-looking woman in her thirties, also in a suit, in the chairs alongside mine. They appeared unselfconscious about their voices, sitting as they were in a place sympathetic to their difficulties and where they expected amelioration. I listened, amazed. I was suddenly no longer "alone" in the world. I was now part of an odd diaspora of twisted, capricious voices. And *theirs* sounded worse than mine. I then realized I was eavesdropping with the self-deception of someone who refused to listen to himself on tape. They were talking about the Reform Party and the upcoming national election in Canada.

When I was called into the clinic my torturer was reassuring. Murray Morrison asked me to remove my sweater, lie down on the table, and undo my shirt. The green-eyed nurse wetted me with what felt like mortician's gel and stuck electrodes to my forehead and neck. My surgeon explained how he would be making two injections into my voice box, one in and up to the left; followed, on the other side, in and up to the right. Thus would my larynx's fragile wings be impaled. I was still snuggling up comfortably against his nurse when I felt the needle go in.

I was prepared for the pain, which wasn't intense, but what surprised me was the gagging sensation each time the glass syringe entered my throat. I experienced a sudden, helpless feeling of being pinned at the centre of my being, where air and food passed regularly without hindrance, but where my voice until now had originated with all the predictability of a butterfly in flight. Each time he inserted his needle, like some lepidopterist, he asked me to say *ahhhh*, by which expression of my amazement or wonder this laryngologist seemed to assure himself (by checking the staticky-sounding screen behind my head) that he had found the tiny nerves of the wing he was looking to inject with his embalming fluid.

But enough figurative description. Speaking more responsibly, I had received a transcutaneous bilateral injection, by a hollow Teflon-coated EMG needle, through the cricothyroid membrane into the mid-portion of my thyroarytenoid muscle. Technology soothed, where metaphor merely stirred up anxiety.

After the injection, Dr. Morrison said vocal fluency would probably reach its optimum in two months. In fact, he wanted to see me again in early December for another evaluation, and to make a second videotape of my reading the Rainbow Passage. He talked cheerfully now about how I was on "the Botox treadmill," and would learn to reschedule injections as my voice dipped again, when, as he explained it to me, the nerve ends had resprouted to form fresh neuromuscular junctions. I might even want to decrease the size of dosage, once the original nerves had begun to atrophy. In the first couple of weeks, aside from trouble swallowing, I might also experience "air" in my voice—"breathiness" he called it.

I was not prepared for what "breathiness" might mean.

That evening, I remember taking a long walk after dark, my usual route from Kitsilano up the hill into Point Grey, and then, feeling light of heart and foot, choosing to continue on down Tolmie to the beach. What I would recall indelibly of that night was the black sky dripping with stars over English Bay and North Shore mountains. I felt an overwhelming sense of self, such as I hadn't experienced since childhood, streaming slowly back to me like starlight from so far away I might as well have been a time traveller who'd just stepped off at the station.

I would be able to talk to friends again without tugging my earlobe to distract spasms in my larynx. I would be able to speak up at meetings without sounding like a nutcase. I would be able to answer customs officers, and know the simple pleasures of persuasion rooted in a kind of vocal pride. I would be able to accept invitations to speak in public, without sleep-eroding fear, anxiety attacks or the humiliation of straining my way through a throttled discourse as a cover-up for an absurd disorder. With reservations, I might look forward to living my life in a way everyone else who spoke fluently took for granted.

Over the next four days, I observed with increasing pleasure what happened to this voice. In the time it took for the poison to block release of the chemical transmitter acetylcholine—to weaken my vocal muscles, by paralyzing all their unpredictable, over-aggressive nerve ends—the pleasant firming-up of my voice allowed me to read aloud to my son with increasing effortlessness. I discovered this was the great gift of botulinum toxin: how the strain and effort of speaking, of trying to avoid spasms, gradually receded. Tremors vanished. The voice, as it lightened in tone and texture, seemed to belong to someone else.

I began to relax in a way I could not before. The anxiety caused by a ringing telephone disappeared. Social chit-chat became the fun it was supposed to be, instead of agony. Sincerity supplanted the quicker urge to irony and the putative laugh. I could now listen to others without worrying how to respond. I learned, through confidence gained by a rehabilitated voice, that it was possible to listen in a new way. Devoutly, sincerely. I experienced for the first time in memory what it felt like to be vocally expansive. No longer did I feel an oppressive effort to manage my unmanageable larynx—just to speak at all. I was beginning to forget I no longer needed to manoeuvre my way around the clumsy aerodynamics of a spasm.

What contributed to my amazement in those days after receiving Botox for the first time was an awareness that I had almost no memory of my adult voice. Since adolescence, I couldn't really remember what it was like not to be aware of having an unreliable voice, and then in later years not to struggle daily to control it. This did not mean that before dystonia developed in my late twenties I had no voice; only that I was conscious of having a voice that wasn't mine. The dexterity and ownership of it now seemed stunning.

Reading to my son from *The Trumpet of the Swan*, I was in awe of vocal ease even as my vocal folds withered under the spreading toxin. I had always enjoyed reading aloud to him, as this was easier than reading aloud to anybody else, including me. Yet in giving myself to his uncritical ear, it had still always been an effort not to "spaz," and there had been nights in the past when I was forced to give up because of the unbearable strain on my throat. Now, reading with deep pleasure, I was genuinely surprised by the odd vocal coincidence in E.B. White. The boy in the story is here talking to his father:

"It's a young Trumpeter Swan," said Sam. "He's only a few months old. Will you let me keep him awhile?"

"Well," said Mr. Beaver, "I think it's against the law to hold one of these wild birds in captivity. But I'll phone the game warden and see what he says. If he says yes, you can keep him."

"Tell the warden the swan has something the matter with him," called Sam as his father started toward the house.

"What's wrong with him?" asked his father.

"He has a speech problem," replied Sam. "Something's wrong with his throat."

"What are you talking about? Who ever heard of a swan with a speech problem?"

"Well," said Sam, "this is a Trumpeter Swan that can't trumpet. He's defective. He can't make a sound."

Mr. Beaver looked at his son as though he didn't know whether to believe him or not . . .

Sam is allowed to keep the cygnet. He takes Louis to school with him, to learn to read and write, since he's unable to speak. The first-graders are expectant, when their skeptical teacher Mrs. Hammerbotham challenges Louis to copy a word she writes on the blackboard. (In a way, this reminded me of my high-school experiences, of trying to read out loud without quaking, unfortunately without the same triumphant outcome.)

"O.K., Louis, let's see you write *that*!"

Louis picked up a fresh piece of chalk in his bill. He was scared. He took a good look at the word. "A long word," he thought, "is really no harder than a short one. I'll just copy one letter at a time, and pretty soon it will be finished. Besides, my life is a catastrophe. It's a catastrophe to be without a voice." Then he began writing. CATASTROPHE, he wrote, making each letter very neatly. When he got to the last letter, the pupils clapped and stamped their feet and banged on their desks, and one boy quickly made a paper airplane and zoomed it into the air. Mrs. Hammerbotham rapped for order.

For me, over the next night or two, the interest of White's story lay in Louis's use of a stolen trumpet, which becomes his voice to woo the beautiful swan Serena. My own instrument, which had been returned to me with a Teflon-coated needle, was now sounding hoarser by the day. Yet I was doing my best to woo whoever would listen to me: my characters on the page, as I read their voices back to them at my desk. Strangers on the phone, neighbours over the hedge. I wondered if these neighbours didn't regard me in the same light as they might have someone who looked different, but for a reason they couldn't quite place. Botox seemed the vocal equivalent of getting contact lenses or shaving my beard.

"Don't have to misuse my voice now," I noted in my diary. "Doesn't hurt any more." It hurt neither body nor spirit the way it had as recently as last week. Stretching my voice now was like straightening a leg that had been cramped into a paralyzed position. My recovery felt life-affirming. I seemed up for any journey. I seemed to possess an instinctive sense of how to make the rhythm of each spoken sentence sound effortlessly *right*. I could delight in exploring with my voice the little culs-de-sac and lanes I would "normally" have kept out of for fear of forgetting where I was going, or how I would sound if I needed to ask the way. I no longer needed to worry about not feeling up, having to crank myself up, speaking each word clearly now without fear of losing words to a broken, impenetrable growl. Speech was now a revelation. This is what talking was like! "Talking," as one of my characters had said some years before, "is a funny language." I seemed a suddenly gregarious person wanting to catch up on a buried past.

Maybe I was deceiving myself, but I started to feel as though I were talking with unfamiliar moral authority. Quietly, securely, from the centre. This commanded attention, if only from my family. I had begun to feel as though the coherence of my voice were guiding a divided self toward integrity. "Can't believe everyone who speaks normally *takes this for granted*." Not even the ominous sounds of hoarseness qualified my optimism. For my voice had begun to lose its resonance, sounding falsetto.

Then, after five days, instead of sound, air began to emerge from my mouth. No one had warned me "breathiness" would get this bad. Was I going to lose my voice entirely, in order to regain it? I couldn't talk above a murmur now, without squeaking like a mouse. I squeaked at the ticket-seller in the children's Planetarium; at my old friend Sinclair Ross, whose faint voice was suddenly stronger than mine. I avoided dinners out and felt more isolated than ever. I felt as forlorn as if I had been struck deaf.

I began wondering if such voice loss after every injection was going to be worth this incapacitation beyond even spasms. I had lost even the vocal identity I'd known as a spasmodic. Indeed, in later years, I would come to think of the worse effects of toxin as resembling what happened to the voice if you thought of it as Swiss cheese: full of holes, through which air issued but no sound emerged. I had quickly gone from a squawking crow to this squeaking mouse. Except I couldn't get any bite at all into the sound of my *ee's*—as in *really* or *cheese*.

All those overactive nerve terminals causing spasms, oscillations of the arytenoids, breaks in pitch and phonation, had needed to be knocked for a loop. Evidence of how many "axons" had succumbed to the poison was usually to be heard in the extent of your breathiness. It was the injection with no side effects you came to dread as much as the one with too many. It was a balance you wanted (a kind of split decision between injected toxin and surviving axons), a functional hoarseness. Ideally, the size of dosage and the placement of needle would combine to give a good result.

My voice seeped back slowly that fall. If the drug had gradually left me voiceless, the restoration of tone slowly revived my spirits. For two or three weeks, vocal tone stayed exceedingly shallow. Forcing the resonance only diminished it. I began to appreciate how a shallow voice was keeping me from my bottom-feeding foes of spasmodic dysphonia. It floated. I wanted a deeper voice, but knew by the time my baritone sank back to its natural bottom, the spasms would return, circling like mud sharks.

As my voice revived, it occurred to me it had been precisely twenty years ago to the week I had started losing it to dystonia, occasional words breaking up as I spoke to a class on "The British Novel." This was in late October, shortly after Lorraine and I were involved in a car crash, when a drunken driver crushed our VW from behind giving me a stiff neck from whiplash. One week I was speaking smoothly; the next beginning to misfire.

I now discovered not being able to raise my voice probably made me a more patient father in the playground around my desk. I was setting a marvellous example of tolerance. Yet I recall wondering on Halloween, as I escorted my son between houses to bag candies, if my not being able to call out reminders to say thank-you could possibly lead him in later years to malaise, social indifference, snivelling delinquency—what the hell, a prison sentence—for unnamed crimes against the community directly attributable to botulinum toxin's incapacitating effects on his father. It was a big responsibility, choosing to sound quieter than I generally did in the questionable hope of sounding smoother. I kept my counsel at his soccer and ice hockey games too. And so I was a stick-in-the-mud and a dull blade besides. A Woody Allen nerd in this tale of the vocally challenged squeaker.

I came to know that a smooth voice and renewed vocal identity would arrive by a slightly different route after each injection, and inevitably decline toward the spasms and dogfish below. Within a day or so of every shot, I could feel my vocal folds smartening up, as if under renewed warranty, though the inevitable hoarseness from a successful injection would not set in for three or four days. At which point, I would begin to sound thin and reassuringly reedy.

Occasionally, if the needle missed and my voice stayed deep and deformed, I would presume to exercise my warranty by asking for another injection. The dread of requesting a reinjection to one or both cords, of becoming a nuisance, wouldn't have been worth it if the panic felt over an upcoming event weren't worse. The easygoing Murray Morrison was always sympathetic, open to suggestions as to the size and kind of injections his patients wanted (either unilateral or bilateral—voice loss was less when only one cord was injected, though a good result might not last as long). He was usually wry about this aspect of his practice.

"What we do is cosmetic surgery," he confessed, when I saw him again in December to see how my first injection had taken. "All we're doing is treating the symptoms, not the disease." I supposed he felt vocal fluency was subjective—in the ear of his patient, who needed to think his voice had some influence over the surgery used to restore it. This otolaryngologist never pretended to know more about a voice than a patient had come to understand on his own.

One of these patients was the affable Lloyd Pearson, a building inspector from the UK, who encouraged me during my first period of voice loss. Lloyd had first experienced spasms trying to raise his voice over noisy construction sites during Vancouver's Expo 86. He had travelled to New York for his first injection in 1989. By the time the rest of us caught up to him in numbers of injections, Lloyd had experienced what he called "a spontaneous remission" from his disease, renouncing toxin and preferring instead to manage on his own with the help of church elders and other medication.

After each injection of Botox, during the twelve weeks or less of fluency that followed, I would forget the chronic nature of dystonia and revel in the deep pleasures of an integrated self. I could sense my own charm, a vivacity I had little known before, and give in to the temptations of casual overtures in public places, or of phone calls to those to whom I might previously have written letters. I relaxed into my "real self" and old tics vanished. Dexterous sentences, pawky or plump, emerged from my mouth. No longer anxious over self-betrayal, over disguising a flawed self, I could enjoy other people because I took pleasure in myself. I was learning how far I could trust my voice. The internecine war had achieved an armistice.

But sooner or later I would need to test my drug-succoured voice in public. In March of the following spring, an invitation came to read at a symposium in honour of the prolific Canadian man of letters, George Woodcock, on the occasion of his eighty-second birthday. George, friend of George Orwell and Herbert Read, was an unassuming man who had always brought out the worst in my voice, when we spoke in person or by phone. Probably, because I had admired him for decades, and because he himself spoke clearly and well, I felt especially diffident about my speaking disorder. Trying to disguise it only made it worse. Had this invitation come a year earlier, I couldn't have accepted it. Now, by my acceptance, I was signalling a willingness to pay public tribute to George; but I was also taking the opportunity to exorcise a very private demon. My voice was working well under everyday conditions—what would happen on stage, where so often it had not worked?

I still didn't know what I was going to say at the event. This was inauspicious, even for someone who might have sounded like Dylan Thomas (an old drinking pal of George's), and I did not. Then, a week before this large civic celebration for Woodcock, a call from John Metcalf, accepting my large novel for the literary press he represented in Ontario, made it seem that the nightmare of my wife's and my drowning might begin to be resolved. Moreover, someone's faith in my work seemed like an expression of belief in me.

But there was something else. It seemed perversely auspicious for Metcalf, of all people, to accept my novel on the eve of this tribute to George; for it had been at a similar tribute to John, some years earlier on his fiftieth birthday, that I had given one of my worst public readings ever, mortifying myself beyond redemption. A tape of this reading had been presented to John for his library, and I still shuddered to think of my having embarrassed him in public.

I wrote out my tribute to George and rehearsed reading it on the living room carpet. If my voice sank this time, when it finally had a lifeboat, that would be it for any future in public. I began to look forward to the celebration. I knew people with normal voices also felt anxious before speaking in public, even acutely so, but didn't develop mutilating spasms. I now hoped the same held true for my "normal" voice. I felt in control of its sound, and this seemed promising.

The evening for me was a levitating experience—one I hadn't had since childhood, when I didn't know it was levitating, coming out from behind a curtain at a Christmas concert in a darkened church hall, and asking two hundred parents to rise while I recited to them our school's pledge of allegiance. Reading my tribute to George, I relished the way I could strike any word like a piano key, and know its sound would glide through the room without quavering or splitting. Whatever humour my words occasioned seemed welcome, and afterwards I was in the unfamiliar position of receiving compliments. In the past, better work than this would have received scant comment because of how poorly I had read it. People would have been afraid to mention it, for fear of embarrassing me the more.

On Sunday morning I was still floating. My senses cherished perfume from the wisteria, a distant train whistle over a churning neighbourhood lawnmower, the yellow roses in bloom. That morning, I helped coach my son's baseball team for three hours, and it didn't matter that I still couldn't yell. I was smelling the out-field grass. I felt reintegrated. How astonishing to think I could now be a "normal" writer, to accept future invitations that came my way to speak in public.

Had I known that weekend what I would learn over the next few years, I might not have felt quite as confident of the future. It wouldn't always be as easy as this past weekend. I was to discover that when my rehabilitated voice held up under public pressure, it would be with varying results. I would need to relearn the art of public presentation several times over, each reading a separate one to navigate, in a voice never quite at the same stage of regeneration as the last. Little about any voice, least of all a permanently damaged one, could be taken for granted. Little about botulinum toxin could either.

By fall, I found myself straining again when I spoke, whether asking for a coffee at Starbucks or chatting with a mother at a children's soccer practice. I became interested in what happened when these chronic speaking patterns began to recur. I seemed to lose dignity, at least in my own eyes, by trying too hard, as if to make up for any real or imagined failure to communicate smoothly, graciously. A kind of encapsulated desperation set in. Toward the end of any Botox cycle, it seemed knowing you were soon to sound less collected, calm, and disinterested contributed to sounding distracted, tense, and personal.

Liberation from this old, divided self, again became the yearning.

I began to plan my journey. Wanting to escape the everyday self was a common enough reason for travel; an uncommon reason was wanting to listen to voices. Setting out around the world, I possessed not a strand of promise that any foreigners with my disorder would be willing to meet and confide the story of their voices. There were so few of us in the diaspora that finding them would be an adventure in itself, like searching for a rare bird in Costa Rican foliage. (I'd once spotted what I thought of as the "bird of voice," when I was scouting a part of my novel set in Central and South America, an uncommon flame-coloured tanager in the cloud forest of Poás Volcano, beyond San José.) Habitual pressure on larynxes in people like me made for shy, unpredictable encounters. I could only hope they might be encouraged to share their stories of how the effect of misfiring neurotransmitters—vocal cords that overclosed, underclosed, jammed and fluttered—had shaped their characters. I was interested in how such people had dealt with the delicate art of themselves.

I was lucky. I was suddenly free to move through the world with a smooth voice and a purpose for using it. It might well happen, upon my return, that the publication and reception of my novel would leave me wishing I had stayed abroad. But meanwhile, in preparing to fly south, I felt fortunate beyond words. It was to words I turned back again, the night before leaving Vancouver.

The house was still and my family asleep. I pulled down from a shelf *The Trumpet of the Swan*. I read aloud the last paragraph, with my own effortless instrument. This instrument, *my voice out there*, seemed part of me and not part of me at the same time. I read the closing aria most people would never have bothered speaking aloud because they took their own wonderful music for granted.

On the pond where the swans were, Louis put his trumpet away. The cygnets crept under their mother's wings. Darkness settled on woods and fields and marsh. A loon called its wild night cry. As Louis relaxed and prepared for sleep, all his thoughts were of how lucky he was to inhabit such a beautiful earth, how lucky he had been to solve his problems with music, and how pleasant it was to look forward to another night of sleep and another day tomorrow, and the fresh morning, and the light that returns with the day.

4

A Leaf of Voices

I NO LONGER KNEW inside from outside. Which is a novelist's way of saying I had flown sleepless from the voices inside my head, to those outside me now as a traveller. "The voice you hear is not my speaking voice, but my mind's voice. I have not spoken since I was six years old." Reflecting on my long flight here, I happened to think of this voice-over at the opening of Jane Campion's film, *The Piano*—set, incidentally, on a beach not many miles from where I was now sitting in a glasshouse in Auckland.

I was interrupted by a silver-haired man, replying to some overture made to him (evidently by me).

"Yes, leafy, isn't it?"

He was sitting on the bench beside me. He seemed happy to go on.

"I like to think I'm here for the photosynthesis, if that doesn't sound too fervent. Mother used to comment on my liking to sniff plants manufacturing their food like fussy little factories—'They'll put hair in your ears.' I used to be here at holidays, now it's more or less every day. The genes in my blood seem quite addicted to tropical leaves. You'd think they were tobacco."

His was a smiling, wry voice I liked right away. Precise and formal, a little reedy, in concert with the relaxed breathing the foliage seemed to encourage in his slender figure. "This conservatory spoils my nose for the subtropical fragrances outside." It was January outside, the height of summer in New Zealand.

I thought about what he had just said. "Blindfolded," I responded, "I probably couldn't tell you right now whether I was in here or out there."

He chuckled. My accent had placed me as a visitor from the north. And so naturally both places, on either side of the glass, would seem equally redolent.

I had just walked over here to Auckland Domain, past the hospital and empty rugby stadium, where a few voices were murmuring across the emerald turf. On this Sunday morning, the sound of doves and smell of shorn grass greeted me along the road, through eucalyptus and pine. I overheard the fading voices of three Asian tourists, exclaiming at hibiscus blossoms. Korean, perhaps, by their quick, birdish inflections: *"Creen! Creen! Creen! . . ."*

Red earth and a saffron sky had made the half-empty bus ride from the airport into Auckland a movement of monkish pleasure. The sleepy novelist awakening into a social self; an abstemious man with a vocal daydream, determined to get off on other voices by importuning them with his own.

"I was starting to think deaf wouldn't be so bad," said my elderly glasshouse acquaintance. We were sitting together, confiding like an old married couple. His voice smiled wider, as if I weren't to think he was taking himself quite seriously. "My sinuses used to clog up. Mother had to keep wiping my nose."

He sounded very happy, remembering his misfortune. "But for hay fever, I suppose I might have lived here, listening to the plants." He was wearing the uniform of a man equipped for adapting to circumstances in the eye of adversity: a yellow knit tie and a tan, unzippered windbreaker.

"Luckily, I had this organ to remind me what I was missing." He tapped his leaf-addicted nose. "It's still my eyes and ears. A dog listens with his nose. Why not an old goat?"

Apparently, a sinus operation had been a recent success, because a pair of earphones now dangled from his neck.

He explained how in winter he would sit in this tropical house, where the temperature never fell below 18c amidst these figs, ferns and fly-eating carnivores. This was because there were heating vents in the floor. Now that summer was here, he often sat outside in the large courtyard. Outside is where he was headed now, he said, having fed his nose a bit in here.

On the way out, we lingered by the round lily pool to admire the barrel-vaulted window at one end of the glasshouse. *R-r-r-r-i-i-p-p-t-t-t.* The voice of a frog bounced up from the lily pads. It happened a second time, and I wondered if the old man was covering up indigestion.

The expansive courtyard outside was enclosed by brick walls. There were trellises covered in wisteria vines, ivy and flowering honeysuckle. Weddings, cocktail parties, receptions for film stars . . . my companion dutifully catalogued for me the kinds of celebrations that happened here on the flagstoned lawn beside the long, stepped pond full of crimson lilies. "I come for the symphony orchestra. They put up stands, for two or three hundred people, over that side of the pond. The gardener turns off the fountains."

"Any singers?" I asked. "I'm interested just now in voices."

Politely, he thought about this. "You know, I can't recall many vocal recitals." He then touched his nose, as if to recheck his memory. "One, I do. I wish I could remember her name for you. A soprano. Her notes danced off the glass at either end."

Off the tall tropical glasshouse we'd just come from, he meant, and off the tall temperate glasshouse at the other end of the courtyard. With this, the smile in his voice died, and he repeated, "I wish I could remember her name for you." The failure of memory, this failure of exactitude to complement his parted hair and Windsor-knotted tie, his consonant-ticking voice, saddened him. "I mean, if I were to dream up a name for you, right now, inside of an hour I probably couldn't tell you if I'd made it up or remembered it. This recovered memory business is the rage just now, but suspect, if you ask me. Is there anything in it, do you think?"

Then, as if in recompense for forgetting the singer's name, he told me the temperate house beyond had been erected from the profits earned from the Auckland Industrial, Mining and Agricultural Exhibition in 1913. It wasn't heated, of course, like the tropical house. The tropical house hadn't arrived until 1928. It was this tropical house he remembered coming to as a child on holidays. "I remember that as clearly as talking to you inside, a few minutes ago."

Glancing at his watch, he excused himself, to repose on one of the stone benches amid Grecian statuary and giant vats of mauve petunias. "If you like voices, try the temperate house. It's different from the tropical house. Full of birds, always chattering. A bit like me."

I left him listening to his Walkman.

I was listening to the children, their voices delighted by fat goldfish, and the lilies as tall as they, calling to parents from the pond's edge. The Winter Garden, enclosed on all sides by the Domain, and framed by plane, palm and flame trees, formed a pocket for the summer voices of its guests. Fernz Fernery beckoned, and I made a walking tour of its climatic areas and hundreds of ferns, before returning to the courtyard. The temperate house tempted me, its glass walls guarded outside by pots of cacti and prickly pear.

Inside, cool and bright, the place was full of brilliant potted blossoms. Birds called through the glassy air. On one of the cinder paths sat a white cat twitching its tail.

The gardener, a young man in his twenties, was watering the flowers with a fine-misting nozzle attached to a plump hose. He was willing to explain how the difference between this house and the tropical house was regulated. They heated the tropical by hot water pipes under floor grates, a gas generator having recently replaced the decades-old Diesel. He found it clammier working there, no question. Steamier. In here was like working outside, quite pleasant in summer with the doors open. "And I like working with flowers that'll tolerate the Auckland winter. This cyclamen's typical enough." Not exactly a lazy voice, but taking its time to measure what it expressed, while also measuring me.

In what I came to think of as his ponytail voice, though his own hair was short, he volunteered that every glass pane in both houses had been replaced four years ago for a quarter of a million dollars. "That's two hundred fifty dollars per pane I reckon. Making up—how many?—a thousand panes, give or take the extras." He glanced up to the glass roof. "The extras being largely to do with glazing bars and such like. The winter rain leaks in, rusts them over time, so the frames get repaired and repainted simultaneous like."

I camped out on a bench to observe the catwalks above. Chains dangled from pulleys; panes stood open to allow for the circulation of the warm morning air. An indiscriminate riot of scents pleased me and I breathed deeply. I indulged my nose among them, as the silver-haired old man evidently did his in the tropical house. I listened for voices.

Twenty years earlier, over a semester of vocal withering, I had taken refuge in a tropical glasshouse in the middle of a Calgary winter. Exotic birds had sung as I entered, air had grown increasingly moist; among luxuriating lemon trees the aroma of rich humus had soothed my lungs. I could breathe again. My body felt centred, straining no more to speak. If my voice had any chance to regrow, if I were somehow to recultivate it from winterkill, I was always sure the wonder would begin in here. I would climb the staircase and stroll the gallery, gazing down on the verdant jungle—then outside, to the frozen river and its hibernating cottonwoods.

Each visit that winter had reminded me of how shallowly I breathed. Outside, in the frozen air, I hardly drew breath. Inside, I realized how much of life I had been dribbling away in little breaths, barely keeping lungs inflated, doing nothing at all to float my soul. My voice, it was clear to me, had frozen up. At every visit, the glasshouse would loom up out of the frigid zoological gardens like Kafka's ice axe to hack open the frozen sea inside me. I had approached it like one of those rare books you came across that changed your life. I read into it my reprieve.

Yet there had been no reprieve. I had been unable to recultivate my voice. In that winter climate, I seemed bound to live in a more or less permanent season. True, the glasshouse existed to come back to, the vibrant illusion of a transformed self, a flourishing voice. Who could dispute this benefit of illusion over disillusion? If only one could have maintained the artifice.

I sat here recalling voices from my overnight flight among four hemispheres. Was there a filter the voices of pilots passed through, down the long pressurized tube of modern airliners, turning even a Mickey Rooney voice into William Hutt's? Turbines whined, noise whitened, the voices of flight vanished into cloudscapes. Skies were adrift with voices, the way oceans used to be, criss-crossed by liners. Except now, time between embarkation and disembarkation had shortened conversations between passengers from days to hours, chapters to paragraphs, deck strolls to small talk over chicken breasts.

The white cat on the cinder path now stood up. It was as if the sounds and flights of small birds, controlling the movement of her tail, had proved arduous and it was time to rest it. She yawned like a hippopotamus. The tilted-up head dropped, a paw went up to cuff her ear, tail lost its erect posture.

I thought again of the radio announcer's voice on the shelf above my narrow bed at the Kiwi Hotel on Queen Street. Stepping out of the shower an hour or two ago, I'd heard him say how yesterday a handicapped woman here had perished in a house fire because she possessed no voice to call for help. No voice to save herself—this was the angle. A mute woman crying for help, like a tree falling unheard in the forest. How could it have happened?

I sat among the azaleas imagining the mime Marcel Marceau enacting this pyre of voicelessness. "I have spent more than half a lifetime trying to express the tragic moment." He'd meant as a mime, of course, but I remembered he was also an articulate man, in command of almost as many voices as faces.

I recalled from CBC's radio archives an interview with this famously silent Frenchman, performing an amusing multitongued anthology of foreign tongues. His purpose had been to show how meaning was shaded in different cultures by the way people used their voices. To understand and thus mimic the characters he created, he needed to *hear their voices*. Body language rooted in vocal language; one dependent on the other for inflection.

Was this interdependency very different from what the rest of us needed to achieve with our own voices, in creating meaningful characters of ourselves?

"Please join me for a moment! I found something that might interest you!" My silver-haired acquaintance had spotted me emerging from the temperate house. He motioned me over to his bench in the sun. Breathing deeply of the redolent air, he removed his earphones and popped a cassette from the Walkman.

"My poet," he said with a tinge of disclosure. Across the tape, he or someone else had printed in black ink, *Leaves of Grass*. "I had forgotten this passage, but I had a hunch to listen for it after we parted." Pleased, he offered me his headset, pressing the tape back inside. "I must have first heard the passage at a poetry reading, at the Y in New York. Circa 1950 . . ." He turned on the tape and checked his wristwatch. I didn't recognize the voice, but it sounded like Burt Lancaster's.

> *Now I make a leaf of Voices—for I have found nothing mightier than they are,*
> *And I have found that no word spoken, but is beautiful in its place,*
> *O what is it in me that makes me tremble so at voices?*
> *Surely whoever speaks to me in the right voice, him or her I shall follow,*
> *As the water follows the moon, silently, with fluid steps, anywhere around the globe.*

"That's lovely," I said, astonished. "May I copy it out?

"Yes," he responded. "I'll show you how to pause and rewind."

And then he sat watching my hand move across the lines of my notebook, pausing now and then to rewind.

"I wish I could remember that singer for you," he repeated, his voice wry. "She's still gone. I feel ashamed, forgetting her." If ashamed, his voice sounded no less than charming about the lapse. I think this charm allowed him to sound thoughtful, at the same time spontaneous. "Her aria, though, was from *Butterfly*. I remember that much."

He also remembered to introduce himself. "Otto Reinhold," he said, offering his hand. "By rights, the thumb ought to be green." He chuckled. His native accent might have allowed him to pass as Peter Lockwood.

R-r-r-r-i-i-p-p-t-t-t.

Turning away, I heard this frog's voice again. Excited, the children peered into the pond, listening. I caught Otto smiling, studying his watch. I concluded the voice had come from him, thrown into the lily pads to please the children. Belching seemed at odds with his impeccable manners. Maybe he lived by himself.

That evening I took a taxi to Birkenhead on the North Shore where David Barton lived. I had his name as someone with spasmodic dysphonia in New Zealand—likely from a dystonia newsletter about voice, remarking on a far-flung correspondent. I had looked up his number that morning in the local phone book. Confidence in my new voice meant I felt no hesitation in ringing him up to request an interview. Such was David's sense of obligation to the disability we shared that he invited me over for a talk.

The modern glass and frame house where he and his wife, Lyn, lived sat on a wooded lot somewhere above Waitemata Harbour. David's moustache was as dark as his suntan and it suited his green polo shirt. We spoke in a sunroom on the lower level, surrounded by the summer garden outside. The room resembled an orangery and I mentioned my visit that morning to the glasshouses at the Winter Garden. Because his voice was a husky whisper, the cultivated stillness in here seemed favourable to a discussion of David's laryngeal dystonia.

"I had a recent injection."

He confessed that after every injection of botulinum toxin he suffered from extreme breathiness. He obviously considered a faint sound more manageable than a spasmodic one, for in eliminating his spasms the drug also took away his voice. David had had seventeen injections so far, "and only one or two have been satisfactory."

From what he went on to say, it didn't sound like a return to "normal" voice was something he had ever really experienced. I didn't divine this right away, from the enthusiastic way he divided the account of his vocal history into before-and-after-treatment by Botox.

Not that our conversation proceeded chronologically. When David began to talk, I found it hard to keep up with his crisp delineation of the years, cycling back to first signs of vocal disorder, then forward to diagnosis of sd after many misleading treatments. Who knew what was relevant to the etiology?

He had had his tonsils out at the age of six months. At the age of two and a half, soon after he learned to talk, he had difficulty with fluency—so his parents later told him. There were other possible origins of his vocal collapse as an adult. He mentioned an allergy, chronic rhinitis, the cauterization of his nostrils as a teenager. I heard about his use of antihistamines and aerosols. Then an unsuccessful operation at the age of thirty-seven, to enlarge his nasal passages, had caused his disorder to worsen.

David's whispered speech was tiring, he now confessed, and sometimes made him hyperventilate if he pushed too hard. "Yes . . . yes . . . yes . . ." he whispered, by way of punctuating comments of mine intended partly to extend him a little breathing room. His was a desire to be thorough and accountable.

He was forty-three with no children, the associate head of math and sixth form dean at Rangitoto College, a co-ed school of some sixteen hundred students in Auckland. He had authored or coauthored several math textbooks, two of which he later showed me in his study upstairs—one a calculus "crammer," the other a thick softcover—earning him enough, he said, to have financed trips overseas with Lyn.

He enjoyed writing textbooks, as he increasingly did not enjoy the world of teaching and administration. Tired of the effort involved—talking to students, parents, colleagues, boards of examiners—he hoped to retire soon and take a disability pension. At the moment, he was on summer holidays.

David had first experienced a strained voice in his mid-thirties. He didn't know why and voice therapy helped little. Oddly, the strain gradually disappeared after a year. It didn't return for six years. He had a successful operation in this period to enlarge his nasal passages and to remove polyps. Then, when his speech again deteriorated, his GP referred him to a psychologist, whose specialty was motivating rugby teams.

As a logical man, with an otherwise healthy self-image, David felt his problem must be physical. Yet he couldn't escape thinking stress was involved. A seven-week rest one Christmas, however, didn't improve the way he sounded. Words broke, normal speech could only be got out on short breaths. His voice shocked his parents, when he visited them in Wellington. David tried a speech therapist again—and a hypnotherapist, who suggested the problem might be his father. A chiropractor advised him to build up the heel in his left shoe. A colour therapist diddled him with pastels. An acupuncturist did the same with needles. Surprisingly, an ENT prescribed tranquillizers. It was a neurologist who finally diagnosed the disorder.

"It was a relief to have all the speculation out of the way."

David's reedy whisper followed him like a shadow voice, without defining him in any way I found in synch with the fit man in the green polo shirt. It made trying to catch the shape and cadence of what he said difficult, when the weight and timbre of his voice were missing. And yet, paradoxically, instead of getting to know the exterior man, I felt I was getting to know the private one. It was unusual to meet someone in this way.

But also deceptive, because David was someone with a public mission.

For each of his first four injections, he had flown across the Tasman Sea, where the neurologist Paul Darveniza had agreed to treat him in Sydney with the new toxin from America. Since then David had helped bring the treatment to Auckland, by pushing for training of the local ENT surgeon. He'd taken part in an Australian-made video, devoted to spasmodic dysphonia and the ameliorating benefits of poison—which, when it played in New Zealand, led to other New Zealanders with the same disorder contacting him. Since then he had helped to coordinate a network of fellow patients with a regular newsletter he mailed throughout the country.

Meanwhile, his devotion to teaching had slipped.

With effort, David explained how colleagues accepted and respected him, and how understanding his students were of his crippled voice. Only one student had ever made fun of him, mimicking his voice in class. (I supposed there was something irresistible about a spasmodic voice to a good mimic. In the years after my journey, I began noticing how my once piping son could now in adolescence reproduce guttural phrases of my own, when I was having a bad voice day.) The problem wasn't others, David felt, but himself. He was not convinced he wasn't short-changing students, even colleagues. In the staff room, his conversations consisted mainly of one-liners. "They're my specialty." He avoided conversations of any depth, and consequently real contact with others.

He was devastated when spasms had returned after his first injection. When breathiness persisted after subsequent injections, he experimented by reducing the amount of toxin he received, and in which vocal fold. He experimented with frequency of injections, and still enjoyed mixed results at best; the poison hadn't proved the panacea he hoped. "But it relieves the symptoms to some extent and enables one to pretend everything is normal."

He drove me back in the dark across Harbour Bridge, the sound of our tires sometimes masking his soft voice. Feeling I had found a fellow traveller, I retired more cheerfully to my closet in the Kiwi Hotel. I thought again of the poor woman who had perished by fire in a room of similar dimensions.

When we ran into one another later that year in Dallas, and two years after that in San Diego, I knew David's sense of dedication to the cause of better understanding his disorder was something akin to a lifelong calling. His comradeship had extended beyond his own country to the world; he was now welcoming newcomers with dystonia to on-line support groups. On the Internet he later published a photo of himself and his new daughter.

In contrast to past journeys, before botulinum toxin, I was now in danger of becoming a vocal flirt, making overtures to others for the rush their voices gave me and for the pleasure of exercising my own vocal charm. For too many years, my unsociable voice had put others off. Unable then to deploy it spontaneously, I now wanted to be heard as a desirable interlocutor. I wanted to abet voices with my own. I wanted to open myself up and reconstitute the world through trysts. I wanted to listen. I wanted to dally among voices, as among tropical and subtropical smells in glasshouses.

At Auckland Zoo one hot day, meeting elephants on behalf of an elephant fancier in my recent novel, I asked a server in Doolittle's for a beer. She was unused to Canadians. "A what?" "A beer. A lager?" "Oh, a *bear!*" A polar bear on exhibit, a few yards from where we spoke, caused me ever after (like some victim of synaesthesia) to *see* her accent as *white*. And just as indelible, to someone keen on voices, became her café's name, as if it were commemorating the aspiring voice student, Eliza, in Shaw's *Pygmalion*.

Outside the art gallery downtown, a young Englishwoman told me in breezy Midland inflections how, after months in Australia, she had recently arrived in Auckland to stay with a male pen pal, only to discover he was a bore. She was moving on. It made me wonder if she had ever listened to his written voice. Still, admirably arrogant in that youthful way of amuse-me-or-get-lost, she was willing to talk to anyone, including strangers.

My taxi ride to Shirley Linton's house passed by the gums and phoenix palms that bordered the barbered lawns of Albert Park and over the harbour again, to Glenfield, on the North Shore beyond Birkenhead. The driver, originally from Lahore, spoke tartly of what an expensive small city Auckland was compared to Sydney, its superior in every respect, and where he wished he were now living with his brother.

Shirley Linton had grown up on a farm north of Auckland. She remembered her father stuttered. This eldest daughter in a family of six had wanted to go to university and become a doctor. Instead, she went to training college for teachers and received a C certificate in 1958. She married young, and then raised four children on her own when an abusive husband walked out on the family. To survive, Shirley cleaned out hostels and clerked in variety stores. When her youngest child was four, she began relief teaching, taking the child with her into classrooms. She took courses every year to improve her academic qualifications.

She had struggled financially and vocally for twenty-seven years without a break. At present, she was on sick leave from teaching and sleeping in for the first time in her life. It was as close to heaven as she had been in living memory.

"I've always had it," she said, referring to her symptoms. "I had a wavery voice when I sang at fourteen in the choir." As one son told her neurologist, after Shirley began tests, "Mom's voice has always been like that." Her second son, now thirty, had not spoken until he was three and a half; he began to speak with the help of a therapist and only after his father had left them.

Hearing of the poverty, drink and violence in her marriage, an outsider might have thought it was no wonder her voice sounded the way it did. Except, as Shirley said, she had "always" sounded this way. Her husband's diagnosis had been to tell her over and over she was "stupid." Quoting him, "'Boy, you're stupid!'" Shirley threw her head sideways, into an awkward posture, as if fending off the recollection.

Her weak voice had long made her vulnerable. It had stigmatized her, undermining her strength as a full-time teacher. In a short *cri de coeur* written for herself ten years earlier, she had observed: "Years of never ending struggles. One income—mine. Three mortgages, one parent. Four high spirited children to support and educate, alone. Unpaid bills, threatening letters, never enough money, bureaucracy, the farce of the matrimonial court, tired, exhausted, worn out, a woman alone." This before treatment was available, when medical science was ignorant about the true nature of spasmodic dysphonia. Perhaps that ignorance still prevailed.

Even now, after paying off four mortgages over the last ten years, Shirley wondered if her modest sickness compensation, which she hoped to receive for a whole year away from the classroom, would keep her. Last year, a brain scan had cost $1,000 because one doctor happened to think her dystonia symptoms resembled those of multiple sclerosis.

Before her diagnosis in the 1980s her voice had junked out: spasms, breathiness, complete loss of sound. She had to take three months off teaching because of panic attacks. She tried acupuncture. When a neurologist diagnosed adductor spasmodic dysphonia, she tried a speech therapist. Her trouble at school continued.

"I found it very, very difficult. My voice lost its authority. One principal told me it was getting lost in the walls."

She believed she was a good, sympathetic teacher, if only parents didn't jump to conclusions about her "funny voice." Pupils responded well to her. And yet "voice" always came up in yearly evaluations from her principal, who went so far as to tell her, "If I were you, I would leave teaching."

She was slowly finding out what leaving meant. Having recently faced a twelve-person board three times, to qualify for social benefits, each of which appearances she found a horrible experience because of her unreliable voice, she was looking forward to her year off. She still planned to return to the classroom—but if unable to, she thought perhaps she could teach remedial reading and ESL, privately.

If Shirley was a woman hanging on, her vivacious nature belied the story she was sharing with me in her modest living room. Song, for example, had been her solace. She had tried to go on singing, despite tremors and failing pitch. "Singing in a choir brought tremendous joy and pleasure to me," she had written. "I loved the harmony, the challenge, the fun, the bringing it all together. Through my years of struggle, music had been 'music to my soul' and so healing too . . ." Singing was largely how she had defined herself since childhood. Five years ago, unable any longer to reach high notes, she'd been forced to abandon her choir.

Her chronic difficulties in public seemed to run parallel with chronic domestic problems. She was finding recent revelations by her children painful to deal with. Her eldest son had come out two years ago as a gay man. She was still getting used to this when her daughter's disclosure implicating the absent father in something truly disturbing had torn the family apart. For her sons, their father could have committed no abuse of his daughter. This was how things stood in Shirley's life. And yet, fiercely: "I'm proud of my children."

Indeed, their rebelliousness and willingness to work three jobs at one time—in the case of the eldest son, to put himself through college in California—seemed to mirror their mother's indomitable spirit.

She didn't think Botox shots had made much positive difference to her voice, though she was willing to try again during her year off when the negative effect, the dreadful breathiness, wouldn't prove a problem in the classroom. After her second injection, nine months ago, she had gone back to teaching after just one day and found it impossible with seventy-six children. That had been her last injection.

Treatment for Shirley seemed even worse than the disease. Besides voicelessness, she also experienced trauma during placement of needles in her throat.

To my ears her voice sounded tremulous and broken, but not unmanageable. I sat listening to this charming, often laughing woman, in her mauve frock and flat white shoes, with a fine silver necklace and wristwatch, and my eyes kept returning to the biblical slogan embroidered into the little wall hanging behind her chair:

> Faith   Hope   Love
> The greatest of these
> is LOVE

How was it, I wondered, the greatest of these was often foremost in those who seemed to have received the least of it?

On my way back to the city, half-listening to a likeable Samoan cab driver describe, in a rolling surf-like voice, Canada where he had never been but thought he might like to go, I thought about Shirley Linton. She was a person from whom goodness shone, when goodness had not always been done to her. Her voice, in spite of its disease, had made me fall in love with her.

"I'm a very shy person. I tend to appear calm on the outside, but inside I'm actually quite nervous."

Faye Bergosi, whispering, was serving lunch in the kitchen of her Hillsborough home, a blossom-crowded, clapboard bungalow looking south to towering clouds over Manukau Harbour. A cat breeze whiskered in through the open deck door. Her revelations had put a strain in my neck as I bent close to listen, an hour, more, waiting for the actual subject of her voice to come up.

Perhaps I was naïve. Her storytelling was intended to reveal a person *with* a voice. Faye was a masterful gossip who seldom paused for breath. It was breath she was running on.

She admitted she was lonely, given what had happened to her voice.

"Another cup of tea?"

We had begun to pull back from her dark but absorbing verbal crochet of vanished jobs and family houses, plots to keep a tyrannical Hungarian husband's furniture business from failing, their marriage from collapsing—which it did anyway, under the weight of lovelessness ("But you don't want to hear about that, do you?"), failure to discipline their children, and deep financial worries culminating in Faye's having to find an inexpensive house to live in, this one, with her adult son and his girlfriend.

Faye, at fifty-two, was an attractive, greying woman of arcing narratives and artistic talents. She drew and painted. "I like fine things." Her grandfather had been a painter of some renown. The work of Augustus John particularly attracted her. But she was practical. As a photographer, she wondered how she might profit from creating her own greeting cards. She currently worked as a secretary to a plastic surgeon, but he was due to retire in two months, at which point she would be out of work again.

Mr. Williams, the surgeon, had become more understanding of her vocal difficulties following diagnosis. Still, his wife couldn't keep coming in to help her out after each toxic injection crippled Faye's voice, could she? So Faye was having to ask her own mother and sisters to assist with patients on the phone and in the office. No wonder she experienced tears and depression, during these extended periods of needle-induced breathiness. She'd felt increasingly imperilled by her disorder, frustratingly isolated by its treatment, a not uncommon occurrence.

An impossible situation now seemed to govern her life. She feared the shots themselves, but worse, the relief of the severe symptoms—the spasms and broken speech—didn't seem to make up for the profound isolation from others she experienced with her voice knocked out.

"Even good friends can't *really* understand why the 'cure' never kicks in." Her eyes moistened. "Why can't people understand?"

She was trying hard to understand for them. "People can only assimilate so much information about other people's problems, especially obscure information."

She had just lost a friend, a neighbour who couldn't fathom what had happened to Faye's voice. Possibly, Faye felt that her own grasp of the neurological entanglements was too infirm to explain her chronic disability to others. She just wanted them to be kind.

At present she was on holidays, making occasional attempts to call people, taking solitary jaunts to parks. She was on Prozac and loved to garden. Her last shot had been a week ago. She spoke of trying to cope with her disease and of suicidal feelings. Once, trying to phone a fellow spasmodic sufferer, she must have sounded like an obscene caller because whoever answered hung up. Faye said her normally deep voice had given its first hint of disorder when she was answering phones in a dentist's office on Healy Avenue. It was "He   aly" that started coming out wrong.

Her voice worsened after that.

A doctor prescribed tranquillizers and she tried muscle relaxants. Chiropractic, speech therapy, X-rays all followed, in the effort to repair her degenerating vocal cords. A hypnotherapist charged $750 for two sessions. "But I only went to one because I didn't think he was acting the way he should." An acupuncturist made her voice worse. She tried relaxation tapes and yoga. She had to give up the job on Healy Avenue.

Finally, three years ago, she found her way to an ear, nose and throat specialist. The ENT's diagnosis of spasmodic dysphonia was later verified by a speech therapist. Not until a year after this did she receive her first injection of toxin; she was among the first in New Zealand to receive the new therapy.

With Faye, there had seemed little sense of watershed in discovering what she suffered from. Her stress over having to take a needle in her neck was acute. The surgeon found it difficult to find her larynx, repeated injections bruised her neck, she feared choking and found it hard to swallow afterward. And the treatment seemed less than effective. Her world had collapsed and, with the prospect of losing her present job, wasn't recovering very fast.

The remarkable thing to me seemed her capacity for hope. The future had possibilities. "I love to garden," she repeated. And indeed the window in her study, where she proudly took me to view her charcoal portraits and watercolours, the nude sketches from a life drawing class, looked out on a stunning fountain of Scarlet O'Hara bougainvillea, King's Ransom roses, and a silk tree.

She also had children to be proud of, adults now, a headstrong ocean-sailing daughter and two sons, one of whom was in computer graphics with two houses.

Faye offered to drive me back via their old family home near Hillsborough Bay, which she stopped for us to admire. Then she drove up the steep extinct volcano of One Tree Hill Domain, for a spectacular sweeping view of Auckland and beyond.

The site on top was the remains of an old Maori fortification, crowned by a single gigantic tree, which was in traction at vast public expense because of a lingering dispute with the Maoris. One of them had angrily attempted to chop down the tree, now surrounded by an iron fence and tethered on all sides by ropes to keep it steady in the wind, "bandaged in canvas and black plastic," whispered Faye, "in hope of somehow healing its heartwood and bark."

The wind blew warmly up here. Later, she drove us past her old high school in the fancy Mt. Eden district. Atop Mt. Eden itself we could see back across to One Tree Hill Domain, a similar island in this hilly city of islands, harbours and peninsulas. Faye pointed out landmarks, distant beaches. She expressed satisfaction in listening to the surrounding voices. Fragrances of semi-tropical vegetation wafted up the slopes.

I wondered how she would make out when she lost her job in March.

At the end of that year, she wrote to me in Vancouver.

Her resilient voice seemed to reflect her creative side, her capacity for joy. She'd "started working at Fletcher Challenge in the lowly position of 'Mailroom Assistant.' It was really freaky knowing my job was finishing & that it was no use applying for any other similar positions as I couldn't cope with the phones & a dear friend who works here heard about this job & thought it would be perfect as it wouldn't matter if I couldn't talk. The 'perfect' part is that there is a fantastic art collection here, including I think, 6 of my grandfather's paintings. There are huge beautiful fresh flower arrangements everywhere I walk & all the best pottery from the Fletchers Pottery Awards. The place is like a plush hotel. I have met so many lovely people. The only thing is that the work can be very heavy as I sort & then deliver mail through 3 complete bldgs. Most have lifts but there are stairs in one part & that is very difficult."

She had begun to receive Botox injections—on just one side now, which had "reduced the trauma for me which was the worst part but [with] the January TX I lost my voice for *10* weeks & the June one for *8!* I also don't have such a good result once my voice comes back." She added, "Everyone has got used to me at work with my 'sexy' voice so it doesn't matter." Her letter was enclosed in a simple, beautifully designed card, her own photograph of orange velvet blossoms pasted to the front. Through a friend's flower shop, she had begun to sell her greeting cards, of which she now had about one hundred designs.

She was, as she said herself, someone who liked fine things.

On the morning I left Auckland, for the seaside town of Napier, I learned of the earthquake in Kobe, Japan, a day or two before. The only news I had caught since arriving in New Zealand was about the local house fire and the voiceless woman who perished in it. It seemed an odd coincidence that I was now heading for a town destroyed by a 7.9 earthquake in 1931.

Known as the Great Hawke Bay Earthquake, it had given rise to the "newest city on the globe," when downtown Napier was reconstructed in the art deco style of the period. It had also given rise to more land, lifted in places to a height of eight feet. Much broader now than it was, the beach extended far out beyond the Norfolk pines on Marine Parade, a road that once had run beside the sea.

Here, where Captain Cook visited in 1789, stood the concrete-pillared Veronica Sun Bay, each pillar sponsored by a local business or individual, as if raised in good faith against any more acts of God shaking local civic spirit. A sonnet to commemorate this spirit was reproduced on a plaque. I thought of Shirley Linton and others, defying no less traumatic tremors on the Richter scale of *voice*: that spectrogram's irregular, wide-spaced, vertical striations instead of spikes, telling its tale of vocal quakes and spasms.

At the city museum, where the earthquake was also commemorated, I watched a video one morning about Maori art. "Where there is art, there is human dignity." The Maori, in other words, prized visual art for its coherence, integrity and understanding. I imagined this proverb was equally true of their oral arts encapsulated in the term *waikora*. It gave me pleasure to think a true oral culture, unlike our own oral culture, would carefully make of voice an art.

I was wondering about this when I visited Broadcast House downtown, a large art deco building with a high-ceilinged foyer and noisy offices. I was looking for an announcer or deejay to interview. I wanted to hear a polished voice wax eloquent on its profession, as I weighed the notion of a true oral culture. Disembodied voices echoed in the building, which resembled a converted bank full of ghosts demanding withdrawals.

"I'm afraid they've all gone home for the day," said the blue-eyed receptionist. "They were all here earlier. Now the only ones left are on air."

It was a curious phrase. So much of our oral culture was summed up in that bodiless "on air." The amplification of voice, the electrical transmission of voices—by radio, telephone, TV, computer, tape and compact disc—into every room, car, and jogging ear—had led to the *semblance* of an oral culture. Yet ours bore little resemblance to any oral culture of earlier centuries, when voices had to be physically close enough to hear.

Bodies behind "air" voices were often taken for granted, I thought. Did we even appreciate, or think it mattered that these voices, when squeezed through woofers, boosted by batteries and bounced off satellites, sounded different "in person"? We forgot how recently electricity had changed how we heard the human voice. Listening to voice today was often the equivalent of smelling a rose over the Internet. It had lost its physical, organic presence. Insofar as the electrified voice had no true sound, but could be fiddled with by bass, balance, treble and volume, communication was artificial. The same voice could range from tinny to plummy. My Uncle Harry sang *White Christmas* with the heartfelt voice of Bing Crosby, impressing us all, on a karaoke machine. It was easy to forget that such voices bore about as much resemblance to natural voices as parking lots did to fields. We didn't come upon them in the same way. Their sound didn't enter us like the smell of grass.

I could only have begun thinking of this in Napier, itself a much smaller and quieter place than Auckland, three hundred kilometres north. Used to cities, convinced I could not live without one, I was puzzled here when, walking through the streets one Friday morning, I encountered silence. I even stopped to ask a woman about it. She was washing a shop window.

I smiled. "Is this the usual amount of traffic in Napier?"

She lowered her squeegee and looked up and down the street, wiping her hair back. "Well. I dunno." She wanted to be helpful. She checked her watch, searching for an answer.

"It's Friday," she said. This apparently meant that she couldn't yet blame whatever quiet I was complaining about on the weekend. So she decided to humour my suspicion, that it actually did sound quiet. "I wouldn't say it's busy this week, no. This week the food is rotting on the shelves."

"Pardon?"

"Next week'll be busy. All the pensioners, the solos, the handicapped, the young—they all get their cheques next week. All over

New Zealand. It's the same all over. Twice a month. The economy depends on it. How long yeh here for?"

She was quick to suggest, because nothing much was happening in town, I might like to drive up a local mountain, you know, for a bit of an adventure. When I mentioned I didn't have a car, she offered to drive me up herself.

". . . Except I got the grandkids. But here, there's a taxi next door . . ." A dispatcher's office, which looked closed for lack of business. She explained with genuine enthusiasm the views to be had from the top of—I forget the name of the mountain—over the whole of Hawkes Bay.

"You should see all the shit from up there."

Shep, she must have said. *Sheep*.

"Just like little balls, way below ya."

It was a town surrounded by fields. A country with more sheep than people, she declared, repeating the national mantra. Yet try as she might, with vehicles running by every two or three minutes, she couldn't quite bring herself to think of Napier as less than clamorous.

It was not as if noise at night—passing traffic on Marine Parade, or an astoundingly raucous train—didn't occasionally interrupt my sleep. But the sound was transient. A burst of noise, then a return to absolute stillness. A kind of default state. I could tell I wasn't in a real city, by the lack of abiding white noise. It seemed to me that such uncommon stillness valued the human voice, creating the main condition for an oral culture. It was misleading to mistake the prattling world I was used to for a vocal one.

That afternoon, Ginny Collinge dropped past my motel on Marine Parade, in an orange BMW approximately the colour of her dress. Ginny had just fetched her "older" sister at the airport. I noticed Caroline, just off the plane from Christchurch, was letting her hair go grey, and for an unrelated moment I thought of Botox. Ginny herself lived some miles south, in Havelock North, but had offered to meet me in Napier after my calling long-distance the other day from Auckland. I was exhilarated to be using my voice and calmly persuading strangers to rendezvous. Like Ginny, I was counting on Botox to keep me sounding artificially natural. A kind of bottle blond.

The three of us drove to Anatole's, a classy art deco café on Browning Street, full of rattan furniture, marble-topped tables and polished hardwood planks. An attractively groomed woman, Ginny looked younger than she probably was. Her son and daughter were now in their mid- to late twenties. Fifteen years ago, Ginny and her husband Jeremy had lived for a time in Malawi. I gathered Jeremy was a chartered accountant.

She wanted me to speak a little about myself before talking of her own voice. When she did, she spoke quietly and without waste words. Three and a half years earlier, working as an occupational therapist in a home for the elderly, she had experienced an isolated incident in placing a phone call.

"My voice was not coming out. I'd been nervous about the call."

A year after that, when she was suffering from a bad flu, her voice abruptly worsened. It deteriorated to a whisper. She consulted a puzzled but supportive MD who sent her to an ENT. This patronizing specialist left her with the impression that he considered her vocal affliction to be psychological.

"I knew it wasn't psychological. It had to be physical."

I was impressed, remarking on her sovereignty of mind to have believed from the start in a physical origin.

Not that the conviction had particularly helped in her job, replied Ginny. Having to force her voice, for the benefit of hard-of-hearing seniors, had proved a great strain. She had also been counselling children of alcoholics. It began to be embarrassing, depressing, finally impossible, to make herself understood at all.

She'd given up her job in occupational therapy.

Then, two years ago this January, she and Jeremy had driven north to Auckland, to see an ENT in private practice. With their family about to go on holiday, and herself reduced to a whisper, Ginny hoped for a diagnosis of what was wrong with her broken, spaced-out voice. Her face now brightened as she put down her teacup. Caroline smiled conspiratorially.

All on the same day, she'd had a blood test, endured a CAT scan, visited a neurologist, and learned she had adductor spasmodic dysphonia. "I was elated! I could finally put a name to my condition." The diagnosis confirmed her conviction that the disorder was physical. It made their family vacation especially sweet that year.

I must have asked about dystonia in her family, or about her voice at a younger age, because this led the sisters into a discussion of how old Ginny was when their mother died of cancer. Fourteen. She didn't remember any change of voice at the time. So far, her son and daughter hadn't appeared to exhibit any symptoms of dystonia either. Caroline then said she'd noticed a change in Ginny's voice upon her return from Malawi, fifteen years ago. Ginny thought about this, but said she didn't recall any change. She picked up her fork and buried the tines in her cake.

Since diagnosis, she had received seven or eight injections of toxin. "Neither of the first two shots helped much." For the third, which she remembered as the best so far, her dosage was increased and the benefit immediate. "I went home singing. My voice lasted nineteen weeks—the longest I've gone between injections."

Unfortunately, subsequent treatments had not been as successful. "The last two haven't worked out well. They were very painful." Her sense of trauma had grown.

For each injection, she and her husband drove six hours to reach Auckland the day before the Monday clinic. They met other patients there—"all sounding very calm, *prior* to their shots"—before she and Jeremy returned home late Tuesday, having missed two days of work.

Seven weeks since her last treatment had now left her sounding poor. Or so she felt. Not that she sounded apologetic, or reluctant to talk on the phone. She tried to speak softly, she said. To me her quiet voice sounded useable and even winsome. Currently, she was running a quilting store as well as teaching high school children how to quilt. She found the young more sympathetic than the old. For example, she said smiling, "If I have to whisper to them they'll just whisper back."

I asked if having SD meant she had developed a greater empathy for handicapped people—people like *us*—and she thought for while.

"Ginny has always been a compassionate person," interjected Caroline.

Ginny then reached down to open her purse. Insisting tea was on me, I removed the bill from the table.

"No," she apologized, "it's this I wanted. David Barton sent me this."

It was a card David had had printed up for members of their support network, to show to strangers in case they ever found it impossible to converse. Ginny handed me hers across the marble table. The message was based on the same principle deployed by deaf-mutes, at bus stations in India, who regularly solicited donations in the aisle of your bus before a journey. But with a difference. Ginny's card was neither faded from overuse nor asking for more than understanding. There was even a touch of whimsy.

Not so long ago a deaf and mute man had come into her quilt shop, gesticulating, frustrated he wasn't making himself understood. Suddenly inspired, Ginny had gone to her wallet and handed him her card:

> I have Spasmodic Dysphonia and I
>   sometimes have difficulty speaking.
> I can hear and understand you.
> My name is Ginny Collinge.
> Patience and good humour will help
>   communication.

Reading it, the man had begun to wave it enthusiastically back at her, delighted by their common ground.

From Browning Street I made my way a mile up Bluff Hill, threading through stacked houses and close tropical vegetation, to the top over-looking Hawkes Bay and lumber-stacked wharves far below. These recalled the coniferous forests planted with great regularity up and down the hills I had travelled through on my way south to Hamilton.

A retired man in short pants had boarded my bus in Hamilton, grabbing the empty seat beside mine. "Anyone sitting here?" I told him no. "There is now, mate." He then talked non-stop the entire way to Taupo. I wondered if a voice disorder might not have saved him from himself. Never had I wished this on anyone before.

My revenge against this bore was in allowing myself to be not so quietly amused by lines I was trying to read in a review of a recent novel by William Trevor in the *New York Times Book Review*: ". . . Mr. Hilditch is the type who spends his Sunday afternoons visiting stately homes and engaging strangers in the sort of mindless chat the English are so good at. He is, it appears, a man of stultifying banality, respectability and mediocrity."

Since he was also, it turned out, a man who picks up young female hitchhikers and eventually does away with them, I was given to vengeful speculations about what my travelling companion himself might be covering up as he glibly chewed my ear. I couldn't have been more delighted when, to my amazement, he pointed out the window at a pair of hitchhikers.

"Would you pick up those hitchers?" Clearly scum, to this Mr. Hilditch. He thought he knew without asking what my answer would be.

"Yes."

"You *would?*" His voice changed registers, going up where mine had gone down, astonished by an opposing point of view. "Not me, nohow."

Nonsense, I thought. I imagined him stopping for the hitchers. I survived his verbal chloroform, the stultifying banality of his voice, by cherishing murderous thoughts of him in collusive tandem with William Trevor's character.

When Mr. Hilditch at last got off by the lake in Taupo, still yakking, he looked like a man exposed to the world. I hoped it would only be a matter of minutes before he was picked up and tossed in the slammer for oral manslaughter.

He left me remembering a lunch I had once enjoyed with the laconic William Trevor, by another lake, in southern Ontario. Trevor was a kindly man who preferred listening. When he did speak, it was modestly, humorously, of his early ambition to be a sculptor and his need, still, to feel the stories he wrote as objects shaped and hewn. You sensed his attraction to the palpable crime writing of Patricia Highsmith, who was savouring her own ciga-rette smoke across the tablecloth, there in Niagara-on-the-Lake, and, otherwise, her own whisky-voiced opinions. His voice was precise and unassuming. Now, in the bus, I thought one could take the Maori proverb about art and alter it just slightly in Trevor's case: "Where there is voice, there is human dignity."

I could see for miles in every direction from atop Bluff Hill. Not a sheep to be seen, however, until the following day.

The next morning on a bus to Palmerston North, and eventu-ally Paraparaumu Beach, I sat watching the bright tawny land-scape screen past, rows of trees instead of hedgerows among fields, sheep and cattle farms. The motion of travel felt as structured as cinema. Travelling, I had probably always sensed this illusionary escape from my movement disorder without even knowing it.

"Keath?"

Marie Allison, in sunglasses and shorts, her granddaughter and a teenage babysitter in tow, was waiting for me at the station in her BMW. She drove us all gaily back to a large, white clapboard house on the beach, where she served me a lemon tea, Christmas cake and tiny waffles, in a living room furnished with a grand piano and a small black dog with a tricky disposition. The disposition sniffed my shoes.

"She likes you," said Marie, surprised. "She doesn't get along with me at all."

"It's probably the food," I replied, putting jam on a waffle. "She's hoping for a handout."

Marie was wearing a sleeveless blouse and her tinted hair neat. Now sixty-six, she had suffered from vocal disorder only since the age of fifty-eight. Eight years ago, around the time Anna was born, Marie remembered catching the flu. She found her voice growing tight, then worse, going into spasms. A family doctor sent her to an ENT, who sent her to a speech therapist in Wellington. Marie attended therapy for a year with no improvement.

As a soprano she loved choral singing, but like Shirley Linton had had to give up her avocation. She explained how "frightening, scary, isolating" it was, as the years went by, to be crippled by a condition no one seemed to have a name for. Telephone calls had terrified her, both receiving and making. "I wanted to cut the phone off." This severely tested her love of conversation. "I'd always *loved* to talk." Yet she refused to give in to fear, forcing herself out to public events.

The therapist in Wellington finally sent her to a neurologist, who put her on tranquillizers. The neurologist, incidentally, was the husband of the speech therapist. "He was later struck off the register in New Zealand for interfering with patients. He never interfered with me," said Marie.

Before leaving for Brisbane, where he was also struck off the register, he'd put her in hospital for a brain scan. When that turned up negative, she saw a psychiatrist, and then, over the course of year, a psychologist. She quoted his counsel: "'If you ever feel like taking your life . . .' I was so incensed by his remark!" Like Ginny Collinge, she had no fear for her mental health.

But you could understand how professionals might want to equate vocal anxiety with depression and nervous breakdown. The diagnosis of dystonia was an elusive one when you didn't know what to look for. I had noticed Marie blinking when she spoke. It was simple to conclude that perhaps her focal dystonia wasn't limited to the larynx. Unfortunately, most professionals had never heard of blepharospasm either, seeing it only as a symptom to confirm a general diagnosis of mental strain.

Desperate, Marie wrote to the *Daily Telegraph* in London—to follow up on an article in which she'd read about a new treatment for a disorder sounding suspiciously like her own. She received back a letter from Dr. Garfield Davies at Middlesex Hospital, with information about his injections of botulinum toxin for laryngeal dystonia. Marie wasn't certain she had this, but wrote to ask if she might come to London for an examination and perhaps treatment.

And so in London her condition was finally diagnosed.

Alas, following her long and hopeful journey, the two injections she received didn't help her voice. "I was terribly disappointed." She returned to New Zealand, after her traumatic ordeal, relieved to know at least she had received a proper diagnosis.

Marie's daughter in Sydney then heard about botulin shots being given there, at St. Vincent's Hospital. And Marie happened to see the 1991 Australian TV program on spasmodic dysphonia, with David Barton. After writing to Dr. Paul Darveniza, she was invited to Australia for treatment.

The day her voice came back was momentous. "I was thrilled. Such a release. I can still remember that day. I called out to my granddaughter, from my bed."

Marie would return three or four times a year to Sydney for treatment. Eventually, after Botox came to New Zealand, she travelled to Auckland instead. But she sounded nostalgic for Dr. Darveniza. "Paul has a knack of hitting the bull's-eye. I can tell right away whether a shot is a success. I don't know what it is. I can just tell." Her last treatment in Auckland hadn't been truly effective, and talking to me, she said, her voice felt poor. "I can feel it packing it up."

Though choppy, she was understandable.

"I feel so sorry for young people with this, like you and David. I'm old. But you have the rest of your life ahead." She was appalled to hear how old I really was and how long I had had the disease.

Keen for me to hear a tape of her singing, made around the time she was seeing the speech therapist, Marie now led us upstairs, past naval charts, to a glass room where we could see the bright beach and ocean beyond. Kapiti Island stood offshore and there were sailboats tacking in the strait. The afternoon sun spilled into the room. A copy of Jung Chang's *Wild Swans* lay on the table. It was like sitting in your own glasshouse, except the vegetation was outside. Marie plugged in a tape, and went downstairs to see about her roast in the oven.

"This is May thirteenth . . ." she began, not thinking to give the year. She then accompanied her voice on the grand piano. *Some day my heart will find you . . .* Her soprano voice swept me lyrically away across the sea, her sweet afflicted sound persisting through several verses, as if at this early stage, before diagnosis, she felt she might still sing herself back into fluency. Listening, one could hear problems with high notes and involuntary closures of the larynx.

Between songs, Marie would speak honestly about the condition of her voice, and how it would perform better at certain times of day than others. This unpredictable quality alone might have been evidence of a movement disorder, had her therapist and doctors not been listening for clues to a psychological problem instead.

I sometimes wondered why opera singers in decline were never discussed in neurological terms, and supposed it more dramatic and therefore satisfying for connoisseurs of operatic palaver to connect a suspect voice such as Maria Callas's to a driven, unsatisfactory life. It was easier to explain a faulty larynx as a symptom of damage resulting from a predisposition to self-destructiveness than as evidence of a neurological narrative that could give rise to no gossip. Neuroses made a better plot than neurons.

When I finished listening to Marie Allison's tape, she took me outside where we sat in the back yard drinking Steinlagers in the shade. She relaxed. I began to hear her as friends would. She talked casually of her children and grandchildren, of the eighty-five-year-old man who still came to do her garden, of the difficulty in keeping an older house in repair. Her late English husband, serving the Royal Navy in the war, had been conservative and proper. Since his death, Marie admitted to getting out more, volunteering and having a grand time—for example, at the writers' section of Wellington's Festival of the Arts. Her lively sense of humour was in full flower, despite all that had happened to her voice in widowhood.

Crimson blossoms of the pohutukawa tree, the smell of roasting lamb, our proximity to the ocean, all made me think I could be no where else but in New Zealand. Driving me to the train station, Marie pointed out the little airport her husband's catering business used to service. When I heard from her by letter, a year later, she was flying to Australia once again for injections. "I find [Paul Darveniza] very quick with the injections & very sure, & it's all done with the minimum of fuss. I have the utmost confidence in him & we have a good rapport." Eight months had gone by since her last injection, and she was missing her next appointment that very day in Sydney because she'd recently fallen and broken her wrist, also crushing her vertebrae. "So by the time I finally get there I'll be practically speechless. This is the most I've been, & the longest between injections. It's amazing how you cope. As I live on my own I have no option. I'm well passed the embarrassed stage. Even the phone doesn't faze me now."

Two years after this, Marie was writing again, this time from Sydney, to say her latest Botox had been very successful following two that hadn't worked at all. "He increased the dosage this time & it did the trick." She added that an ENT in Sydney was looking for volunteers to operate on, to separate their adductive vocal cords, probably with silastic wedges, but she was going to wait till the guinea-pig stage was over.

I caught the local electric train that afternoon, and made a slow drowsy tour south through the coastal landscape of small towns, stopping at each one along the way as if it stood for the end of time. You could see the ocean off to the west, shining, till at last the land heaved up, and we began tunnelling back into time. After one last tunnel we burst out the other side of a mountain. Wellington Harbour now lay on the opposite side of the train. The intense blue sky seemed very different from the monsoonal sky I could remember, entering Wellington by ferry ten years earlier from Picton.

I barely understood the voice of my Cambodian taxi driver, who drove me from the station to Trekker's Hotel. His soft vowels were all wrong for his new language. I managed to make out that his educated relatives, "those with knowledge," had been killed by the Khmer Rouge. When I tipped him, a little extravagantly for such a short ride, his chronically anxious face broke into an unexpected smile, as if I was his first conquest in Wellington since his arrival in a country that discouraged tipping.

In the morning I rode Wellington's cable car up to the university. I was hoping to visit an old colleague from Canada, a stutterer who'd once advised me to see a "shrink" about my voice. His was the expected response at the time, when damaged voices, including his own, were still usually traced to the nurture side of the ongoing debate about causes. I now wondered how much his thinking about our voices might still be governed by the notion of psychological abuse.

I also wondered how stuttering had shaped him as a social being. Stutterers seemed to possess a disarming if unsought ability to ingratiate themselves with others. He did, anyway (not that he was aware of it). People were somewhat more familiar with stuttering than other vocal disorders, more willing to listen sympathetically, whereas spasmodic dysphonia threatened them, its alarming guttural sounds suggesting you might be a mental case who was better avoided.

This attitude no longer included me, if it ever had. I was pleased with the warm willingness of people so far to welcome me, and not just people with voices like mine. I had spent the previous evening having coffee with an ESL teacher I'd met in Napier. She lived here in Wellington, was interested in yoga, and had a deep philosophical interest in how the "core" self differed from the "chatterbox" self.

I had hoped my former colleague might help me carry on this conversation over much catching-up. Having tried to contact him ten years ago, on my earlier New Zealand visit, I'd discovered he was out of the country on summer holidays.

Alas, I now found out from his office colleague he was away again.

In the Botanical Gardens I phoned home, where it was still yesterday. Travelling in the future was an aberration I never got used to, coming as I did from one of the last time zones in the west where there remained opportunities for revision and the second chance, after the rest of the world had moved on. Vancouver, in this sense, reminded me of a novel as much as a city.

I walked from there to Katherine Mansfield's family home on Tinakori Road. In the small rooms I listened for voices. KM's work is distinguished by its voices. From the back yard, on this perfect day, I peered down a bushy ravine to the harbour. I made it to the wharves in time to catch the catamaran to Day's Bay.

This was where her family had summered, and where she set two influential stories. Vocal sketches in "At the Bay" include that of an infant as well as insects and animals impersonated by the story's children. For Mansfield the art of voice seemed to exist, as in Maori culture, in its evanescence. Perishable (hence cherishable) voices haunted her, as they did the writer she influenced most with these fictions (including "Prelude"), Virginia Woolf.

It was very hot at Day's Bay and I wilted under a manuka tree. The sea was now flat, the sand blinding, the crowds in a holiday mood. I took tea in the old pavilion and had no luck finding a summer cottage once owned by Katherine Beauchamp's family. It didn't matter. The surrounding bush and gullies felt too sticky for loitering.

Next day as I crossed Cook Strait to Picton it rained as heavily as it had ten years earlier when I came over in the opposite direction. This time I sailed aboard the fast new catamaran, a wide-bodied shuttle with stewardesses. It left at 8 a.m. and encountered rough passage and poor visibility. Lifted above it by hydrofoils, reading *The New Yorker*, I barely noticed.

Two hours later, in the Lynx Express, I left Picton in a cramped club-car seat reserved for me in Wellington. The locomotive ahead jolted and squealed. A wet landscape of forested mountains eventually gave way to drier hills, scantier vegetation and sheep farms. Reaching the east coast, we continued south to Canterbury.

At Blenheim I was joined by a tall blond American in a plaid shirt, who had the narrow seat facing mine. We chuckled at the coincidence of our adjacent reservations in an otherwise deserted car. Clearly, a rugby team was expected at the next stop. He offered to move across the aisle, but I said why risk imprisonment? His composed and ingratiating manner resembled a land economist's from Boston, with a voice like Robert Kennedy's. He was, in fact, a land economist from Massachusetts who had studied at Harvard. His three-week vacation, camping and hiking around the South Island, was now ending with the return of his rented motorcycle. From the grape country here in Marlborough, he was returning south.

We began a long, intermittent conversation ranging over ecology and North American culture, literacy and bad journeys, this country and India. Once the conductor had checked our tickets for compliance and good behaviour, she offered us quieter, wider seats with large windows in the following carriage, where we encountered other passengers, including a talkative farmer who raised sheep and deer and was getting into emu. A grey sky hung low over the sea. The sheep on the hills looked soiled.

Entering Kaikoura, we noticed none of its ocean's famous sperm whales or dolphins, only a few crayfish boats alongside red-painted sheds. My friend said the scene reminded him of a New England town, and, staring at it, you could see how a picture of it might have been hung in Winnipeg, say, to entice visitors to either the New England coast or this one. I wondered whether the exotic (now we were inside it) was ever present when you were actually there.

We didn't arrive in Christchurch until 3:45 p.m. A little regretfully, I said goodbye to my friend from Boston. I was interested these days in how the fleeting friendships of travel seemed to score the memory deeper than similarly casual encounters at home. Did the movement of travel have something in common with the imagination of dream? Did having a movement disorder, moreover, mean you moped about it more than was normal? I rode into town with another American, this one from Australia, visiting her sister here on the South Island. Her sister was scheduled for a tricky operation on the inner ear. The taxi stopped to let her out, and I knew I would never see *her* again either. I was becoming the Rachmaninov of itinerant conversationalists, with special emphasis on the Preludes.

The drizzle seemed to be letting up.

Settling into a reasonably priced motel on Worcester Street, I called Melva McIlroy. She invited me over to her house in Hornby, as soon as I wanted to come.

I walked the mile into the centre of Christchurch, ate a quick supper and caught the public bus. I stepped out of it some time later, in the middle of a flat suburb ruled by power pylons. Lost, I wandered up blockless streets and looped into crescents. Bungalows had been set down in a manner calculated to confuse alien intruders in the overcast, fading light. Whole neighbourhoods were devoid of people and dogs. The humidity felt electric. I saw a cat, but it turned out to be a pail. No one of interest lived here.

Blind luck let me blunder into Lomax Place and up to a brick bungalow with a patch of lawn, a date palm and a small conservatory enclosing a front porch. I had no idea how I would find my way back, or whether taxis came out to this side of the moon. My only hope was a Honda Civic, with racing stripes, parked in the garage.

Unfortunately, the tiny old lady who answered the door in a broken voice appeared largely immobile. Melva McIlroy had a sweet humorous face and obviously no awareness of the world beyond her flower garden. I already regretted the visit. Settling into her favourite chair, its antimacassar at the level of her white hair, Melva folded her navy skirt to one side and waited for me to begin.

I must have mentioned the disorder we shared.

"I been there and back," she said, twinkling when she said it. "Everything happened to me at sixty."

"Why don't you tell me about it? How old are you now?"

Seventy-six, and she had had adductor spasmodic dysphonia for just eight months. Mercifully, then, her story would brief and I could be out the door before dark. Another damaged voice, though this one couldn't have had time to engage the heartache, affliction, poverty and violence I had been privy to on the North Island.

I learned that Melva, at sixty, had taken charge of her life following the death of an alcoholic husband. This had been a distinctly positive development, even if it meant working three jobs for the next four years. During these years she had risen at 4:00 a.m. to work as a janitor at the airport, before beginning her regular day job at the chocolate factory. To fill the weekends, she'd secured her licence to drive a taxi.

I sat up.

She had needed work to survive, but also to save for a trip abroad.

She was pleased in retrospect about her career as a cab driver. And tickled that at the same age as getting her taxi licence, she learned to play the church organ. But she was downright delighted to have made a trip to Maui, where she received a certificate for visiting Father Damien's chapel at an old leper colony, after riding a mule down a two-thousand-foot mountain.

"I been there and back."

"You really came out of your shell, didn't you?"

"I really did," she said, smiling.

Her so-called shell, I now discovered, had begun to enclose her after leaving her Woolworths job in Christchurch at age seventeen. Melva had been working since she was fourteen, but decided to enter a convent with the Sisters of Calvary, a nursing order, who had promptly shipped her to Australia. There she felt isolated, homesick and often ill for the two and a half years she lived in a Sydney convent. Her mother had had cancer before Melva left New Zealand. And died after Melva was away only six months. Yet this news was kept from the girl, as she was forbidden to read letters from home. (Was this the saddest story I had ever heard?) Melva spent her first six months as a postulant, wearing a small headscarf, and then twelve months as a novice in a white veil, never allowed to visit the hospital or practise the nursing vocation that had drawn her to the order in the first place.

Convent life in the 1930s had included silent retreats of up to a week's duration. If you spoke so much as a word, the "goodie-goodies" would "snitch" on you. Even if you *hadn't* spoken, said Melva, there were those who snitched for the sole purpose of testing your resolve. You could not *deny* you had spoken, as you were supposed to learn humility, and that meant accepting penance without complaint.

"Many's the time I had to be disciplined for something I didn't say," said Melva with resignation. Even later, walking as a postulant in the colonnade between novitiate and hospital, spies waited to snitch on her. This test of convent life had proved severe.

Punished for using her voice on occasions when she had not spoken at all, she was forced to lie prostrate on the stone floor in church for long periods kissing her hands—an unbearable public humiliation for the girl. Or else she was required to eat her meals off a chair, watched by her superiors from the head table and by sister postulants.

Retreats meant complete silence at meals. Even when retreats finished, talking was still forbidden at breakfast. Further punishment for Melva included extra chores, and any kind of low-grade humiliation designed to prepare her as a bride for Christ (I imagined her convent drudgery as not dissimilar to picking oakum in Reading Gaol).

"I been there and back. The young women today wouldn't put up with it."

I wasn't certain Melva entirely approved of today's young women.

Her spirit, meant to flourish in this nursing order, grew sick. Constrained and isolated, she found herself breaking into boils as her health deteriorated.

It was decided to ship her back to a New Zealand hospital.

Once home, Melva refused to believe her mother had died. No one had told her. Heartbroken, she spent a year in hospital— yet instead of resting as prescribed, she was made by the nursing sisters to run up and down stairs with trays for other patients. During this period her vocation began to slip away.

A man who worked at the hospital took an interest in her, and eventually persuaded her to marry him.

He had been careful not to drink on the job. So the young Melva had no idea what she was getting into. He was able to keep up the pretence by day. "But you knew it was trouble if he had a whisky bottle in his pocket." His drinking became chronic. "Once he even went to Sunnyside—the place for mental people—but when he came out again he fell into the sherry."

Together they bought a small paddock where Melva looked after the pigs. On her own she raised their seven children. Violent when he drank, her husband broke both her arms on different occasions and once he broke their son's ribs. Melva learned to hide under a bridge or a hedge at night, waiting for him to go to bed, before she snuck back into their house. He caught her once and nearly took her head off with his blows.

"I been there and back."

Melva's small living room was stuffed with the mementos of a lifetime. Scores of family photos, statuettes, craft knick-knacks, glass-boxed souvenirs, commendations for volunteer work. She now had twenty-three grandchildren and thirteen great-grand-children. Beside her was a CD player atop a huge TV set.

"I *just love* to listen to Pavarotti. Domingo."

Melva had long loved music and the singing voice. Like other victims of SD, such as Shirley Linton and Marie Allison, she had had to stop singing. Melva had belonged to a singing group for thirteen years and become used to performing in old folks' homes. "It was a terrible blow to give it up." She missed singing with her group so much that they thought to include her at concerts. So now she went along with them, dressed in her costume of red skirt, white blouse and scarlet sash, to sit in the front row where she lip-synched as the others sang. They sang "all the old songs," including favourites from the war.

Regarding what had happened to her voice: "It just happened, all of a sudden."

Less than a year ago, she had climbed out of a swimming pool and found herself coughing and unable to breathe. That night she'd driven herself to a medical centre where they put her on Ventolin and oxygen. Then they sent her to hospital where she spent the next two weeks. She was prescribed a regimen of several daily puffers and capsules. She later wondered about the effects of all these on her voice.

"It was uncanny when I came out of hospital. It all happened so quick. I got such a shock when I started to talk. It was real weird. I thought, 'Heavens, what am I?'" Melva's speech was more broken than this—but I was writing it down in my notebook as though its effect on me was whole and continuous.

For fifteen years before this, talking had been an effort for Melva, what with coughing and laryngitis. She would get "fits of the cough" and "nearly die for coughing." Her coughing still remained a problem. It had now got so bad in church she carried a glass of water to mass. She thought maybe her asthma had been responsible for her cough. But she hadn't had asthma since her spasmodic dysphonia started. This new disorder, altogether dif-ferent than anything before, had made talking far more difficult.

Melva's diagnosis had proceeded smoothly. But the two injections of Botox she then received from Canterbury Public Hospital had made no difference to her voice. She seemed resigned to this bizarre disease, which she didn't fully understand. As recently as this past Christmas, she thought she might have cancer of the throat, although her family physician had told her no. She was scheduled for another shot next month.

I asked her a few questions about convent life. Listening to her broken voice, I was fascinated by how it would suddenly become smooth and fluid when she told me of her ordeals during those silent retreats, endured almost sixty years earlier. It was as if the neurological damage responsible for her disease, perhaps even responsible for her chronic coughing in church, might somehow go back to the public humiliation and severe injustices done her as a shy, homesick girl.

Who knew? Wasn't health a tissue of contingencies governed by a plausible narrative? Melva's story was complicated. She had nearly died of a bladder infection ten years earlier, in a Brisbane hospital, where she had flown from Vancouver after visiting her daughter in Washington State. "It was touch and go." Was this the same daughter, married to an American sailor on an aircraft carrier, whose hospitalized children Melva had found herself stranded with in Japan at age sixty, where she didn't speak the language or know a soul?

"I been there and back."

She kindly offered to drive me back to Christchurch, in the Honda Civic with racing stripes parked outside.

This tiny old lady drove quickly through the night, struggling to tell me how she used to hate sitting round in her taxi waiting for customers, because she was a doer and not a sitter. That was why she gave up hacking. Hearing now I wanted to be dropped in Cathedral Square, she warned me with an old cabbie's knowledge to watch out for the backpackers, and to keep clear of this seedy neighbourhood at night. It was already getting late. Melva McIlroy reminded me of my maternal grandmother who, when she retired from working as a janitor, and at the same age as Melva, had still been driving her own car.

The next afternoon, invited for dinner, I took a cab to the novelist Allan Sealy's house on Champion Street. It was really his wife Cushla's house, Allan explained in his light tenor voice, and they alternated every two years between living here and in his own house in India. Having just completed the biennial cycle, they and their small daughter were planning to rent out Cushla's house and move on soon to Dehra Dun, in the Himalayan foothills, where Allan planned to begin his third novel. India was where he was born and where he located his stories. His books sold mainly in his home country, he said, and insofar as he was known at all in New Zealand it was as an Anglo-Indian writer.

We had met in Vancouver three or four years earlier, when Allan was setting out on a North American trip he planned to turn into a travel book. I had since wondered how his journey and narrative had gone. The answer, on top of a shipping trunk in the living room, among other colourful covers, was a copy of *From Yukon to Yucatan*, just published in London. We talked about his trip, and I took the opportunity to glance through the first chapter when the author went out to open a bottle of Chardonnay.

It was sobering to see our long, half-remembered conversation reduced to a page or two of questions and answers. I sounded very talky. I recalled our meeting after a week of workshop teaching, at the University of Toronto, where I must have managed my disorder well enough to let me think I could submit to an interview. Maybe I thought the "roll" I was on there would continue at home. This was a year or two before I finally found out what was wrong with my voice, and two or three years before treatment, so the effort of trying to sound natural was chronic. When we'd sat down to coffee, I was relieved Allan had no tape recorder, only a notebook.

He now returned from the kitchen with his sister Janet, to whom he had dedicated his book. Tomorrow she and her daughter were returning to their home in Australia. So we both toasted our forthcoming return to Australia. Rubbing his salt-and-pepper goatee, Allan mentioned house break-ins and drug addicts here in Christchurch. I countered with my recent visit to Cuningham House, in the nearby Botanical Gardens, a grand curvilinear glasshouse dating from 1923 and wonderfully immune to the thorns of modern life.

Soon Cushla came in with roast lamb and sweet potatoes. Cushla, a school teacher, had an admirably languid voice and an entirely relaxed demeanour, as she joined us in conversation. These seemed at odds with her disclosure that she wouldn't be travelling with Allan and their daughter back to India. She feared travel by air. Instead, as customary, over the next six weeks, she would take a freighter to Bombay via Auckland, Sydney, Indonesia and Hong Kong, accompanied only by their shipping trunk.

The family planned to attend a play that evening, and invited me along. The "theatre" turned out to be an outdoor stage beside the Avon River. Along with hundreds of others, we sat on a barbered lawn near the town hall, and tried not to lean off our blanket into duck droppings. This production of *The Tempest* was sometimes hard to hear in spite of miked actors. I cupped my ear for Miranda's "abhorred slave" speech to Caliban, in Act 1. To someone with laryngeal dystonia, she sounded a bit like an unsympathetic speech therapist not keen on an incurable patient:

> . . . *I pitied thee,*
> *Took pains to make thee speak, taught thee each hour*
> *One thing or other. When thou didst not, savage,*
> *Know thine own meaning, but wouldst gabble like*
> *A thing most brutish, I endow'd thy purposes*
> *With words that made them known.*

On my last night in Christchurch I spoke to the composer and choir conductor Stephen Leek. I had never heard of him until an hour earlier. He was on tour with St. Peters Chorale, the Lutheran College choir from Brisbane, giving its final performance that evening in New Zealand.

It so happened I was walking up Worcester Boulevard after seeing Krzysztof Kieslowski's film *Blue*, pondering its rather thrilling voices in the unfinished composition of a composer killed in a car crash—a composition possibly written by his wife—when I was drawn inside Christ Church Cathedral by similar-sounding voices.

Massed voices had always moved me, making CBC's *Choral Concert* every Sunday morning at home my favourite radio program. I had not sung in a choir since childhood, but like Shirley Linton and other choristers who had fallen prey to laryngeal dystonia, I was perhaps excessively attracted to the sound of human voices in harmonious endeavour.

Inside, the cathedral's timber ceiling gave back gloriously the voices of sixty-four teenage girls and boys. I sat down in a pew, enraptured by their rendition of *O Magnum Mysterium*, by sixteenth-century composer Tomas Luis de Victoria. The boys in red bow ties and red cummerbunds, the girls in white dresses, made me think of seventy-six-year-old Melva McIlroy in her white dress and red sash, lip-synching as her own choir sang.

The sound of the children seemed to transcend their age. When they sang Australian Sarah Hopkins' *Past Life Melodies*, with its sinewy harmonics, their grouped voices rang wiser than would their adolescent, individual voices. I thought this ageless Aboriginal chant they interwove, its high tones chiming like a wineglass, partly responsible for this. When an indigenous voice was threatened with extinction, it seemed enriched by the ecology it once defined. Possibly, too, this explained young Australian composers' attraction to it.

Stephen Leek's own *Songs of Passage*, commissioned by the

choir for their New Zealand tour, was structured in homage to five Aboriginal words. Each song's title was the word that its music negotiated and embellished. "Ngana"—"creatures in the water"—was one. "Ceduna"—"waterhole"—was another. While the first song somewhat echoed Orff's *Carmina Burana*, the next one, "Ngayulyul" ("hawk dreaming"), possessed a transcendent legato, endless in its drifting finish. Voices here went beyond voices, into pure sound.

When I spoke to the composer afterwards, he explained how he preferred to work from a prior text. "Because then I don't have to deal with words." A text like the minimalist one of *Songs* enabled him to concentrate on the music. I asked him if there was a difference between speaking and singing. "None at all," he said. "For me a sound is a sound is a sound."

I wondered aloud why some people with speech impediments, such as stutterers, could manage to sing fluently, yet not speak fluently. He thought about this. "I don't know. Perhaps it has something to do with the emotion of singing, rising from the entire body and spirit."

Hearing his own work had clearly invigorated him, his songs as restorative to their creator as breathing from the navel. We spoke in an empty pew at the back of the cathedral. In his mid-thirties now, tall and suited, Leek had been a composer for thirteen years, composing music and songs for choir, ballet, theatre and opera. He took his librettos very seriously—however much he would prefer *not* to bother with words when composing. This evening's songs, once native to the decimated Aborigines of Tasmania, he had respectfully excavated from a library. He worked a lot with Aborigines. And with young people, including this choir and the Australian Voices Youth Choir, which had recently toured America to acclaim.

I had been reading of the savant Stephen Wiltshire's success as a brilliant auditory mimic, a classical pianist as well as a pop singer, and asked Stephen Leek how he heard the world as a composer.

"Do you take notes? Do you have to hear something outside yourself first?"

"I never really hear anything until it begins to come out at my desk. I don't consciously listen to store up sounds or memorize them. I don't really know what I hear till I imagine it."

I recognized in what Stephen said the kernel of what I'd long felt. The artist (unlike the mimic) doesn't see or hear anything until he remembers it as it never really existed. Does not see or hear the world—instead he re-sees it, re-hears it.

Outside the cathedral, I walked up the street with one of the departing young choristers, discussing the concert, when I caught her Lutheran escort viewing mistrustfully my worn sandals and Humbert Humbert enthusiasm. Their ride was waiting by the park, just where the sycamores began to shade out the streetlights. So I waved goodnight and continued on to my motel.

The following morning, up at 5 a.m. for the airport, I heard a knock on my door and thought the van had arrived early. It was a policeman, looking for Humbert Humbert. No, he was looking for a prowler. A call had come in. My light was on, he wondered why.

It didn't help my case later, as I waited outside in the dark, that a tracking dog was investigating the nearby vacant lot with all the reserve of a rabbit-sniffing basset. When the airport van arrived, two morose male passengers suspected me of being mixed up in whatever the noisy debacle outside was about. They were tired, I was tired. I felt my voice wouldn't work at all well if I tried to dispel their misgivings.

At the airport, after check-in, looking around in vain for St. Peters Chorale, I settled in to await my flight to Australia, opening Christchurch's daily paper, *The Press*. A small story entitled "Fond and Final Farewell" caught my attention:

> A British singer gave a solo performance of a song called "Goodbye" at his choir's annual dinner. Then he dropped dead. Charles Davies, 67, collapsed as fellow diners applauded

his rendition at the annual dinner of the Cotswold Male Voice Choir in Eckington, western England. "He was a real trouper who will be greatly missed," said Leslie Burgess, the choir's director of music.

This voice, like others I had heard in New Zealand, became a story by its loss.

5

The Talking Cure

I N THE AIR over the Tasman Sea, I thought of a novel
by the Australian writer Murray Bail, whom I had discovered on my last trip to the continent. Notionally to
do with a flock of Australian tourists jetting between continents,
countries, cities, *Homesickness* had taken as its central metaphor that
Mecca of earnest sightseeing, the museum, and enlarged bound-
lessly upon the context of eligible exhibits. Legs, for example. The
Museum of Legs in Ecuador, approachable only on foot and run by
a one-legged director, contains plaster casts, Achilles' heels, songs
about walking, amputation kits, ballroom pumps, specimens of
athlete's foot, a live waitress on exhibit with varicose veins, legs of
journeys—one got the idea—not to mention the museum's subtle
gradients and bland walls, intended to increase fatigue and draw
attention down to (what else?) the legs! The imagination, it seemed,
might make of any fact, or object, a fiction in order to celebrate
better a world we took for granted. Not that fiction with this
purpose pleased all. Several years earlier, after receiving his permission to excerpt a chapter for my anthology of bad journeys, I
encountered strenuous objections over it from New York editors,
who hated the particular game-park museum Bail had created of
Central Park.

I now thought of calling him up in Sydney, but remembered the
Australian novelist Peter Carey once mentioning *he* hadn't met

him, so if Bail was as private a man as that I doubted he would be interested in discussing which exhibits he might include in a gallery devoted to the human voice. A Joan Rivers monologue? A Dame Joan aria from *L'Elisir d'amore*? I could remember sitting among thousands in the grassy Domain, exactly ten years ago today, Australia Day, listening to a blue-gowned Joan Sutherland perform alongside her white-tuxedoed husband Richard Bonynge. This afternoon I now found myself across the road at the state library, two or three hours after landing, for the launch of an anthology of sex stories by young Australian writers.

The room was close and crowded. A man in sunglasses, dressed in the scarlet cassock of a Roman Catholic cardinal, spoke at length in a dead-on Italian accent about how this salacious collection should be added to the Index of banned books. A clever parody, because not only was the Pope visiting Australia this month, he had recently spoken out in a similar way about whatever indigenous moral waywardness he had unearthed here. His presence had also caused the drought to end farther north. The murderous humidity in Sydney seemed to suggest it wouldn't be long before he influenced the weather here too.

I crossed Cahill Expressway to visit two new glasshouses I could see in the Royal Botanic Gardens from the library. The Exotic Glasshouse proved cooler than the tropical gardens outside it. This was the most modern glasshouse I had so far visited, having grown used to the idea of glasshouses as peculiar to earlier centuries, when the technology reached its elaborate summit in Joseph Paxton's Crystal Palace. I did not expect to find, least of all in the southern hemisphere, space-age structures devoted to the original end of relocating small islands of tropical plants. Australia itself was a large island, naturally full of such plants.

The Pyramid and the Exotic Glasshouse were both designed with the latest laminated glass and tubular steel. You could stand at the apex of the slightly newer Exotic and view the surrounding trees of the Botanic Gardens as well as Sydney's towering skyscrapers above. In the other direction, down the sloping gardens outside, spinnakers in the harbour. This curvaceous, barrel-vaulted glasshouse cascaded away to lower elevations, its design tipping its glass toward the western light. Various levels and platforms allowed for points of view unfamiliar in the traditional glasshouse with similar palm trees, lianas and epiphytes. Stubbornly, I tried to walk against whatever flow the architecture imposed. The tubular handrails of polished steel reminded me of the comfort afforded by the profession—very little, I thought, reluctant to grip these anacondas. There were no benches. You weren't meant to contemplate existence or anything else in a building like this one; you were meant to contemplate the building. And it was beguiling the way light fell into it. I admired these varied views and the tumbling green spectacle. I just didn't feel *my* voice had any place here, although my breathing smartened up, as it always did, inside the scents of a rain forest.

In the Pyramid, by its ancient Egyptian shape, you would have expected a classical opposition to the romanticism of the Exotic Glasshouse. But no, it too deployed platforms and staircases, aspiration and process, in a somewhat more pedestrian fashion. Also known as the Australian Glasshouse, and devoted to the country's tropical plants of the northern monsoonal forest and Queensland coast, it wanted you to walk clockwise, which is why I went counterclockwise. Again, no benches.

"Hello? Testing, testing? 'Do breath tests test the breath?'" Repeating from memory, a self-imposed vocal exercise: "'Yes, that's the best of a breath test. So the best breath stands the breath test best.'"

I had read stories of how plants loved to be spoken to. The toxin now lubricating my words had never worked so well. I had to admit I liked what I heard. This botanical audience was fortunate.

"Can you hear me, plants?"

I didn't see two women descending from behind. They seemed quite taken by Tarzan addressing the jungle from his perch, and I noticed them smiling as they passed down the staircase. They were careful not to look at me. I felt I had reverted back to the vocal status of a mental.

I happened to be carrying a seven-year-old wire service story to do with an unidentified flying object—reported in Southern Australia—which, when it swept down upon a family car on a lonely highway, not only lifted up the car and covered it in ash, but, more interesting to me, had scrambled the voices of a mother and her three sons inside. Their speech had changed. They couldn't understand one another—as if the Tower of Babel had toppled onto them. Skeptical, the police became believers when they heard from the crew of a tuna boat, fifty kilometres off the coast, that they themselves were buzzed by a UFO minutes later. Their own speech had grown similarly scrambled, unintelligible.

"Hello?" I repeated. The two women had now left the building. "Testing, testing?"

Smooth, not a scrambled syllable.

It was the "withinness" of verdant glasshouses that seemed to encapsulate my voice and to contain and protect it from conditions outside. This withinness resembled, it seemed to me, what happened when toxin allowed my voice to grow naturally into the smooth space it created between previously collapsing cords.

I was within myself here, even in the Pyramid. In this "unnatural" environment of glass and forced culture, breathing smoothly from the diaphragm, I sounded paradoxically natural. Yet as each treatment had worn off over the previous year, this range of "within" always began to shrink. The glass walls would contract like my throat. The air would go out of my diaphragm. I would start straining again to speak—feeling as in the past outside myself. I would start to worry all over about locating the next glasshouse. Only another injection kept my vocal folds from sounding withered.

I did admire the Australian insistence on designing and building its own glasshouses, as though dislike of a colonial heritage encouraged it. British firms once commonly prefabricated glasshouses and exported them to the colonies and the United States. I had suspected this was the case with the structures I visited in New Zealand, and it was certainly true of the classically designed palm house shipped in 1879 via Cape Horn to Golden

Gate Park, San Francisco. This building had interested me on a past visit because of its Palm House model in Kew Gardens, London. In Adelaide, again in Perth, I would be impressed by the current Australian desire to create its own glasshouses—even if the ones I visited were all New Age.

With my voice in tune, then, if not exactly in synch, I spent that evening on the phone back in my ground-floor room at a hotel in King's Cross. Cynthia Turner was indisposed, but willing to talk at a distance. I had got her name from the speech pathology department at St. Leonard's Hospital. Cynthia, her accent middle-class English and assured, was the leader of the Sydney support group for people with laryngeal dystonia.

I learned it was while playing Lady Bracknell in Wilde's *The Importance of Being Earnest*, in her final year of an acting course, that she first heard her voice beginning "to break up like an adolescent boy's." Having dropped her pitch for the role, she found it wouldn't come back up. "'F   ound!'" Her voice cracked on separate words. Cynthia was now seventy-one, and had started acting classes fifteen years earlier.

For the first two years of classes she had done very well. She had hired an agent and begun acquiring bit parts in the booming Australian film industry. She had a small part in a Jane Campion film. She began speaking her way through television commercials. In her third year, a stressful year when both her parents died, her voice changed. Her speech teacher scolded and prodded her but it made no difference. Confounded, Cynthia dropped out of acting school.

"When SD developed, I nearly became a social outcast. At functions with my husband, I always chose the end seat if I decided to accompany him. Friends (or should I say acquaintances) called less often. Our marriage went through a very rocky patch, and I felt he was drifting away and looking for other stimulus, as it was such a struggle to converse. He and people he confided in felt the voice problem was psychological and related to our deteriorating relationship. If I really wanted to, I could make my voice recover!"

Throat nodules, she thought. But an ENT found none. He dealt her off to a speech therapist. Followed by several years of chiropractors, acupuncturists, yoga masters, herbalists, psychologists, blood tests and brain scans. It had to be mental, she decided. "The whole feeling was that if I could conquer my psychological problems I could rediscover my voice." A psychiatrist put her on pills, which made her fall down an escalator in Honolulu and spend a week in hospital. In London, she saw more ENTs and a neurologist (who told her the problem was not neurological). Few specialists had come across such a disorder; fewer still recognized the symptoms.

"I was frustrated and desperate. I had a fairly severe case. People would patronize me and make me feel like I wasn't all there. Or they would raise their voices. Every day I would go to a shop and the girl would ask, 'What's wrong with your voice?' Or I would ring up a friend and I'd hear a teenage boy saying, 'Mum, there's a very old lady on the telephone.'"

Not until a speech therapist at St. Vincent's took up her case was Cynthia finally diagnosed with "spastic dysphonia." And so she began to meet once a month with a few others suffering the same incurable fate. In 1990, the neurologist Paul Darveniza finally introduced the group to the idea of running a clinical trial here in Sydney of a new drug, recently introduced in America. Cynthia and six other outcasts became Botox guinea pigs the following year.

"When I finally had Botox, and the voice returned, my husband was reduced to tears. For the first time he came to realize the problems I had been battling. He had never realized how pleased he would be to hear me chattering away again!"

She became part of the program *Good Medicine*, made about botulinum toxin for Australian TV. Cynthia, a social animal, could now return to society. Instead of scurrying round to the rear door of her apartment to avoid people, as an actress she found the front entrance again.

When I met Cynthia in person, two and a half years later in California, she struck me very much as a woman of the world. A kind of soft-hearted Lady Bracknell, used to having her way around words, and who wouldn't be wholly comfortable mincing them. She spoke effortlessly. She was an ideal recipient of Botox, whose results disguised all past self-doubts, vocal crackings and heartache over having lost control of her life for a period of years.

I fell dead asleep in the late-night heat, dreaming of a policeman at the door looking for a burglar. Had this really happened to me, early that same morning? This same year even? In another country, perhaps. When the telephone rang toward midnight it tore through me like a fire alarm. I might as well give up now and confess to Lolita fantasies.

It was Rohinton Mistry, calling from the Canadian High Commission in Canberra. He had recently won the Canada-Australia prize and was jetting around the country on a reading tour. I had tried calling him at the Sydney Writers' Festival, where he had appeared the day before. The sound of his voice, resonant yet reserved, reminded me of how far he had come as a public author in only a few years. I had first met him at a conference in Kingston, Ontario, where several of us were modestly courted as fiction writers to watch. Rohinton had become the most watched, in the briefest time. Even Rohinton was amused and incredulous at the ease of his public accession and his literary prizes. His second novel would go on that year to much acclaim in Canada and abroad.

His speaking voice, I thought, was what saved him from the customary envy and jealousy among writers. As the morning newspaper had put it, he "speaks quietly and precisely and clearly finds self-revelation and self-promotion uncongenial." I remembered his public voice in Kingston as less inflected than it would later become, a little boring. My own voice that same evening had been spasmodic and amiss. Three or four years later, when we again shared a platform with other writers, to honour a columnist in Toronto who had taken his own life, Rohinton read a passage from Joyce's *A Portrait of the Artist* and demonstrated, at least to me, how much euphonious yearning even a "quiet" voice could declare without breaking mould.

"What are you doing in Australia?" he asked.

Listening to voices, I wanted to say. Talking to myself in glass-houses.

"Travelling. Looking into a non-fiction."

I was sorry we couldn't have got together for a drink, or whatever my abstemious acquaintance favoured in this hot country.

That earlier night in Toronto, incidentally, I had used a beta blocker for the first time at a public reading and it gave me enough confidence to get through my allotted time without the disaster I feared. But this drug never worked well again. A couple of years later, in Strasbourg, France, when I still thought I could survive such public presentations, I read with another author who would soon break through internationally, Carol Shields, and found myself wondering why I bothered to stand up and read when it depressed me afterwards to have done it badly. "What's the matter with your voice?" asked a brusque Scottish academic, as some of us strolled back that night after dinner through the city's lovely streets. This was some time before I learned what the matter with my voice was. That I was regarded (even by myself) as someone in need of a shrink seemed evident in another stroller's crossing the street to avoid embarrassing me further, should I summon the will to answer.

Carol, incidentally, had been somewhere behind us, in earnest conversation with another of our dinner companions. I remembered her calling me two or three years earlier in Vancouver, and my being almost unable to speak for reasons of unpredictable spasms. You would have thought by now the practice of trying to cover them up might have got me into an acceptable, if cracked groove. But no.

Next morning in Sydney, I chatted with a honey farmer from Washington State over breakfast. Nancy was a voluble, wide-eyed woman soaking up the city, her first foreign city. It was, it seemed, the bee's knees. Open to culture, to the metropolis, she had been to the Writers' Festival. "I just love Rohinton Mistry. I just love Sydney." She didn't think she would bother travelling outside

Sydney before returning to Seattle in two weeks' time. "There's so much to do here. I'm going to take it slowly, day by day. Isn't this lovely marmalade?" She asked it as though in her holiday from honey she had found an unexpected bonus in the substitute.

I glanced through that morning's *Australian* and was bemused by "the lesson" evidently learned by children of a suburban Sydney school, from visiting singers. The Song Company had been sharing its appreciation for vocal range and harmony, for different kinds of songs and singing. "The point of the lesson isn't lost on nine-year-old Victoria Springett. 'Anyone can make music,' she says. 'You only need your voice.'"

Only!

Victoria's attitude, I thought, did not seem exactly conducive to treasuring the instrument. On the same page, I noticed where a production of *Patience* was playing that evening at the Opera House. I made up my mind to go, as a kind of anodyne to this latent corruption of Australian youth.

Perhaps I mentioned to Helen Brake, a speech pathologist at St. Vincent's Hospital in Victoria Street, this musical lesson learned from nothing more complicated than the voice. That afternoon I'd walked along Darlinghurst Road to the deserted hospital, where she agreed to leave the door open to her department on this de facto holiday (sandwiched that year between Australia Day yesterday, and the weekend tomorrow). She was genuinely interested in music. "In fact, by this evening my husband and I have to decide whether or not to go with friends on a classical music tour of Eastern Europe."

Helen worked with singers who might be hoarse, fatigued, unable to prevent inflamed throats. She treated them in prepathological stages. She listened to the technical production of their voices and prescribed accordingly. "I've had reasonable success . . ." The singers who came to see her came in every week, for a month, before reassessment. Then every fortnight, for maybe several months. I decided the peripatetic Song Company might have done well to employ one or two of Helen's unhealthy singers, if only to encourage greater respect for the voice's ability to make music at all.

Helen, a tall blonde in sleeveless blouse and shorts, likened the loss of a voice to the loss of a limb. Pathological voice altered personality. Her role in helping stroke victims involved looking at the whole person. She explained how there were exercises to strengthen the vocal muscles of a person struck speechless. In order to rebuild a voice, you first slowed the speech down. *Speech sounds precede words.* (This sounded like the composer Stephen Leek.) She worked on intonation. She developed strategies for naming objects a patient no longer recognized. She worked with family, encouraging them to use short, slow sentences, even gestures to help the patient relearn his voice. In effect, to help him relearn who he was.

From St. Vincent's I caught a taxi down Oxford Street, eventually to the Pitt Street Mall. Maria Gerakiteys worked in a modest tea shop in the Strand Arcade, a multi-galleried, teak-toned, glassed-roofed structure amidst Sydney's busy canyons. Her willingness to talk to an unexpected stranger endeared her to me immediately. She led us back out to Pitt Street and into a quiet cafeteria.

Maria wondered if the origin of her vocal dislocation didn't go all the way back to an injury done to the top of her vertebrae by a bone-cracking mother when Maria was a child. Her mother had fallen over a suitcase during the war and become interested in chiropractic as a result of a bad back. This was the first time I wondered about a connection between my own whiplash, from that car accident many years earlier, and a voice that began to develop spasms two weeks later.

A high-strung woman by her own account, Maria had been doing yoga for the past twenty years. When that didn't help her relax she took Valium, but only two or three tablets a year. She also visited a Malaysian acupuncturist. She had been going to him for the past seven years. And she listened to relaxation tapes. She was now forty-nine.

Maria seemed not to have bought into the notion of a neurological disturbance as the cause of her bad voice. I wondered why.

While she accepted the neurological verdict as a way of explaining her voice to others, including family, she still appeared to retain the psychological verdict for herself. If she could relax and control her emotions, she could control her voice. She wouldn't *need* a needle. In the several years since Botox had come to Australia, she'd had only two shots. After the first she couldn't swallow any liquids; she went three weeks without swallowing, and experienced earaches and tooth-grinding worry. She was off work for six weeks, under care of her neurologist.

To embrace a psychosomatic cause of her dystonia, therefore, justified her avoiding surgical intervention.

Her last injection had been over a year ago. "I'm trying to string it out as long as I can." She said this without acknowledging that the benefits of the poison had clearly worn off. Instead, she seemed to have reached a stage of self-accommodation with her voice. "I'm in the moderate group. I find myself in the intermediate range. How do *you* find me?"

We said goodbye in King Street against rush-hour traffic. This small woman reminded me of Judy Garland in appearance. I was moved by her passion to speak, regardless of her claim to have abandoned "vocal life." Having a voice, she instinctively knew, made her human, who she was, and she refused to give up on it as she refused to give up on her family when it responded badly to the way she sounded. There was a generosity of spirit in these people I was meeting and would meet in the months and years to come. They came from all backgrounds. As with characters in any novel faithful to its society, their voices were not so much social and convivial as singular, coping.

The de facto holiday wasn't for office workers. In a river of them, each skyscraper spilling its tributary into the street, I drifted to Circular Quay. People were also crowding the buffet at the Opera House, where I found myself at dinner after buying a ticket for that evening's Gilbert and Sullivan production. The prosperous droves were as numerous as at London's National Theatre or Barbican Centre.

I treasured the broad staircase climb to the opera theatre, assured those sails somewhere above guaranteed me a memorable voyage, however much the blond-wood seats inside might remind one of IKEA. The last production I had seen here was of *Tosca*, with the Brazilian soprano Celine Imbert, whose legato and messa di voce had floated me through the evening. Tonight, I had a cheap seat in a side loge for *Patience*.

By intermission I was convinced that what Gilbert and Sullivan celebrated, by dancing round it as if it were a maypole, was the *playfulness* of voice. Exactly what I needed this evening. For all the production's delightful physical dexterity (and this G&S production was choreographed more interestingly than most), it was the *playful voice* that its music and book came down to, mocking solemnity, decadent art, pretension—and dicing diction like a knife. The audience, spread in summer colours across the stalls below, loved and clapped this vocal spectacle of Bunthorne's Bride.

At intermission I went outside to smell the salty wind from across Sydney Heads. Skyscrapers stood in their vertebrae of light, car lights necklaced along the Cahill Expressway. Later on, between symphony and operetta throngs, I found myself headed back toward Circular Quay, listening to Luciano Pavarotti up ahead. A red-costumed puppet danced on strings, lip-synching the aria "Vesti la giubba" from *Pagliacci*, before crumpling to the sidewalk. Voice voice voice, I was thinking. Wasn't the performing voice all about projecting oneself into a new association with the world? At the train station, a song by Gilbert and Sullivan's descendants, Lennon and McCartney, was coming through tinny speakers. I noticed a woman dressed for the opera, singing along. Unlike the waiting teenagers, she was old enough to remember the words to "Things We Said Today."

After a change at Town Hall, I ran into the bee farmer from Washington on the escalator at King's Cross. She was returning from the Opera House, too. "I'd never heard of *Carmina Burana* before tonight. I just loved it! It was on a double-bill with Beethoven's Seventh." And so we walked back together through our seedy, raucous-voiced neighbourhood, to our hotel on Ward. Nancy said, "I might stay on an extra week."

In the morning, I paid thirty dollars for a hepatitis A shot in the bum on nearby Springfield Avenue. Learning I was Canadian, Dr. Raymond Seidler spoke fondly of travelling in Europe once with a girlfriend from Kamloops. Earlier, his German-speaking father had emigrated to Canada to work on documentaries for the National Film Board, before internment in a Winnipeg detention camp during World War II. He was used to travellers here in King's Cross. "I like to listen. It's not a bad life."

I returned to my hotel and phoned Greg Partington. I could hear young children in the background. Cynthia Turner had told me he played cricket on Saturday morning. But when I called earlier he was "down at the shop." I pictured a wiry man in shorts, and a responsible T-shirt imprinted with a Disney duck, or a logo for Beaver Lumber. Greg spoke quickly, offhand, with an unpolished accent.

He'd been a primary teacher in the mid-1980s when he gradually lost his voice. Having worked his "backside off for a year, eighteen months," preparing for a promotion to the next level, "I missed out." Another teacher was successful. Greg then came down with laryngitis. "That's the way it often starts."

He recalled giving a speech to the assembled school, something he had done many times before, and feeling a catch in his throat. His voice began to tremble. It deteriorated into raspiness and harshness. When I spoke to him, he hadn't taught a class in six years, although he was working with small groups and helping to set up an in-school computer system.

Greg had been the first toxin "guinea pig" in Australia. He was now a veteran of a dozen injections. If his shot was Wednesday, by Monday following he was inaudible for a week. Then his voice was "very soft" for another three weeks. Eight weeks later and he was back for another shot, and the same vocal cycle. It was easy to see why he would have difficulty facing a class over ten months. Still: "Seventy-five per cent of the time my voice is fine." And, what was helpful now: "Everybody knows what's wrong with my voice." Although he had suffered the humiliation of losing his classroom, Greg had learned to deal with his disorder in an open manner. He preferred to be forthright.

"Listen," he said, "do you mind if I ring you back tomorrow. We got people here."

The night before I flew to Tasmania, I sat in an open-door Italian restaurant on Victoria Street getting mildly high on a half bottle of Bolla Valpolicella, when the Pope's revenge struck in a torrent. I had never seen such a downpour outside Lahina or Rangoon. It came down as heavily as a curtain in the Vatican, slamming in among us, drowning the voices at surrounding tables.

Then a dreamy thing happened to these voices. They grew in a moment to leafy crescendo, as if bursting into uncontrollable growth from the overdue monsoon. You could smell the photosynthesis. You could hear the seething of cicadas. All about seemed an organic process of unpredictable result, a kind of structured chaos, in a community of voices animated by the prospect of renewal.

That these young voices were discussing nothing more urgent than a ventriloquist comic—and whether, for dessert, to have the chocolate mud cake or the strawberry and kiwi crêpes—had made me think of Gauguin's paintings from tropical Tahiti. I thought of how often Gauguin painted the human voice in community. He was one of few painters who actually heard what he saw. Mute pictures were not the same as ones without voices. Like Marcel Marceau, he knew how to intensify the visual by enhancing its muteness. In paintings such as *Words, Words (or Gossip); What, Are You Jealous?; The Market; Where Are You Going?* we overhear the voices of his subjects. They are his subjects. These are aural as well as visual works. Gauguin even said of his pictures, they should be looked at as "operas without librettos."

When the rain let up I walked back to King's Cross, listening along the way to Saturday-night voices outside the strip clubs. These were the Tuesday- and Wednesday-night voices as well. "You wanna go?" "Step right this way, sir." Flat voices, harsh voices, raucous ones. From plain-looking hookers in miniskirts, tattooed "security" goons touting their clubs, grandfathers dressed in biker gear, the pissed bums without teeth, drug pushers offering cellophane pouches while looking the other way.

Who ever went *into* these clubs along Darlinghurst Road? The Pink Bushy Cat, Fuller Brush, Dork Dong, Pussy in the Well, the Gear Shift . . . I went on making up names, or maybe even remembering names, till I fell asleep, faintly conscious of the honey farmer's loud voice somewhere in the hotel extolling Bondi and Manly as Riviera-type beaches not to be missed. I pictured Nancy's newly sunburned knees, while all around her lay uncovered breasts as brown as honey.

What I particularly remembered about Hobart, even before I left Hobart, was a badly rhyming hotel called Bop's Coupe de Ville Bar & Grill. On paper it went by the name of the Prince Regent Hotel, which might explain my difficulty finding it, after ringing up from the airport and catching a bus into town where apparently I could not miss it. There was no door, except to a pub.

I thought the bus driver had dropped me at the wrong intersection. "Excuse me," I called, to a man waiting for the traffic light to change. As it was a Sunday, there were no cars in the street. "Do you happen to know where the Prince Regent Hotel is?"

He turned and I saw he was wearing a maroon vest and a cleric's collar. "Naaoo," he doubtfully drawled.

Together, we could make out curtained windows along the upper floor of an adjacent building with a pub. Reverend Bittles walked up and tried the pub door. It was locked, of course. In a worldly, shepherd's voice he then said: "You'd better come with me to the rectory. Yes, come with me. The rectory is just up the block."

By now the traffic light had changed back to red. We stood waiting for it to change back to green, before proceeding through the deserted intersection.

"Yes, we're all part of it," he said vaguely, when I asked if his United Church was related to the United Church in Canada, founded in the twenties when Methodists and Presbyterians merged. We had reached the rectory. His study, when we entered it, was full of worn volumes and an old computer squatting on his desk, its cables braided to one side like a pigtail. Reverend Bittles began riffling through a telephone directory he had removed from its drawer.

"Yes, the Reverend Bittles here, from the United Church up the street. I have an American with me who says he has a reservation at your hotel, uh, but he can't seem to get inside . . . Yes . . . Yes . . . I see. Fine. Yes. Your name? Good day."

I had, it seemed, to ring a buzzer at the end of the block.

"Is there a door?"

"Evidently."

Reverend Bittles felt his remaining duty was to see me back down to the intersection and through it safely.

"There it is," said Bittles, pointing out a door halfway along the next block, where a long head was sticking out. "Wait for the green. His name is . . . Leonard."

A young man of nineteen or twenty snickered and touched a tiny red buzzer on the outside wall, where I was meant to have buzzed him in the first place. "Cool, man," said Leonard. By cool he meant my American voice. He was only slightly disappointed to learn it was a Canadian voice.

"Studebaker."

"Pardon?"

"Studebaker's from Kinada."

"No," I said. Was it?

He looked disappointed. "That's what I read."

Leonard was a fifties freak, with American culture inescapably on the brain. It didn't help matters that he seemed a prisoner of his residence. Extending down the entire side wall of Bop's Coupe de Ville Bar & Grill, where I had just walked, was a mural of lovingly painted, classic 1950s American autos, with young women's limbs dangling deliriously from their windows.

He now tugged at his black T-shirt. It was a size too small, hanging loose above his Levi's, like a glove on a Popsicle stick.

The tiny lobby where we stood was a kind of stopping stage between the pub and the toilets. It reeked of urinal disinfectant. A staircase went up—apparently to the hotel.

Leonard led me through to the pub. It was dark and deserted. Over the bar he switched on a neon light that began to buzz like a fly caught dozing out of season. Dropping down behind the counter, he re-emerged with a large ledger. Opening it, he proceeded horizontally to track the recent history of a room.

"Ite's your best bet. Numo uno's only free two days. Didn't you say, from the airport like, you wanted three?" He spoke, of course, from the American side of his mouth, where enunciation required, but did not receive, extra attack to give it more chew. It was as if he were smoking a Tootsie Roll.

He turned the page, following the availability of number 8 with his finger into the foreseeable future. "If you wanted Ite, you could stay two weeks." I immediately wondered if the unavailability of number 1 wouldn't make that room a better choice. Not according to Leonard. "Quieter at this end. Numo uno's over the intersection." I remembered the pastoral serenity of the intersection, and sensed he was saving number 1, a better room all round, for zoot-suited friends of management.

But taking it would mean having to switch after two nights.

I accepted number 8, and followed Leonard out of the pub and upstairs. The windows were tall and bright, but the carpet looked left over from the fifties, and the lamp was broken. There was no telephone. "Downstairs," said Leonard. "Phone booth." I wondered if calls were still a nickel.

I was unable to open the bathroom door, except with my shoulder. Inside, against the welcome natural light of the bedroom, shone a forty-watt bulb. I wouldn't be able to negotiate the toilet without first closing the door.

The guide book had promised large, modern rooms at the Prince Regent. What it didn't mention was that the pervasive smell of disinfectant from the washrooms downstairs attested to a long, corrosive affiliation with Bop's Coupe de Ville Bar & Grill.

At least it was quiet.

That evening, after a long walk along the empty docks, I had to knock on Leonard's door to ask about the odd double-lock on mine. I didn't understand how it worked. I noticed a girl inside on the sofa, sitting in a pond of amber light. She was wearing a crinoline under her semi-formal dress, hooped waist-high, as though she'd been unable to beat it any lower when she sat down to fence with Leonard.

Leonard had slicked his hair back and changed into a white T-shirt, just like Jimmy Dean's, along with strides and polished bankers. "Cool, man." It sounded as if he had changed his voice too. It was deeper. Smoke could do that to a voice, caress your throat like honey, then drop it into the tar. I checked for a box of Camels between his sleeve and skinny bicep.

The couple was either preparing to go out for a soda, or else reliving Saturday night. Sunday night in Hobart, as I had just discovered, was shut tighter than the Pope's mind. From the perspective of the fifties, where Leonard and his date were coming from, this would have had to be Pius XII's mind. Not a lot of room to jive in.

I fell asleep watching an Italian film I was unable to shut off with the battery-dead remote. It had been about a deaf yuppie in Milan who is seeing a speech therapist. Not a lot of give and take, but who was I to slander a vocally challenged script?

I must have wakened briefly around midnight, believing the same film still in progress, because I saw where the scene had shifted from Milan to the Australian outback, where Aborigines were preparing "a cure" with their striped and stippled paintings. I was convinced the Italian characters had come to Australia in search of vocal rehabilitation.

In the morning, lorry traffic in the street below woke me. The TV screen, still lit, was perky with morning voices interviewing each other about the stock market in Sydney, and the weather in Launceston. I got up and pulled the plug. Looking out the curtain, I noticed my windowsill hadn't been dusted since 1954. There was a sign on the nineteenth-century building across the street: The Hobart College of Music / Tuition First Floor.

A man on the sidewalk, carrying a black-and-yellow airplane with a five-foot wingspan, made me wonder if I was stuck in an Antonioni film where dialogue was not the point.

I shouldered into the bathroom. Unfortunately, the tiny bulb had died quietly in the night, so I was forced to leave the door open. This of course made using the toilet impossible, so I had to shut it and pee in the dark.

My stay at the Prince Regent included breakfast. As no one else appeared to be living in the hotel, except for Leonard, I was uncertain I had the right location for breakfast. It smelled of ashtrays and spilled beer. "Yeah, I'll getchur flakes," said the young woman behind the bar, in a Victoria's Secret bra. "Milk?" Her tone made me wonder if there might be a surcharge, if not on dairy products then verbal excess.

I sat down at a table. With the lights up, I noticed for the first time the pub-wall décor. Emerging *from* the wall were fins of a black Ford Fairlane, circa 1956, and the even larger fins of a pink Cadillac Coupe de Ville, circa Elvis. Also on the wall, between full-size cutouts of Buddy Holly and Marilyn Monroe, hung a pink motor scooter.

A wooden jukebox stood in pride of place alongside the bar. In the corner was a red Texaco gasoline pump. I beheld a set of stoplights from an American intersection somewhere in the Midwest. A neon sign advertising Lone Star beer. More than one American flag. More than one guitar.

The gumball machines I remembered indelibly from child-hood.

It was like breakfast in a mausoleum. Along the wall, under the Fairlane's fins, were classic wooden booths, indigenous to a soda shop, and sitting inside one of these booths was Marlon Brando in a cap. He appeared to be looking for something, possibly, I thought, a Tootsie Roll. I now noticed on the opposite wall a full-size Harley-Davidson motorcycle—or at least its Antipodean equivalent—complete with spoke wheels, racy handlebars, and leather saddle bags with Roo decals.

The napkin dispenser on my table was a baby Coupe de Ville. In a nearby glass case, key chains lay embalmed, together with model cars of the DeSoto line, trading cards of Duke Snyder and Pee Wee Reese, and a pair of stained Fudgsicle wrappers. Running away from the bar, lit up at either end with Cadillac taillights, was a rolled Nauga-hyde bench, once white. Overhead, nailed to the pub's Tudor beams, flew emblems of American eagles. Everywhere, coloured posters of vintage Chevies had yellowed over time from smoke.

I listened. I expected to hear the Crickets. Instead, on the radio behind the bar, played some homogenizing girl-band from the 1990s, clearly favoured by the young woman in Victoria's Secret underwear, charged with setting out cornflakes and heating water for the powdered coffee.

Leonard was nowhere to be seen. When I mentioned him this milkmaid seemed surprised. "Who, mate?"

"Leonard?"

"Nah. Never 'eard of him."

Later that morning, I learned of a civic controversy surrounding the automobile mural on the side of Bop's Coupe De Ville Bar & Grill, from the security guard in the City Museum's deserted art gallery. "They must have painted it over," she said, when I couldn't recall the panel with a man's arm reaching up a woman's skirt.

Rose Cupit, a slim pretty girl with nothing to do except read books, was an artist herself, having graduated last week in fine arts from the University of Tasmania. The museum owned one of her photographs. It was not on display, among all the nineteenth-century oils. Her shy voice, misplaced in its role of a museum guard, seemed to yearn for the iconography of the outside world.

"You should visit Salamanca Place. It's about as chic as we get in Hobart."

Salamanca Place was an old district of warehouses curling along Hobart's waterfront on the Derwent estuary, now converted to bistros and galleries and boutiques, looking out on nineteenth-century schooners permanently at anchor. For sale in the antique shops were butter churns and French provincial furniture.

I noticed a flyer taped to the window of one boutique, announcing "VOICE VOYAGING. You are invited to 'a journey of discovery through the voice.' A special day for women to come together and rediscover the power of their voices. A time of personal journey and re-awakening as the voice is renewed and reclaimed. An opportunity to experience the joy of exploring your vocal potential. . . ."

As the date for this one-day course had already passed, I went inside to ask the proprietor if I might take the flyer. "Of course. Be my guest." We started to talk about film. She was able to tell me what happened in the Italian movie I had fallen asleep watching last night. Her husband, she said, had also fallen asleep. It didn't seem anything but natural, in a small town like Hobart, for us all to be watching the same film in bed on a Sunday night. "After the yuppie young man befriends the deaf girl, he starts learning sign language, and then they rescue an Oriental mime from a beating by thugs. Were you awake for him? He insists on being taken to a theatre. . . ."

Outside, where it was humid and overcast, I tried calling the Voice Voyaging workshop from a box, but there was no answer. I had nothing else to do, so I followed the cascading bells to St. David's Cathedral, dating from the 1830s. Hobart itself dated back to 1804. I dutifully admired the church's timbered ceiling and parquet floor. It had now begun to rain. I then visited St. Michael's

Cathedral, a smaller structure half a mile away in the Battery, the city's original fortification. This was another upscale area of cafés, galleries and refurbished row houses. Waiting for the rain to stop, I fell into conversation with an ingratiating, middle-aged minister dressed in a green shirt with crosses on his collars. He seemed eager to be of assistance, geographically, architecturally, even morally. I felt I could probably take my pick.

"How many parishioners have you?"

"Sixty."

This seemed not exactly a large congregation, and I wondered aloud whether his parish was in competition for members with the slightly older St. David's downtown.

"I'm only in competition with evil and the devil," he responded in a smooth English voice, refined by a century and a half in residence.

I liked him. I was supposed to like him. This was his job, to impress and recruit members to his congregation in an age less and less susceptible to a smooth English voice, refined by a century and a half in residence.

He knew about literature, of course, yet I could have mentioned botany or outboard engines without pushing him outside his parish of familiars. Modestly, he lived in a world where it was still possible for one man to encompass all of human knowledge, at least in competition with evil and the devil. I began to think that between him and the Reverend Bittles it was unlikely that a single citizen of Hobart would not experience, at some point in life, kindness or assistance from one of them; but more likely on the street than in church. Their pulpit voices from the last century had diminished in sway and audibleness.

I returned to the city museum that afternoon and asked Rose Cupit to have coffee. She remembered me because there had not been another visitor to the roof-lit room since morning. She was sitting comfortably in her chair, reading a collection of Peter Carey's stories. She had recently finished *The English Patient*.

On our walk along the harbour, we talked about David Hockney, fax art and reproductions. Then, at a café in Salamanca Place, about private schools (she had gone to one) and her mother's car crash yesterday, because of which she needed to be home by seven. This, however, would not prevent her from accompanying me to a small Indonesian restaurant she knew, where we could talk some more over supper.

Rose was twenty-one and hoped to travel soon to Brisbane, Sydney and Adelaide. She might try for a graduate degree in Brisbane, she wasn't sure. Her younger sister was training to sing classical music. She possessed a large voice. Rose's voice, refined if a little faint, made for a demure yet adventurous conversationalist. She recommended I see *Pulp Fiction*, playing that evening up the street. "John Travolta even dances."

"How does he do?"

"Not bad, for an old guy. I think you'd like it."

I did. Later that night, walking back to the Prince Regent through deserted streets, I felt jumpy. The film's violence lingered like a nightmare. Reaching the door of my hotel, I found the smell of urinal disinfectant seeping up from the Coupe de Ville's washrooms familiar and reassuring.

The film had hooked me early on, as someone with SD, when the two principal gangsters are on their way to avenge an unfortunate man who has been dropped out of a fourth-story window, and who has, according to Travolta's sidekick, "developed a speech impediment." I listened to the film's other voices, natural-sounding in their vulgar ejaculations, delivering at the same time a highly artificial script of arch vocabulary and evangelical burlesque.

When I thought of the Theatre Royale in downtown Hobart—the oldest theatre in Australia, dating from the 1830s—and St. Michael's Cathedral, with its sixty parishioners in attendance, I later wondered at how far the public voice in these had declined relative to the public voice heard electronically in films. I guessed it had declined to the point of quaintness. Like the handwritten letter, as opposed to the keyboarded letter or e-mail, the voice sounded different when it was filtered mechanically.

Margaret McKinnon's did. When she met me at the bus stop in Perth, she sounded like another person compared to the one I had phoned in Longford.

My journey north, climbing beyond the rolling brick-bunga-lowed suburbs of Hobart, was an unsummery cold one, passing through barren and treed landscapes, and small towns like Oat-lands and Tunbridge. By Ross, the sky was still overcast, though the temperature had climbed. The river here was swollen, fields swampy, a hawk hunting. After Conara, there was a bushy land-scape of gums and no more fields for the first time that morning. Before Perth, however, the landscape opened up into large sheep farms and blue distant mountains.

Then the sun came out, warm and seasonal.

Margaret was dressed in a pink-striped blouse and navy-blue skirt, topped with attractive white hair. She sounded tremulous, and yet her appearance bespoke a younger woman. In fact, she sounded younger in person, but it wasn't her appearance so much as an intelligent vivacity that contributed to this different voice. I was hearing a fuller range of person than over the phone.

In her new blue Ford she drove us into Perth, past an attractive stone church, stopping at the chemist's to pick up her prescrip-tion—pills, from her neurologist in Launceston, I found out later, to reduce her head and neck tremor. The swollen South Esk River ran brownly through town.

Margaret was talkative and unconcerned about the tremor in her voice. She drove us to her brick bungalow in Longford for lunch. Here, surrounded front and back with "therapeutic" flower gardens, and a pergola with grapevines off the patio, she admitted to feeling cramped by her low, eight-foot ceilings. She and her husband, who had died thirteen years ago of a stroke, had once lived in a nineteenth-century manor house, on a three-thousand-acre sheep farm outside Campbell Town.

She indicated a painting of that house hanging on the wall, a seventieth-birthday gift commissioned by her children. The house in the painting was dwarfed by the surrounding gum trees, rolling open spaces, and a mountain with a Scottish name. As a young woman, Margaret had come from Sydney to study science at the University of Tasmania, because she couldn't get into science at the University of New South Wales. "I could have studied medicine if I wanted, in Sydney, but I didn't want that." In Hobart she studied physics, but only for two years and without completing a degree. She had married instead and soon had three children.

Margaret poured us gin and tonics, which she admitted to fixing herself often, to "relax" with. She said she felt very relaxed with me because she didn't have to worry about how she sounded. Such worry had made her a shy, but not retiring person. Obviously well off, she was used to dinner parties and donating her time to visiting the elderly in hospital. She had travelled to Hawaii, San Francisco, Vancouver—from where she still hoped some day to embark on a cruise ship to Alaska.

Her vocal troubles had started with "a catch in the voice." She remembered going to a party, after the death of her husband, and afterwards ringing up to thank the hostess, who asked what was wrong with her voice. There had been other recent deaths in her family. "So it never occurred to me to go to a neurologist." It was her gynecologist who eventually sent her to a neurologist.

Margaret served us quiche at the dining room table. Saying her name, she explained, was the hardest thing for her to speak. "Margaret McKinnon. I have a hard time, even when I phone my accountant." She spoke often to her accountant, who needed to be reminded of the difficult time she also had signing her name, on cheques. She couldn't control her muscles.

It hadn't occurred to her that dystonia, in the form of writer's cramp, might have something to do with her arm, as well as her voice and trembling head. I mentioned the shame I sometimes felt about my own handwriting, how chronically immature it seemed. Something had happened to it in grade four. An extra stroke had got into my *n* and my *y*. I'd also developed a slight vocal hesitation, reading aloud that year. I had concentrated on reading smoothly and it went away, at least for a few years. But not the handwriting, it was never smooth. I just learned to control it better than my voice.

"It's an embarrassment," agreed Margaret, about her voice. "I'm not sure the Botox is doing me any good." Same thing for the voice of a friend she had made at the clinic in Sydney. They had since flown around the Australian outback together, in a ten-seater plane, as though in reckless consolation. Whether it was her age or her tremors, speaking had not got much easier since injections began three years ago.

I had not intended to stay all afternoon, but our lunch and conversation ran long. We were enjoying ourselves. Each of us had found a sympathetic ear. Margaret offered to drive me to Launceston, where she suggested I could visit the town and take the late bus home.

On the highway again, I grew a little concerned about the unsteadiness of her new car. Her tremulous steering, like her tremulous speech, took getting used to. I did wonder what had happened to her previous car. Yet she managed, as she was doing valiantly with her life, to keep us inside the line of acceptable flux.

She continued to tell me her story. Possibly because Botox had done little to help her tremors, she was also seeing an acupuncturist and a chiropractor. "I like the chiropractor. He shows me X-rays."

At this my alarm bell went off and the car wobbled. I had just finished writing a novel in which one of the principal characters was a chiropractor, who had lost faith in the profession because of its illusions. I mentioned to Margaret how chiropractors traditionally tried to enhance the legitimacy of their profession by using the X-ray machine to impress patients with pictures.

"It amounts to one of the worst abuses of their profession."

"Oh, dear," she said. But I wondered if she felt injecting botulinum toxin was any less of an abuse. Margaret seemed to find alternative medicine and the kind administered to her by neurology all more or less of the same cloth. The only thing about dystonia she knew for certain was that it embarrassed and debilitated her. She was sympathetically disposed to whatever treatment might take her mind off the effort of living with it.

"I just hope, before I die, I can have a good voice for a little while so I can sing again in a choir."

On the bus back to Hobart in the early evening, I saw her old ranch house and its vast acreage washed in a golden light. The mountain behind this ranch looked identical to the one in the painting. Thousands of sheep tumbled into view. Wetlands shone. We followed a gleaming, narrow-gauge railroad through flocculent spaces and blue eucalypts. Chopin was playing in the bus. No one spoke. Long shadows darkened, slanted still further, faded away. I wondered what people without children dreamed when they travelled. I could no longer remember. I was dreaming of a son singing inside a white church, before I awoke in the dark to scold his father, myself, for wishing upon him the liturgical equivalent of a white picket fence. I would be happy if he could speak without spasms, to whoever shared his apartment in the years to come.

The Prince Regent Hotel, with its "large modern rooms," promised relief from nostalgia. Having just inspected the early nineteenth-century buildings in Launceston, I knew my Hobart home would clear up any lingering homesickness by gathering me into the bosom of modernity.

That night, letting myself into number 8 and turning on the light, I thought I had the wrong room. There were two suitcases I didn't recognize, their contents spread all over the twin beds. Pantyhose, a man's walking shorts, an elegant sash or else a whip. I returned to check the number on the door. Back inside, shouldering my way into the bathroom, I noticed lotions and toothbrushes had supplanted my own whip of dental floss. The light bulb had been supplanted by one that worked. A drying undergarment was dripping in the shower.

All trace of me had now vanished from the Prince Regent. For some reason, my belongings had been thrown out.

There was no answer when I knocked on Leonard's door, so I descended to the roisterous Coupe de Ville, now full of smoke and shouting voices. *Wake Up Little Susie* belted unheard from the jukebox. Behind the bar, I found the milk-maid from breakfast pulling a lager tap toward her nearly naked bosom. I blurted out something about my room. She had no idea who I was. It suddenly occurred to me she was the demure fifties girl in the crinoline I had glimpsed inside Leonard's room that first night.

"Bop," she called down the bar. "Fella 'ere wonderin' about 'is room." She said to me, "My father'll take kere of ya."

It took Bop a few seconds to comprehend the connection between his Coupe de Ville and the Prince Regent—that there was one. Then, cheerfully, he said, "Oh yeah, we were wondering where your key had got to. We needed it like. Didn't know where ya'd gone."

Bop wore striped overalls, the shoulder-harness variety with metal buttons usually worn by train drivers, now manufactured in Shanghai with buttons impossible to slip through eyes without slicing a fingertip. I wondered, having negotiated his way into them the first time, if he had ever taken them off. His beer belly seemed to have grown into the generous pockets and beyond. Bop was blond, in his mid-forties.

"We only had ya booked two nots," he called. He put down the lathered mugs he was carrying and held out his pudgy palm for my key. "Ta, mate." He then removed the Prince Regent register from under the bar, rested it across the mouths of the overflowing mugs, opened it, slapped through some sticky pages, before stopping to show me where my name had been erased and two others written in.

"That's weird," I said. "Leonard give me number 8, so's I'd have a clear run, in case I decided to hang out two weeks like. He said it was free, man."

I could hear my voice taking on the protective camouflage of an American gas jockey's, from the open, Coors-littered spaces of western Arizona. Far safer than sounding like an imperious

guest, in case Bop decided he had no other room for a presumptuous twit.

"Ah, yeah," said Bop. "Leonard would say that." Leonard, he
reluctantly conceded, had been taking care of the place on Sunday
when I arrived. And not doing a bang-up job of it, either. "He's a
little casual is Leonard."

"OK, man, but where's my shit?" I had started to whine.

"It's cool," said Bop. He then bent down to the floor and reappeared with a canvas bag, nearly upsetting both book and beer as
he pushed it across the bar. As evidence of haste in its packing, it
now bulged in several unfamiliar places.

Bop said he was glad to accommodate me if they could find a
free room. "Hell's bells, you paid for one. Marilyn!" His daughter
was dropping mugs of beer onto a table, beneath a photograph
of Richie Valens with waterfall hair. "Run up and see if number 1's
avylable." What he meant was, see if the bed was made. And, possibly, pack up the belongings of any guest not personally in the
room. He put his hand inside his overalls and brought out a key,
which he tossed to her. She missed and it landed inside Victoria's
Secret, where she fished awhile, to the beery delight of several
onlookers with waterfall haircuts.

My mood had suddenly improved. But I was reluctant to let
my voice revert to its normal Botox-induced eloquence until I was
sure of Bop's good will. We awaited his daughter's return.

I was now inclined to like my landlord. He might have removed
me from my room in the transparent interest of renting it out as a
double, at twice the rate, but he was willing to go out of his way to
reaccommodate me when they were overrun down here in the pub.
He even mentioned, since I was leaving in the morning, his willingness to drive me to the bus station.

He had returned to pulling on taps, like levers on a locomotive.
The precise diction of the Everly Brothers had been replaced by
slurrings from Elvis. I wondered if Bop's name was a diminutive for
the Big Bopper. Not that Bop's voice much conjured up a playful
baritone. It sounded more c.&w. Moved to song, my host would

probably sound more like Hank Snow droning "Movin' On" than his namesake knocking off "Chantilly Lace."

To keep on his good side, while awaiting news of number 1, I asked if he had seen *Pulp Fiction*. I told him about the 1950s restaurant in it, with waiters dressed up like Buddy Holly and Marilyn Monroe.

"Yeah," said Bop, pushing a tap back up. "I been told I should see it."

Marilyn now reappeared, through cigarette smoke and the odd wolf whistle, to say number 1 was empty.

In her double life, Bop's daughter obviously had two sets of undergarments, a Victoria's Secret bra for the coarser life down here among patrons of the Coupe de Ville, and a crinoline for her imaginary life upstairs in the Prince Regent with Jimmy Dean. I had to assume Leonard was learning the hospitality business as Bop's future son-in-law, but that he might be having a hard time ignoring what sometimes went on downstairs—wolf whistles, the wandering hands of tattooed motorcyclists, etc.—in the interests of Bop's profitable and cohesive enterprise.

I found myself right over the intersection that Leonard had warned me about that first afternoon. Mufflerless hot rods were now accelerating through it. The smell of urinal disinfectant had faded at this end of the long corridor, replaced by cigarette smoke seeping up from the bar. The curtain wouldn't close, so the street light shone in like a beacon of salvation managed by Reverend Bittles up the street.

Nothing in here was not more worn and dirty than it had been in number 8. The bed, when I pressed it, would not come back up. The toilet was running a marathon. The operation of the bathroom door was smooth, mercifully, yet the air inside was not. Little fresh air had been introduced inside for perhaps a decade. My old room began to smell like paradise. I yearned to be back in number 8, with its wonky remote control and its bathroom door that stuck like honey.

The sound of crashing metal beer kegs woke me early. A hungover labourer, grunting at the unwelcome light of day, was unloading a lorry. When I touched it with my fingers, a moth on my pillow fell to dust.

I made my way downstairs for breakfast, and sat in the booth next to Marlon Brando. "Sl'ip good?" asked Marilyn. Sounding positively refreshed herself, she could not have had more than four hours' rest after the pub closed—maybe fewer, if she'd visited Leonard's room later on and changed into her crinoline.

"I could hear the jukebox."

"That's enuff to put anybody to sl'ip." The girl band was again playing in the background. "Flakes?"

"Stale. I mean—yes, I'll have some."

"Milk?"

"Why not?"

After breakfast, when I returned with my bag, Marilyn had disappeared and Leonard was standing behind the bar. "Yer timing's cool," he said. "Just finished unloadin'." I would have expected him to be dressed in overalls, but he was wearing his black T-shirt and Levi's. He put a cigarette between his lips. "Bop's busy. Ask'd me to run yeh up to the Redline."

Leonard had forgotten removing my bag the night before and denied any part in my room change. "Thatcher yer bag?" he asked, waving his cigarette inculpably.

We went out together, down the sidewalk, past the vehicular cartoons caught in the time-warp surrounding Bop's Coupe de Ville. I stopped by the vehicle Leonard indicated, waiting to be let in. He just stood, grinning. "Cool," he said, exhaling smoke through thin nostrils. I had mistaken his driver's door for the passenger's door of an American car that drove on the other side of the road.

The vehicle he let me into was a late-model 4x4 Range Rover from Britain. I opened the window and Leonard asked me to close it. He switched on the air-conditioner before gunning us away from the curb in time to run the red light, rocketing us past the United Church on our way up the hill to the bus station.

"Wouldn't you rather be driving a '55 Chevy?" I asked him.

Leonard was surprisingly circumspect. I wasn't sure if this was because he was driving Bop's vehicle, although I would have felt compelled to ask Bop the same question. Bop especially, as the owner of the Coupe de Ville, would seem out of character in a young urban professional vehicle.

"In Austr'lia," said Leonard, "I read they once tried to bring b'ek the 1964 Holden. Manufactured it with original pa'ts. Niva caught on."

Stubbornly, I persisted. A Holden wasn't a Chevy. Wouldn't a mint reconstructed '55 Chevy sell like beer?

Leonard again hesitated. He adjusted the Rover's cooling system. He then wondered if the Chevy's steering wouldn't be a bit stiff. Certain conveniences, he supposed, would be missing. "Would *you* drive one?" he asked.

This, coming from Leonard James Dean, but also Bop, who had recreated in loving detail an entire generation of American culture for colonials on the fringes of the remote Tasman Sea, men who rented out for profit rooms from the 1950s, along with dust and toilets from the same decade, with no mod-cons such as air-conditioners: *They would both rather be driving a yuppie wagon.*

I answered his question with a brief spasm.

"My d   ad once had a '54 Chev sedan delivery. I learned to drive in that."

"Cool, man," said Leonard, suddenly fascinated. "Stick shift. Ya' know how to drive one?" By now he had stopped in front of the Redline Terminal, waiting for me to climb down. "Love that American accent."

Not only had he forgotten moving my bag last night, and his fifties principles when it came to transportation through the world, he had also forgotten where I came from.

I flew to Melbourne seated beside a Hare Krishna couple. They were each doing something with their hands under their respective long white dhotis. Over the short flight, we talked easily of our lives. They liked living in India, outside Calcutta, on the banks of the Ganges. At the moment, however, they were heading for Surfers Paradise. I thought this an odd destination for Hare Krishnas at home on the Ganges. But I supposed begging might be profitable in a prosperous Gold Coast resort, which I remembered mainly for a shark alert, on a day trip once from Brisbane.

"It's all connected."

The young man was well spoken and worldly. I learned he had been born and educated in Hobart, at the University of Tasmania. His middle-class voice seemed slightly at odds with his beads and the long pigtail curled up on his neck like a dozing snake. He and his wife had been staying with his mother on Tasmania's east coast.

"Tasmania is the birthplace of the Australian ecology movement. There's even a wealthy American executive who gave up everything to come and live in Tasmania's rural paradise in a small house. It's all connected. Giving up worldly possessions and a love of the planet."

Followed by a volley of motion under their dhotis.

I learned he had joined "the society" in Hobart in 1980, the same year he left Tasmania and the year his wife had lived for a while in Vancouver.

I looked at her. "So it's possible I might have seen you, chanting on a street downtown?"

"I love consanguinity," she replied. "We're probably related. The rain forest. It's all connected."

"Spiritually, she means."

"Do you miss India?"

"We love India," she said.

I mentioned CIVA, dedicated to rural projects there. I expected them to disapprove of middle-class Canadians helping out in places they knew little about and had no intimate understanding of. Instead, their interest was whetted.

"Village aid," said the young man. "Do you have to be a village to qualify?"

"Yeah," I said. Adding, to be on the safe side, "We're non-denominational."

"Which means you don't discriminate on the basis of religion."

"Yes. I mean, no. It does mean that."

He turned and smiled at his wife.

I caught a glimpse of his active left hand. He was pumping and squeezing a small sac. They seemed in touch with one another through their sacs.

"Do you have a card?" he asked me.

They both seemed surprised to meet someone without a card.

"But we can contact CIVA by fax? That is, if we hear about a village in India with a good project?"

"No problem."

You had to admire their entrepreneurial spirit. I could imagine upon my return to Canada receiving from a Ganges-based ashram of the Hare Krishnas a project proposal for an administratively viable goatery devoted to the material uplift of sac-squeezing members. It would be self-sustaining, empowering to women, and ecologically sensitive. It would all be connected, of course, and the sacs made from goat leather.

When they changed planes for the Gold Coast, I did the same for Adelaide.

Listening to them had reminded me of how ecotourism was being marketed in Tasmania and New Zealand—wilderness camping, kayaking and trekking expeditions on offer to places as remote as Antarctica. The buzz phrases were as pervasive as those of international development. You could become a more sensitive person, help to save the wilderness, and cut down on pollution, by investing a large sum of money in whale-watching, rain-forest monitors, or penguin-sketching. It amounted to a new religion. The natural world, or what was left of it, was big.

The unnatural world was also big, at least in Adelaide. The Bicentennial Conservatory had opened here in 1989, for ecotourists who, like me, preferred to stay in cities. It resembled a giant space-ship, and hummed into view like the eighth wonder of the world. As a confirmed glasshouse stalker, I'd been looking instead for the original Palm House, constructed from German design in the 1870s, here in the Botanic Garden. I had found it standing rib-naked, stripped of glass and divested of plants. Proposed renova-tions had surrounded it with a fence and temporary wall. It was like an archaeological dig at the site of dinosaur bones. Maybe they had run out of money. Disappointed, I waded on through the 34C heat of mid-afternoon.

I heard the sound of powerful engines coming from the steep metal walls of the new curvilinear conservatory. Somewhere high up on these walls began the high-tech glass. The whole ship seemed about to lift off.

Inside, control of the climate was in the brains of machines. I was safe in here from any extremes of temperature or pollution. I had left the jurisdiction of earth and entered a rain forest like none other known to man. Everything had been created anew. In such surroundings, Frederick Delius would have had to rewrite *A Walk to the Paradise Garden* to accommodate the rhythms and tempos of a new garden and age.

I stepped farther into the forest.

Then watched and listened in amazement as a computerized misting system came on, its nearly one thousand nozzles spewing billions of water molecules overhead in what resembled clouds of carbon monoxide, until visibility gradually disappeared in a fog over the forest, and great drops of water, now condensing at a rapid rate, fell on me in a downpour. The machinery making all this happen—further evidence that this natural world was anything but natural—abruptly changed gear, whirred itself slowly into a declining coda and retreated into the giant bays of the spaceship.

In this glasshouse, I had no time to test my voice. I was too busy ducking down paths through dripping foliage. I was too busy climbing a winding wooden walkway into other zones. I was too busy being an ecotourist.

"Awesome," I heard an American say to his wife. They were wringing out their Tilley Endurable hats. "Never seen anything like that before."

"Wetter than the whales at Water World," said his wife.

"Hootier than Hooters."

The sound of excitement in their voices resembled the good things you listened for in children, including wonder. I sat wondering at one of the brochures I had picked up at the door, full of facts about computerized weather stations, flow rates, sensors, treated soil and toughened glass. No mention of birds or insects. Itemized instead were tonnage of steel framework and cubic metres of concrete. Engineering sophistication seemed to tower over any other reason for the place's existence. Indeed, the "educational" purpose of the conservatory seemed more attuned to the structure itself than to its contents. (In this it resembled the Exotic Glasshouse in Sydney, times a hundred.) I had no problem with inventive glasshouse architecture per se. But when the structure merely took your breath away, as this place did mine, how were you expected to breathe down deep into your lungs the tropical scents of the cloud forest?

There needed to be a correlation between style and content, for a proper marriage of soul and voice. The energy consumed by building and then maintaining the place shouldn't have sounded like a cosmic wheeze.

This space-age, post-modern design felt onerous where it ought to have felt light. I would have welcomed the chance to compare this Bicentennial Conservatory with the nearby nineteenth-century Palm House, now undergoing its makeover. I had come to think of glasshouses as resembling inverted crystal bowls placed to the ground of cities. I liked to listen inside them for voices, including my own. I knew mine was an illusion, but what sort of illusion, and why did I not hear it here? Possibly because the BC had deliberately forgone illusions. The uplifting weightlessness of the traditional glasshouse, on its cast-iron pillars as unnoticeable as bones, was meant to allow its glass skin to breathe. This glasshouse had forgone most of its glass. It had lost sight of its aesthetic balance in the engineering spectacle it had become. The oasis of tranquillity, in which voices could be overheard, had been replaced by an eco-forest nurtured by the breathing of machines.

Returning from my spaceship visit, slowly because of the afternoon heat, I walked past the venerable Royal Brisbane Hospital, deep among shade trees. Maybe its offer of coolness attracted me, but I was also unable to resist a visit inside to look for a speech pathology department. I found one, and although it was near time for staff to be going home, Sandra Given (not her real name) was willing to take me to her office and talk. She should have been at a meeting.

What had impelled her to go into voice work? "I can't remember," she said, a pleasant woman in a blue print dress. "It was twenty years ago. More or less, I suppose, it was because I didn't have a lot of options." Sandra's main work now included stroke and cancer victims who had lost their voices to surgery and circumstance. "I don't do speech pathology. Rehab, rather, helping patients develop strategies for dealing with the loss of their voices."

I asked about her own voice.

"To be honest, I can't remember ever being conscious of my voice. Either surprised or disappointed: since that's what you're asking. I never think about it even now. Well, perhaps I'll overhear it on tape, talking to a patient, and think how lucky I am. Or something . . ." Here she seemed on unfamiliar ground, as if telling me what she thought I wanted to hear.

I thanked her and made my way out of the hospital, wondering why I should be surprised that a wonder about voice wasn't a requirement for anyone in the field, any more than a love of literature was among those paid to teach it.

The following afternoon, on my way to Ann Laidlaw's house in South Plympton, I met a Londoner in maroon walking shorts waiting for the bus. He'd travelled halfway round the world three years ago to find himself and his vocation here in Adelaide.

"I teach in a Bible college."

I asked about the vocal demands of teaching there. He was pleased to say he regarded his voice as an instrument to "play" the score of the Bible. His son, incidentally, had recently won an elocution contest at school and he was proud of the way Terence spoke the word of the Lord.

"He has the throat of John."

I'd called Ann Laidlaw earlier from my hotel on Hindley Street. "Oh, shit!" I heard. She had dropped her papers all over the floor. "I'll just put the phone down for a minute." When she picked it up again she said, "Damned if I know what I've done with Jan Hooper's number. You realize, of course, you won't be visiting the most glamorous woman in the world. I've just had all my hair cut off. I'm taking swimming lessons these days."

Ann lived on a busy four-lane road, in a not insubstantial house, but with a pedestrian bricked-in yard and burglar warnings on the door. Two tiny dogs started yapping when I knocked. "Rolex" and "Gucci," she called them, waving me in with her cigarette. "Watchdogs," she said, in a deep smoker's voice.

Settling into a sofa in her living room, beside an ashtray, she lit up another of many cigarettes. The small room was already hot with afternoon sun. She was wearing green shorts and a green top.

Ann, who was fifty-five, called herself "Ann of Green Gables" and would probably have welcomed any visitor from Canada where her fictional idol had originated. She was also partial to writers, fancying herself one, and sending out letters and long poems about her rare speaking disorder to sympathetic American newsletters.

We visit our Doctors, in hope and despair,
And we try, very hard, to explain why we're there.
Some Doctors, at first, are kind and concerned,
Then they diagnose "Psychosomatic" and so we are spurned . . .

"I have a gift, so why not use it?"

Perhaps her greater gift was for bringing people together. "It's the gift I've been given." As self-appointed coordinator of a small support group in Adelaide, she wanted those with vocal cord dystonia to feel "normal" in society, where she sometimes arranged meetings in restaurants.

I learned her own husband was a physician who had never heard of spasmodic dysphonia. Not that they were married when her symptoms first developed. She had been living in New Zealand, where "I'd disposed of my husband of the time," and undergone a couple of "botched" operations for stomach ulcers. She'd returned to Australia because her condition looked terminal and she wanted to see her grandchildren. She weighed forty-two kilos. During this desperate illness her doctor had reminded her of something else.

"He always used to say there was something wrong with my voice."

Four years later, and twelve months after marrying Bill, she began having trouble with her handwriting. Bill had the sense to send her to a neurologist, who told her she had "writer's cramp." No consensus about her voice, however. General practitioners diagnosed laryngitis and prescribed "tablets." As her husband's business manager, meanwhile, Ann found talking on the phone was killing her. "It was so frustrating, I would burst into tears at the end of the day." Her health deteriorated. "I had a couple of heart attacks, so my voice lost priority again."

Doctors, to whom she did talk about her voice, thought she enjoyed medical attention too much. One sent her to a psychiatrist. "He made me wonder if I *was* bonkers!" This didn't help her strained, choked voice at all. Not that she encountered blanket sympathy at home, either. "'Oh, for God's sake, Mum, don't tell me you're putting on that bloody voice act again'." She was quoting her thirty-three-year-old son. But Ann tended to be a tolerant mother. "My own mother was a vicious, vindictive bitch. She brought up me and two brothers on the end of a stock whip."

She knew of families who had split up as a result of this vocal disorder. She considered her marriage to a sympathetic physician fortunate. "If I wasn't married to an MD, the voice would have cost me my job *and* my husband." Still, it hadn't been easy. "Bill is going deaf," she said of her seventy-year-old husband. "And when I was losing my voice, the tension was incredible. He would yell at me and not admit he was going deaf, blaming it all on my voice. Now he's got a hearing aid and I've got Botox. You wouldn't believe the difference it's made."

I had never met someone so grumpily cheerful about her various afflictions. Air thick with cigarette smoke kept her spirits cooking and her voice manly. She took a "tablet" for epilepsy (to control her writer's cramp), a "tablet" for Parkinson's (which she didn't go into), and an "occasional" Valium for nerves. She had had no real trouble with her handwriting since her first diagnosis for dystonia, unless she wrote too many Christmas cards, at which point she took a tranquillizer and a glass of Scotch. As for writing her newsletter—to send out to fellow SDs—she said she tried to make it "half fact and half fiction."

I wondered if I were getting both halves too. Her health sounded too awful to be taken seriously, which I think is how she meant it to be taken.

Two or three years later, I received in the mail a typewritten, thirteen-page single-spaced letter from Ann, detailing a lengthy struggle with breast cancer. It was a feisty, upbeat letter she had sent out to all her friends, often graphic in its description of her treatments. I remember thinking that her voice had lost priority. She didn't mention it. She had also suffered a stroke. "I must be a cat, I think, or else it is the Leo in me, because I have nearly died two or three times—I don't know how many of my nine lives I have used up. Maybe God is scared stiff of having me in Heaven! Do you think that this is the reason why I keep on keeping on?"

She was glad her hair had now grown back, and "that Breast Cancer was not a death sentence." She managed to make it seem like she enjoyed her highly unpredictable body, a constant adventure and an unending source of wonder. She was now glad just to be "alive and happy, and Bill still loves what is left of me and that is the most important thing as far as I am concerned!"

She signed it "Ann of Green Gables." In a shakily handwritten P.S., she added: "Smear test showed more cancer. Hysterectomy next week. You came to our house a long time ago to meet people with Spasmodic Dysphonia. Remember?"

I wrote back. A year or so later I heard she had died.

In Adelaide, I found I liked to sit in the open-doored Blue Iguana Café in Rundle Street. I would admire the scrollwork on wrought-iron balconies across the street, and admire, too, the women strolling by or sitting inside, smoking. The waitress told me Rundle cafés didn't discriminate against smokers in the way of more established restaurants, because most of their clientele were young women who puffed. I was beginning to feel I had come to a city full of women. Except for the Bible teacher, everyone I met in Adelaide was a woman.

It was certainly true that among the SDs I was meeting so far, here and in other cities, more of them were women. But this uneven ratio of cases, also noted in the literature on the diaspora, had never been accepted as gospel. Men were perhaps less likely to seek diagnosis in the first place or to talk about a bizarre vocal flaw, especially if they had decided that an unmanly weakness had caused them to speak the way they did. I did find more women than men living *alone* with SD, as though the supporting mate with the aural patience to be loyal was more likely to be a wife.

The handsome waiter at the Iguana, who clearly felt himself to be a rooster, I avoided meeting. He liked to stomp across the varnished planks in black patten gores.

His smarmy voice claimed superiority among us lunching hens, inflating its sleekness into a bloated syntax in an attempt to impress us. I listened, amazed. "Will there be anything else at your table, madame? Another latte to round you off? A special dessert for an auspicious occasion, perhaps? . . . Then may I arrange your account, madame? Sir?"

One morning at my table over coffee, I read of the death of Donald Pleasence. The obituary's headline read: "Movies lose the 'chilling villain with staring eyes.'" I would have thought his sinister *voice* nearer the truth. That nasal voice, placed precisely in "the mask," had made the film of Harold Pinter's play *The Caretaker* an unforgettable experience. "I don't jabber, man. Nobody ever told me that before." *Pause.* "What would I be jabbering about?" I could still hear his voice. He was seventy-five when he died.

If any actor deserved to have applied to him a passage I had long puzzled over in E.M. Forster's novel *The Longest Journey*, I now thought it should be Donald Pleasence, posthumously. Of one of his characters, whose life is about to change, Forster had written: "In the voice he had found a surer guarantee. Habits and sex may change with the new generation, features may alter with the play of a private passion, but a voice is apart from these. It lies nearer to the racial essence and perhaps to the divine; it can, at all events, overleap one grave."

One afternoon, instead of the Blue Iguana for lunch, I went to Johnny Rocket, the exception to the rule in Rundle Street, where sienna-coloured walls and Italian fusion food were fashionable. Johnny Rocket was a fifties diner. After Bop's Coupe de Ville, I was unable to resist a glance at how pure and unadulterated such retro places were *supposed* to look: chrome walls, counter jukeboxes, red-plastic stools that swivelled on their floor-bolted pillars, the soda jerk waiters in white sailor hats and black bow ties. Elvis was singing "Don't Be Cruel." I ordered a soda and a hamburger. I thought of a girl I'd once taken to see Johnny Mathis, on a first date. "I just love his voice." On our second date, she stood me up, preferring to go off instead with someone else to hear the Beatles in concert at Empire Stadium.

Fried onion rings were a pleasant change from rigatoni. I chewed them, thinking about a Wim Wenders film I had seen the night before, *Faraway, So Close!* "We are nothing, they are everything," says the angel-protagonist, in a voice-over, reflecting on mankind from his unassailable perspective. I liked how, when he decides without thinking to rescue a little girl falling from a building, Cassiel acquires "gravity" in both senses of the word, diving from the great angel monument into Berlin, where he suddenly loses his angel's voice and also his wings. Now among the fallen, he wanders the newly unified city to a celestial sound of choral voices, until . . . But the cinema's air-conditioning was broken and I had nodded off in the humidity.

I lunched another day at a Malaysian restaurant called Twains. In a suitably Asian mood, I then wandered off to the zoo and found myself listening to the siamang, their necks puffing out with air.

I knew these robust gibbon voices from the five years I lived beside Vancouver's Stanley Park. They would boom across Lost Lagoon, from half a mile away. It was a little like living in Sumatra, I imagined. The local conifers had simply replaced the jungle. I would listen, astonished, to the variations of these voices: empty, bottle-blowing huffs, sliding suddenly upward into ear-splitting *ow-ow-ows*, with plangent cries thrown in like the warm-up exercises of a Greek soprano.

Judy Tregilgas was not a Greek soprano, but she would have loved to be a lounge singer. She imagined herself as a cross between Barbra Streisand and Cleo Laine. Her theatrical heritage went back to her grandfather, who would take her backstage at the Theatre Royal, as a child in Brisbane, where she met ballet dancers such as Robert Helpmann. She remembered meeting Katharine Hepburn, starring in *The Taming of the Shrew*. Judy grew up wanting to be either a great singer or a great dancer. After her parents divorced, her father became a producer in LA, London and other cities, and when he was dying of cancer two years ago, having come home to die, famous actors would telephone from overseas to ask how he was.

Her heritage was important to Judy. Pride in it seemed the chief antidote to what had happened to her voice. Her kind of vocal cord dystonia was even rarer than the adductor kind. "You common lot of adductors," was how she wryly put it, when we met later that week. Vocal cords like mine clamped shut, leading to broken, guttural sounds when my breath couldn't push my words past my throat. Judy's abductor dysphonia meant her vocal cords jammed *open*, causing her to sound hopelessly breathy. Speaking with any volume required a constant, equally exhausting effort, for which botulin injections had so far proved ineffective.

Much else had happened to Judy, now forty-six, besides losing her voice. Ten years before her father died of cancer, she had undergone surgical operations for uterine cancer. During one of these, her heart had actually stopped beating. Before her voice ran out, her struggle for survival had already been long. She left school at fifteen to start working. A marriage in her early twenties lasted just three years, during which her husband kicked and punched her, broke three ribs, strangled her, and kicked to death her two-month-old fetus.

She had no other pregnancies, no children. She was living with her mother now. After developing cancer, she was no longer strong enough to continue at the radio station, where she'd looked after research and advertising. As part of this job she had once recorded commercials.

I could understand Judy's success in the business world. She was a beautiful, large-eyed woman with rich full hair, who knew how to command attention. She wore a pretty summer dress, pearls and tasteful make-up. To look at her was to see an apparently composed, self-assured woman of the world. To hear her was to understand the deceptive, even theatrical nature of her appearance. Her role in the world had changed.

"I'm shy and introverted now."

It was hard for her to *be* in the world. With such an unknown disorder, she wasn't crippled in any conventional way that might arouse sympathy or understanding. Except when she laughed. "My larynx lifts and I sound better. I have a sick sense of humour that's helped me survive." Talking, she could sound unpredictably smooth, and then unaccountably voiceless—huffing across spasmodic chasms, delivering nothing but whispers of air.

"My voice started getting softer and softer about five or six years ago." She described a familiar mad circuit of medical ignorance: GP sending her to ENT, who recommends neurologist, who delivers her to speech pathologist, who recommends psychiatrist, who thinks second psychiatrist might help, who then unloads her onto a hypnotist.

"I'm a good hypnotic subject," said Judy, laughing. "I rather enjoyed it."

Her voice got progressively worse.

"The first time I heard a tape of my own voice I said, 'That's not me.' I knew I sounded bad, but that's not me I thought. I couldn't believe it."

I wondered aloud about such disbelief. It seemed those of us with spasmodic dysphonia, and perhaps other vocal disorders, would often claim after listening to ourselves to sound "much worse" than we thought we did when recording our voices.

"That was me," said Judy.

"Maybe we're so desperate to be thought normal, we think we sound whole when we don't. The saving illusion."

Like Ann of Green Gables' hair, I thought. Ann Laidlaw had touched her shorn head the day I saw her. "It still feels long." In the same way that amputees still felt an absent arm or a leg—a legendary and ghostly presence—so those afflicted by vocal spasms still heard the voices they used to have.

In Judy's case, it was someone else's tape, arriving from Boston two years ago, that led to her diagnosis. Since then she had received unilateral injections of Botox once a month. Of these, only the last two had worked at all. Judy recalled for me what happened at the breakfast table after the injection before last.

"'Pass the milk,' I said to my mother in a normal voice. And then I burst into tears. It was the first time in years I sounded normal."

A rare oasis. The devastating effects of Judy Tregilgas's inconstant voice had continued—she couldn't telephone or shop. Social functions defeated her. "Such an effort to talk. I get very tight in the chest. I've put on weight, because I'm too tired to exercise. At the bank I write out what I want." Even the dry cleaner, losing patience, had recently turned against her for not having a "normal" voice. Recalling this encounter, the intolerance of someone she had trusted to be kind, Judy came close to tears.

But she was patient with herself. Even theatrical. She wryly listed for me her different voices, which she appreciated for their nuances. She had a voice for her Welsh corgi, a voice for lovers, a *non*-telephone voice, the voice of a daughter . . . She went on itemizing these. What made Judy's appreciation of her voice especially unusual, and not unlike the Aborigine's boundless gradations of desert, or the Inuit's of snow, was that she was describing what some might call a tiresome, limited voice. She seemed to be carrying around inside her a sense of drama about voice itself: much too common a subject for most people to bother over with fine distinctions. Her vocabulary for voice, her sense of wonder about it, seemed enlarged by the disease.

Judy offered to drop me off at the beach resort of Glenelg, four kilometres away, where a breeze off the Indian Ocean might help moderate the humidity here in South Plympton. She drove a tiny yellow car, inherited from her father. He'd had a good voice, she strained to say, over the sound of her popping motor.

We said goodbye at the tram terminus. Glenelg was a beach and retirement resort, with a three-block high street leading to the public ferry pier. I walked out on it, thinking of our conversation. Children fished from pilings. Seawater rolled underneath in long green hills. I glanced back. The beach was full of bathers, straw-hatted volleyballers, people prostrate in the heat. Beyond, a children's amusement park and a revolving Ferris wheel. A wedding party, making its way onto the pier for photographs, resembled a wake.

I tried to recall what the voices of freshly married couples were like, from my young years as an altar boy. I could not recall a single voice. Newlyweds never spoke. They smiled and whispered a lot, as if touch were the password. In the sacristy, where they came back to sign the registry, I was more interested in the best man's voice. From the best man would come cash, inside an envelope. This was why he was called the best man. "That's for you guys. Divide it up, between you."

I turned and noticed a woman in a suit and sunglasses, gazing out to sea.

"What do they sound like?" I called over.

"Pardon me?"

My presumption, as someone with a smooth voice, was that I could use it to ask any irrelevant question on the assumption that it might lead to conversation, thus making up for past journeys when I was too uncertain of my voice to let it help me overcome a chronic muteness. Besides, I was so accustomed by now to strangers willing to tell me their stories that I somehow expected, like the country doctor, to hear more than I bargained for.

I asked her in which direction Kangaroo Island lay. And so we fell into casual conversation, staring out to the horizon, and periodically back to the wedding party making its slow way out the pier, stopping for photographs. I learned it was her mother's birthday today, except she had died the previous year. I wondered if this accounted in part for her mildly tremulous voice. A voice at odds with the chiselled cheekbones, and blond hair cut stylishly short. Her Australian accent was tinged with some other accent. At times her words gapped, or else she would miss a word.

I wondered if I was hearing a voice that wasn't there. Laryngeal dystonia was so rare, I had never happened upon anyone with it except by prior arrangement. Had I simply got to a point in the diaspora where I was hearing what I wanted to hear? Maybe my world did not exist in any other way, and so I wondered if the anthropic principle shouldn't be rewritten: "I hear the universe the way it is because my peculiar voice exists."

Billi Corbett seemed willing to indulge my need to listen, by indulging her own need to talk. She worked for the Australian

Civil Service. She lived in Parafield Gardens, some miles north of Adelaide. She was commuting lately from Glenelg. The marriage party reminded her sadly of her own marriage. She had left her severely "obsessive-compulsive" husband seven years ago, after twenty-one years of marriage, and she didn't know why she had stayed so long. She had married at nineteen.

In white dress and black tuxedo, the newly married couple made their way closer, smiling dreamily at the bossy photographer, who would wave them one way and then the other like a man making up for a dearth of summer weddings. Whenever Billi removed her sunglasses to peer in the direction of the newlyweds, I noticed lines around her eyes.

"I've become mildly neurotic," she confessed. Meaning, it sounded like, she needed to talk more than she needed to stand on ceremony with a stranger. She told me the story of her younger daughter. When she was little, her husband had often committed "verbal incest" with her—words so awful Billi couldn't repeat them, but which eventually put the six-year-old in hospital, near death from anorexia. The mother had gone every day to help force-feed her daughter. "It was awful. My life changed then."

I wondered if her voice had too. Like Judy Tregilgas's voice, it seemed at odds with her attractive worldly appearance.

We could see the bride whispering in her husband's ear. He pumped her lacy elbow. The shutter whirred like a cicada. Billi replaced her sunglasses and turned back to sea.

I was surprised by what she continued to tell me. I probably shouldn't have been. I had been working through the unfashionable notion of Freud's "talking cure" in fiction. Why should a real person sound any less forthcoming than a character? It seemed to me that the flow of one's voice was as crucial to a healthy life as the movement of one's bones. Though unnamed in my novel, the talking cure had been important to a chiropractor's feeling that his patients needed to talk as much, if not more, than he needed to listen.

When I presumed to ask about her voice, about the odd misspoken word, Billi attributed this to her tendency sometimes to think of the Dutch equivalent for a word and thus to mispronounce her English. She had spoken Dutch as a girl. Leaning over, she pointed to her right ear. She was wearing a small, flesh-coloured hearing aid, and suggested this might also affect how she spoke.

I began to wonder if stories resistant to smooth telling weren't the stories I most wanted to hear. I listened for an hour. When the sky began to cloud over, the wedding party began its retreat back down the pier. The bridesmaids and the groom's mafia were now strung out along the railings, bumping hips, twirling like waltzers. Even the photographer had surrendered to sultriness, by taking off his jacket and rolling up his trousers. Showing off, the flower girl continued to skip past the fisher children, who ignored her.

I returned to Adelaide by tram. A storm was boiling up out of the humidity that had massed all afternoon over the ocean. It blew in through the rattling frame windows. Voices rose, arms rose to pull down blinds. I loved this streetcar with its swaying straps, clanking wheels, reversing seats and folding doors. It seemed to tow the suffix *–ing* like a caboose. My father used to be a conductor on one just like it, plunging his changer with a thumb and welcoming passengers with the disarming voice of a leading man.

Next morning, a woman in a blue blouse and white skirt was loitering near my hotel on the corner of Gilbert Place and Hindley Street. Her blond hair was done up, but there were tendrils dangling attractively down. Was this Val Zeunert, cautiously looking me over before approach? But it wasn't her. The woman I turned away from resembled the American actress Suzanne Somers.

"Keath?" It *was* Val. "I came early."

Nothing the matter with this voice, I thought. We shook hands and went into the adjacent café for cappuccino, doughnuts, a conversation. Val was determined to put herself at ease, by pumping me first, so I did my best to sound unthreatening, knowing she was a reluctant participant who had preferred to meet on neutral ground.

"I'm a shy person, but not nervous."

She wasn't shy at all, once she warmed to you. When she began to tell her story, she was forthcoming and vivacious.

By now I was so used to men and women developing spasmodic dysphonia later in life, that it was unusual to hear of someone who got it as a child. I myself had been twenty-eight, with a dystonia vocal tremor that stretched back to adolescence. But Val had developed what sounded like full-blown SD at the age of fourteen, the youngest of anyone I had met.

She'd first become aware of how she sounded as a girl, when she and a friend made a tape of themselves singing and fooling around. "When we played it back, I was hurt and embarrassed at how I sounded." She heard tremors, spasms, distorted words. She had no idea. And began to be teased at school for the way she spoke.

Around this time, Val was removed from a very violent family and placed in a foster home. "I hated it." Because other children tormented her there, she wished she could go back home to her family. Unfortunately, her wish came true. At fifteen she returned to her parents. "It was a bad idea." The next year she left school.

She tried training as a nurse. Because of the great difficulty she had talking to patients, she lasted just a year. She then went into typing and bookkeeping. Again, voice determined her fate. Unable to stand up in class, to read back shorthand dictation, she was forced to quit the program.

"But I wasn't going to let this stop me from *being* something," said Val. She now broke into a radiant smile, recalling her craziest ambition of all. "I decided to become an air hostess." By now, in spite of her best efforts to resist its decline, her voice had got steadily worse. "'This is ridiculous,' I said to myself, 'I'll just *make* myself speak normally.'" A speech pathologist had told her it was all a bad habit she would have to overcome on her own. "But I burst into tears, and made a big fool of myself at the airline interview."

Val was wry about her failures. "Can you imagine me, in an airplane emergency, trying to shout instructions to passengers? For me to apply for an air hostess job was like a one-legged tour guide applying for a job at Ayers Rock." Val had a flair for apt similes, and I soon regretted my inability to remember more of them. I was concentrating on the excellent quality of her voice, waiting to hear about its metamorphosis. It continued to amaze me how small variations on a vocal theme could lead to such divergent biographies. "I felt I *had* to succeed. I've got lots of confidence. I always have. I don't really know why."

She went on to say what happened in the long years between her youthful idealism and the appalling accident that almost cost her life. No stranger to childhood violence, Val had since left three husbands. "I won't put up with any abuse. I won't let anyone treat me like my father treated my mother. I'm a very gentle person." She confessed her attraction nevertheless to violent men like her father.

Maybe her gentleness arose from a tendency to value the bright side of life. Her first son, now twenty-eight, was happily married with three children of his own. This made Val a grandmother. Such perspective on her life encouraged her to think it had been a good life.

"I always had loads and loads of friends and boyfriends. And I'm still on good terms with my ex-husbands. One of them helped me fix up the mechanics on my van."

I now learned how the mechanics on her voice had nearly never been fixed up. She had lived almost her entire life with a severe case of adductor vocal cord dystonia, with no clue to why her voice was broken, other than that this voice was simply her voice. "I couldn't even read to my children. I had a severe speech impediment. I couldn't say my name. I should've married someone called Smith, because I could say Smith."

The turning point in her life came one day while she was watching the influential short feature made for Australian TV about botulinum toxin and spasmodic dysphonia. "For the first time in my life," said Val, "I heard someone else who sounded like me! I remember the exact date. It was April 12, 1991. I wrote a letter straightaway to this doctor in Sydney, explaining what I had."

That weekend, after posting her letter, she took her surfboard out on the ocean and lost it in a big wave. The board went straight down. When it came straight up again, it struck her head like a rocket. So severely that she lost not only the whole left side of her face but her memory as well.

Reconstructive plastic surgery followed, to replace her face.

Replacing her memory was more of a problem. She had lost her ability to spell even an easy word such as *dear*. When she told me this, perhaps Val was thinking of the last thing she'd written before her memory disappeared, the letter to Paul Darveniza. The neurologist had replied by return post, but she didn't read his letter until three years later.

Val, who had barely touched her coffee, paused to sip from her cup. The woman in the next booth leaned closer, to catch what happened next.

"It was the loveliest letter," said Val, "encouraging me to go to a neurologist and get a diagnosis for my voice. That very moment I rang up and got an appointment."

She was sent on to a speech pathologist, and an ENT, who diagnosed her lifelong speaking disorder correctly as SD. A medical condition, finally, to account for an affliction she had always believed to be unique, hers alone. Her relief was huge, her self-blame a little less.

But with the treatment of choice still only available in Sydney, Val waited another four months before toxin injections arrived in Adelaide. Her first was cathartic. Val's mother, her son and his wife, and two of her ex-husbands came to the hospital. "They *all* had a tear in their eye, because when I came out speaking, a little huskily, it was such a *dramatic* difference they could tell as soon as I came out."

Except for her mother, when Val was a small girl, none of them, including her sons, had ever heard her real voice. And now friends couldn't believe it was her. "They genuinely didn't know who it was, when I phoned. One of my friends passed the phone to her husband, who wouldn't believe it was me either. With friends and relatives, nothing changed after the Botox, they said it made no difference to them. 'We always loved you.' But it did have a marked effect on people who didn't know me. Who couldn't understand me. It was just incredible!"

She was suddenly free to use the telephone, talk to bank tellers, make new friends. Not that she had allowed her previous life to cripple her. She said she had never felt depressed. You could tell the elation of recovery interested her more than the despondency of affliction. "I would like to write a book, and Steven Spielberg to make the film, about someone with a speech impediment like mine."

To Val, Botox surgery must have seemed like play-acting compared to the reconstructive surgery on her face and eye. Even her most recent treatment, when she had to put up with a total of eight puncture holes in her neck before the doctor found her larynx with his needle, was a small price to pay for a voice.

At the time we spoke, it had been eight weeks since her last injection and she still sounded fluent—one of the smoothest of afflicted voices I had heard on my journey—especially when I credited the severity of her disorder. "I've always had a perfect result. I love it. For a couple of weeks I'll sound hushy, like Eartha Kitt. Then it's perfect for four months. At the supermarket, before Botox started, somebody would ask me, 'How are you today?' 'F i i i ne,' I used to say. All my life people thought I was very shy. I didn't go to more than a dozen hotels in my life, because of the noise."

To parties and dances, she meant, where no one could have heard her let alone understood her. She could remember how she had been affected by a blinky eye, along with her wonky voice, and this had caused one man at a party to ask why she was winking at him.

Later, when we were sitting in her VW van, in the scorching asphalt lot of her speech therapist's office, she asked if I could see how the shape of her left eye was different than the right. She pointed out how she had fewer wrinkles around her left eye, because of her operation. Definitely a woman whose cup was always half full.

By Sunday morning I was ensconced at the City Waters Lodge in Perth, a motel not far from the Swan River where it opens wide into Perth Water. This motel, with its facing terraces of cat-walks and cells, resembled nothing if not an old-fashioned prison block, such as Reading Gaol. Oscar Wilde wouldn't have found it unfamiliar.

"It's an incredible voice. She has the ability to sing like Patsy Cline if she wants. It's an amazing instrument. It's a transcendental and extraordinary voice."

This from a bearded pundit on the wall-mounted screen, com-menting on a singer whom we then heard strumming her guitar and vocalizing, before the program cut away to a church choir singing Handel's *Messiah*.

I turned off the TV and the worn air-conditioner. Then wan-dered across the city. I had always loved Perth, even before I first arrived here ten years ago, on a flight from Bangkok, hauling around my usual half-a-voice and preference for solitary confine-ment. It wasn't the city so much as its location I loved, the remote edge of a remote continent, its dry climate and vegetation, the Mediterranean feel of its landscape and illimitable ocean.

There was something sad about stepping-off cities like Perth. Vancouver was another. Colombo, too. Dreaming cities, situated on these edges of the world. Their historic distance from capitals of empire meant they were doomed to be unattended by easy recog-nition, unremembered in popular myth, more suited to a future that would come slowly and after we were gone.

Along with its natural setting, I admired Perth's architecture. I could remember reading an article by George Woodcock in a Canadian magazine, some time in the 1980s, commenting on Perth's architecture as recommended to him by Arthur Erickson.

I was struck by how even the public parkades seemed gracefully designed, often of creamy hue, and framed on different levels with flowers and vegetation. Unique skyscrapers downtown, along St. George's Terrace, spoke of a civic imagination made restless by the still impressive colonial structures at their feet. It was as if the year-round fine weather allowed these older buildings to go on in pristine condition, a little like vintage Chevs in Havana, or classic Austins in Kerala. And it seemed like an ideal city for glass. Across from the Transperth Bus Station, in the middle of the skyscraper district, I found a handsome conservatory, open-sided and still unplanted, with the latest tubular steel and curving tempered glass.

George Woodcock was on my mind for another reason just then, besides Perth's architecture. For it was here, upon calling home, that I learned he had died two weeks earlier. As a model for young writers, George had shown how a lifelong commitment to the writing life could be a distinguished endeavour—first in London as an anarchist during the war, and then in Vancouver as a humanitarian, author and traveller for the last forty-five years. The mild Shropshire voice of this gentle anarchist had long counterpointed a strength of character and generosity. Even at meetings or on the radio, when his voice began to waver at the end from emphysema and a bad heart, it never lost clarity or incisiveness. I felt the loneliness of travel again. There was no one to talk to here about his death. I was left on my own to cast back to the previous May and the public celebration of George's eighty-second birthday.

I was saved at least from isolation by a new civic by-law. That Sunday happened to be the first shopping Sunday ever allowed in Perth, and so instead of a deserted downtown, I could walk on the shady side in record heat and not feel I had come to an inhospitable planet, as one sometimes did visiting conservative foreign cities on weekends. I could surround myself with voices. I visited pedestrian malls, crossed the tracks and ate in Northridge, toured the art gallery. I remembered seeing the carved wooden motorcycle there before, by an American sculptor, but looked in vain for the astonishing wooden carvings from South Indian temples. I spent time listening for voices in Australian Aborigine paintings, with their pointillist style and variations on dreaming, water, landscapes. I heard only the silence of the Outback.

"It's a little like your first lover," Helen Sjardin said fondly, the following afternoon. "You never forget."

The chief speech pathologist at Royal Perth Hospital was sitting in her cluttered office, out of which I could see intense blue sky. She had begun to tell me about finding her vocation. She knew as a tiny girl she wanted to be a speech pathologist. Her mother had been nursing Helen's grandmother in their home in Tasmania, and the woman assisting her had a daughter with Down's syndrome. Helen indelibly remembered helping this child say her first word.

"I guess it was in my nature to be a helper," she said.

In their neighbourhood were cerebral palsy victims, and Helen and friends would put on plays to raise money for them.

"I had an interest in speech," she went on, "so I did well in speech and drama." Her drama teacher later asked her to consider speech pathology. Helen remembered going along to meet "Shirley," from England, who encouraged her to train in Melbourne. Afterward, she returned to Hobart and worked in educational speech therapy, as the only speech pathologist in Tasmania. She and her husband were also oyster farmers, before their marriage dissolved, after which this lively, bespectacled woman brought her two daughters west to Perth where she established herself.

Colleagues elected her national president of the Australian Speech and Hearing Association. That week I would learn of the respect and affection she also commanded among patients. Today, this afternoon in fact, she'd just had her photograph in the weekend *West Australian*, along with two of those patients, to accompany a brief article entitled "Poison Restores Lost Voices."

Even as we spoke, the influence of this article was affecting at least one woman Helen had yet to meet. Some years later, I read a short account by Joan Fletcher in the newsletter of Perth's local support group, in which she told of first learning about her condition this same weekend, after living in ignorance of the reasons for her spasmodic voice for twenty-seven years.

Helen had been crucial in building an energetic support group in Western Australia, having persuaded a local neurologist to begin using Botox on patients with vocal cord dystonia. Over the last three years, her group had grown to over two dozen. Unusually, there were more men than women by a ratio of three to one. Loath to generalize about gender, Helen did feel the disorder was perhaps more a problem for men, at least where the kind of public jobs they had traditionally held caused loss of face, which made them more likely to quit. Her two severest cases were male.

Afterwards, the stone pillars and pinched light inside nearby St. Mary's Cathedral caused me to prefer instead the inside of St. George's Cathedral, where I had rested from the heat that morning on my way over to the hospital. Architecture Anglican seemed somewhat airier in Perth than architecture Catholic. At St. George's, while noting the brick and timber construction, I had spoken to a balding, raspy-voiced vicar, who told me that the garrah wood of which the pillars, panels and roof beams were made was from local trees, and had been soaked in the Swan River to seal it after the trees were cut down. This rich wood now glowed like rosewood.

The wood-and-stone pulpits in both cathedrals resembled cockpits. Here the captain of souls would climb to speak the word of God into a microphone attached to a black snaky cord. To see an underworld serpent, plugged into an instrument of spiritual amplification, as I was inclined, you needed to inhabit a speech disorder smacking of original sin. No faith had ever seemed persuasive enough to slay a boa constrictor voice.

Over dinner that evening I read an announcement of the death of Patricia Highsmith, at the age of seventy-four, in Switzerland. I recalled how she had once written to me saying she was too busy trying to help Palestinians "find their voices" (this is how I remembered her words) to write anything in support of villages in India. I had admired her unfashionable independence.

On the same page of *The West Australian*, I noticed a review of the novelist Elizabeth Jolley's new collection of radio plays.

Jolley lived in Perth. Back in my cell that evening, I called to ask if she would care to talk to me about voice in her work, distinguished, it seemed to me, by its eclectic understanding of the speaking voice. I was nervous as I spoke and didn't sound convincing. In a small, tired way she replied that she was busy preparing for an ABC interview and would call back later that week.

I bought a copy of her book next morning for the air-conditioned train ride to Midland, where Gordon Tompsett sat waiting in his new V-6 Holden to drive us back to a capacious bungalow in Glen Forrest. The house sat on a half-acre lot surrounded by towering gum and wattle trees. Gordon said they'd planted the palms themselves. I noticed his voice sounded very smooth. Brenda, Gordon's wife, offered us tea and biscuits, then sat quietly in their large living room while her husband told me his story from a couch across the room.

Gordon had immigrated to Perth from England thirty years ago. Ten years ago, when he was fifty-five, his problems had begun. "I was aware of this catch in my throat. Then in about a year Brenda and the family started to notice. My voice manifested itself as very high"—before it began to sound "pretty awful . . . getting to a stage where I couldn't get any vowels out at all." Cancer of the throat, he speculated, a tumour on the brain. A psychiatrist thought it was all in his head. "He suggested hypnotherapy," said Gordon. "So I went to relaxation classes. I went to speech therapists at Curtin University. None of it made any difference."

At Curtin, they CAT-scanned his brain and sent a recording of his voice to the Mayo Clinic in America for diagnosis. From there he found out he had vocal dystonia, for which there was no useful treatment. A local surgeon, who had observed the recurrent nerve section operations in the States, told him such surgery had only a 30 per cent chance of "coming off," and even then it might regress.

So Gordon had another kind of operation, which spread a Teflon coating on one of his vocal folds. "I got this terrible echo."

Six weeks later his voice was good, then it deteriorated irretrievably. A year later, in 1989, he quit the workplace where he had been a successful building consultant for decades.

"From the age of fifty-nine, I was resigned to becoming a hermit," said Gordon. "I used to work from a display centre. My job was to see what houses people would like to build for themselves. I used to liaise with people all the way through. It got to a stage where I could no longer get the message out. People would say, 'Sorry, I don't understand you.' I went from being the top salesman in the state to one of the lowest. It didn't do much for the self-esteem. Brenda had to phone people. People used to look at you as if you were brain-damaged. I knew what I was saying, it just wasn't coming out that way."

I asked Brenda how she had coped with Gordon's forced retirement and increasing despondency.

"I was frustrated for his sake. I would always let him start a conversation, and see how far he could get, before I had to take over. It was a complete role reversal. Gordon used to be the outgoing one and I was the shy one. I tried to talk him into giving up work sooner than he did."

Gordon had been a gregarious man who shone socially as well as domestically. Brenda had stayed home and brought up their four children. When Gordon's voice finally made it impossible for him to communicate, Brenda answered the phone, dealt with business transactions, led family discussions, even went to work part-time in order to supplement Gordon's disability pension. For someone of her generation, said Brenda, it was a revelation.

"Spasmodic dysphonia brought me out."

Of course, the women of Brenda's generation *with* spasmodic dysphonia—at least those on their own whom I was meeting— were far less fortunate than their married male counterparts in receiving the kind of domestic help given by Brenda.

Gordon, dressed casually in slacks, now bounded from his chair and offered to play me a videotape showing him "before" and "after" his first treatment, three years ago. He had had to endure rumours of a miraculous new drug abroad, and a long wait, before the national government permitted its introduction into Australia.

In the video, Gordon looks youthful in a pink polo shirt, sitting calmly in an examining chair with his hands quietly folded. Then Helen Sjardin asks his name, how long he's had spasmodic dysphonia, how he came to give up his job.

The severity of his chopped, choking, strangled voice shocked me. If I had become complacent about my own voice, even the voices of others with the same disorder, this sound was a sharp reminder of what my trip was about. Botox had lulled me into forgetting the awful struggle to speak at all, the tremendous social and personal dislocation people underwent with the onset, and chronic presence, of this disease.

At the train station I'd met Gordon as he used to be, socially respectable and convivial. I was suddenly seeing another man who bore little resemblance to that one. My response was typical of most people who couldn't fathom what had happened to him. I sat wondering: "Why can't he help himself? He's just putting on this voice."

On screen Helen asks him to say "Ah." A sound of sorts emerges from the patient.

"The call of the mating antelope," Gordon wryly observed, watching himself. "It's amazing the stomach pains, the neck and chest pains, when you try to speak. The pressure used to give me headaches." He worried I might be bored and kept offering to fast-forward the tape.

His responses to other requests from Helen lead to more incomprehensible sentences. Clearly, pathologist and patient are both engaged in making this video for the hopeful purpose of contrasting his smoother speech, following imminent treatment, with this amazing vocal mess.

"You know, Keath," said Gordon, "*I* can't understand what I'm saying. It's no wonder people looked at me with a blank stare."

He had enough and skipped ahead to the week after his first injection of Botox, when he and Helen had got together for another session. His voice is reedy but coherent. Two weeks later Gordon's voice has more body to it. Seven weeks later it's resonant and deeper.

"It had an effect pretty well straightaway," remarked Gordon. Indeed, the vocal transformation was astonishing. "Magnificent," was Gordon's word. "After eight weeks, my voice was as good as it had ever been. It was like getting your life back. It was like getting your legs back. I went to a cricket match and yapped so much I lost my voice again. I was in rapture." His grandchildren had begun to say, "Come and listen to grandad! He's got the same voice we do!" Ah, the elixir of youth.

"That injection lasted about six months, before it started going back. You can feel the old golf ball in the throat starting to come on. Your voice runs down and you get this laryngitis. What really annoys me are these people who get a cold and say, 'I'm losing my voice.' They're not losing their voice at all."

Gordon had had eight injections over the last three years. Usually he had three days of breathiness, before his voice began growing stronger and deeper. He credited his neurologist with knowing exactly where to go with the needle.

Returning to the station through John Forest National Park, we could see the far-off skyscrapers of Perth beneath a fierce blue sky. It was going up to 35c today. I would not meet a man happier in retirement than Gordon, unless it was Earle Reeve. Both men, because of shattered voices, had been forced to resign early from jobs they loved. Both had since experienced miraculous vocal transformations. And the two men lived at either end of the same train line.

Later that week, on the morning I travelled to Fremantle, I woke up without a voice. I was unable to make a sound. My immediate sense was of acute chagrin and disbelief. How would I talk to people I had already arranged to meet? My plans seemed in peril.

Suddenly I was no longer the relaxed traveller, welcome in drawing rooms; I was the voiceless prisoner of Reading Gaol. I was surprised at how humiliated a malfunctioning voice could still make me feel. I was supposed to be exorcising the shame that had been visited upon me by the episode of my wife's putative death two years earlier, by learning how others coped with their disorder. Now I was scrambling once more to cope with my own. Convinced I'd learned nothing, I began guzzling water from the bathroom tap.

Clearly, no amount of knowledge about the physiological origins of my disease would ever dislodge all of its psychological repercussions. I began to think that the inherent shame of the original fall of my voice, many decades earlier, was never going to disappear, no matter how smoothly I hid it under a drug.

This morning it was another drug—a decongestive pill taken last night for a head cold—I now suspected to be the source of my aphasia. But I found it easier to blame the clattering air conditioner. (Two or three years later, I was not surprised to learn that antihistamines were implicated in exacerbating pre-existing cases of dystonia.) The head jailer at my motel was an abrasive woman, tired of taking phone messages and stuffing them in my key box. When I tanked up at her water cooler, before setting out in the morning heat, she seemed pleased to hear I was now paying for my liberties as a gadabout.

I bought bottles of fruit juice in shops along the way to the train station. I kept sounding for my voice. By the time I took my seat on the train I had emitted a short bark. I was ecstatic. I tried again. This time a honk.

The new commuter train was nothing like the boneshaker I remembered between Perth and Fremantle. Smoother, it allowed me to sound, bark, honk and to actually hear myself along the sixteen-station ride. We passed through posh-looking Claremont, a Californian-looking town of tile roofs, where I knew Elizabeth Jolley lived and was going to have nothing better to do than invite over a stuffed-up stranger who claimed he was travelling the world talking to people with funny voices.

By the time I stepped off the train in Fremantle, I had managed to hum a bar from a Patsy Cline song, hoping for some continuity of sound so as not to spoil this interview with a man who hadn't really wanted to submit to it. I looked around for someone who had described himself as five feet ten, sixty-three, and balding.

Earle Reeve was dressed in sports shirt and slacks, about as pleasant looking as you would expect a TV anchorman to be without posing a distraction to the news. His relief seemed palpable when we got into his car and he learned I wasn't carrying a tape recorder. Not that he couldn't have smoothly carried off an electronic interview, but as an ex-ABC broadcaster, humiliated by a deteriorating voice and forced into retirement ten years ago, he was still acutely aware of the power of audio tape to remind him of how the voice that had launched his career in radio back in 1949 had also ended it on TV in 1984.

"My wife suggested we might drive into town for coffee, to save us travelling five miles to the house."

He was already telling me of his rural background in New South Wales, before he moved north to Brisbane as a cadet announcer for ABC at nineteen. He was unused to talking about himself. I later learned he preferred interviewing others, including Elizabeth Jolley.

We parked on the corner of South Terrace, where Earle indicated the coffee was good at the Dôme, an attractive two-storey building with a carefully preserved façade, including a large covered veranda along the second floor. We order lattes and sat inside on the main floor, where Earle resumed his story, occasionally ducking out to plug fresh twenty-cent pieces into the parking meter.

On the radio, he had read news and sports; and introduced classical music. In those years, said Earle, you needed a British accent. In 1954, for example, he had reported on the Royal Tour, and listening to a tape of that today he didn't recognize his own voice. Transferred across the country to Perth, he began reading TV news for ABC in Western Australia in 1960. "I enjoyed it." He was still in his mid-thirties when a commission for the network commended him for his "remarkable voice"—a compliment Earle now thought "a bit much," but an "outstanding" commendation nonetheless.

He read the news on TV until 1975. As early as 1973, he began noticing words not coming out of his mouth quite right. "Pr emier," for instance. "P urpose." Over the next three years, along with increasing spasms and strangled sounds, he also developed a noticeable tremor in his speech.

We were now interrupted by a blonde Earle knew. I got the feeling he might have asked her to drop by, in case he needed an excuse to escape. Christine Gossfield sat down without ordering coffee and casually let me know Earle had set the tone for a whole generation of announcers at ABC. She then proceeded to talk about a recent robbery, the police who did and didn't come, and a dyslexic son. By now Earle, looking at his watch, was anxious to get back to his own story.

When Christine left he told me her husband was one of the top ten steel guitarists in the world, leader of a famous country and western band called Lucky Oceans. Did I know it? Earle had got to know them while hosting a c.&w. music program on the radio, something he continued to do after he was taken off television.

"I found informal chatting was relatively easy. You know, you could skip around certain words. But reading news was a lot more difficult. You couldn't avoid the written word."

His removal from television news had been a tremendous blow to his self-esteem. Required to read the news on radio, he would sometimes get other announcers to fill in for him, particularly in the early morning. For some reason, he felt easier reading in the evening. This, however, did not prevent listeners from phoning in to ask if the announcer was drunk. For a proud man, aware of his commendable broadcasting past, Earle found it mortifying to be betrayed by his own voice.

I asked for another glass of water and continued listening, amid a talkative crowd of young caffeine drinkers who did not recognize

Earle, his disappearance from television having occurred before their time.

As early as 1973 or '74 he had been to a speech therapist, a hypnotherapist and a neurologist who prescribed heavy tranquillizers. He used them once, could barely read the news, went home and flushed them down the toilet. One doctor asked, "Why don't you have a couple of drinks before you read the news?" But Earle found alcohol dried up his sinuses. At Royal Perth Hospital he tried biorhythm relaxation exercises. He tried everything possible. "I was desperate to continue the work I loved."

He was taken off the air altogether in 1978.

"It had never happened before, to an ABC announcer."

For a while he worked at the network as a producer. In 1979, he was allowed to return at public request to his old Tuesday night c.&w. program, "and this seemed to go fairly well." It remained informal and he could relax. Then unexpectedly, in 1981, he was again rostered to read the news. He did so, in fifteen-minute bulletins, with great reluctance.

"These next years were the toughest time of my life. I found it increasingly difficult to be positive. At night I began to have nightmares about not being able to read the news. I yearned and prayed to be what I once was, highly regarded and good at what I did. I loved to read the news."

In August 1984 Earle was asked to step into his boss's office, to be told they were taking him off air. He recalled vividly for me how the man's hands shook as he read the letter from ABC's Sydney head office. Tapes, it seemed, were sent regularly back east for review.

During this period, unable to rescue his voice, Earle had begun to listen more closely to others. "I became a much keener student of announcers, the way some read well and others didn't. I became a student of presentation. A keen student of the English language."

After leaving ABC in 1985, he began lecturing to broadcasting students at the Western Australia Academy of Performing Arts, a job he enjoyed. Here he was able to confess to his classes that he had a voice problem, for which there was no cure. He knew he had something called "spastic dysphonia," but of course it did him little good to know this, since the disorder was even more obscure then—still unlinked to dystonia and the brain stem, still untreatable. At the academy, Earle adopted as his motto *Ars celare artem*: Art conceals art.

In other words, said Earle, "Something is better said than read."

In teaching voices how to read, he would go into the importance of phrasing, pitch, colour, emphasis, cadence, pauses, and the "round" voice. "Eighty-five per cent of people can hit a golf ball," said Earle. "But only the top few percent can read the news." Having a voice was not enough to communicate well. It had to be trained. And he taught the importance of good *writing* for the voice.

His students appreciated his wealth of experience, and would sometimes persuade him to be interviewed for their student broadcasts.

"Listening to these tapes of myself, I would cringe at having succumbed."

He remained "terribly frustrated" about his disorder, and there were other "crushing" moments in his life before he submitted to his first botulin treatment, in January 1994. He told me of being invited in 1993, as an after-dinner speaker, and afterward of thinking he had done very well. He was witty, and people had seemed to enjoy what he had to say. Only later did he hear from somebody who hadn't been there, who heard from someone who had been, that Earle's voice had sounded "terrible."

"I was crushed. I'm a pretty strong person emotionally, but . . ."

I drank more water and offered Earle, in a fading voice, a similar experience of my own, before an audience at the International Festival of Authors in Toronto, thinking I sounded not too bad after overcoming a hesitant start. I later sent for the audio tape, wanting to share the triumph with my wife in Vancouver. Turning it on, I too had been crushed. I couldn't listen beyond a few sentences. I remembered having received a strong ovation, but now felt this was more like the response for the performance of a wheelchair athlete. The audience's relief was that I had been able to carry off speaking at all. A scheduled CBC interview was promptly cancelled. Like Earle's, this humiliation concerning one's own hubris, the poor ear for one's own voice, had never gone away.

Earle feared losing his voice entirely, when he agreed to his first injection of toxin. It had not turned out to be quite the watershed he hoped for right away. He was still wary of the drug's side effects, something even worse than the strain he'd grown used to. After his second injection, last August, he had lost his voice for six weeks. Then in November, still worried about his voice, he'd had to testify before a tribunal on behalf of a friend charged with sexual harassment.

"How did it go?" I asked.

"I did amazingly well."

Indeed, the smoothing effects of the drug still sounded much in evidence. A word here or there might break, but nothing unmanageable. He was stretching out his last procurement, for as long as possible, to avoid the kind of voicelessness that was much on my own mind this morning.

Earle was now employed part-time by a local TV channel, as an adviser to newsreaders, journalists and announcers. Life with his "wonderfully supportive" wife seemed to have reached rounded retirement. And he was proud of his thirty-three-year-old son, Simon, who was travelling the globe these days with Olivia Newton John, making short films for the program *Wild Life*. Earle suggested I might care to tune in that evening, for the latest instalment.

That afternoon I remembered what it was like to be in society without a voice again. Mine had grown increasingly mute, after coffee with Earle. I could not keep it lubricated, functioning, or audible. Calling from a phone box in Fremantle, I was unable to speak to a man in Safety Bay, and had to hang up. Back in Perth, when I returned to the Qantas office to arrange my trip to Johannesburg, I recognized the agent's cool and suspicious response. She was reluctant to deal with someone in obvious emotional distress. Two days earlier, she'd been exceptionally cordial. Had I been sporting a neck brace instead of this voice, or walking in leg irons, I would have felt welcome. Somehow, sounding strange is much worse than looking abnormal.

Aliens had scrambled my voice and nothing would bring it back.

I was too stuffed up to do more than plod back to my cell and turn on *Wild Life*, with Simon Reeve. Unfortunately, the show I saw seemed little more than an excuse to film attractive scenery by provoking animals into unnatural acts, in sometimes unnatural habitats. In Simon's segment, he narrated and participated in a wagon race of Siberian huskies over sand dunes in Oregon. Tall and blond, he sounded lighter and less "trained" than Earle, more Australian.

Two or three years later, Simon would narrate an updated documentary on spasmodic dysphonia, for *Good Medicine*, on national TV. It would focus on his father's broadcasting career and his medical treatment. Robyn Mundy, whom I also met that week in Perth, wrote to me about it: "It was well done, and as a result of that, the hospitals were flooded with enquiries from prospective patients from all over Australia. One 45-50 year aged lady, who lives on a farm in the wheatbelt area of WA, has had symptoms since she was 15 years old and simply decided she was the only person in the world with this 'wonky' voice. On seeing the programme, she made contact with Royal Perth Hospital, was subsequently diagnosed with SD, and has recently had her first botulin injections with great success."

This documentary wasn't Simon Reeve's first piece on Botox. A couple of weeks later, waiting all day for a bus in Grahamstown, South Africa, I happened to catch his piece on women in New York and Los Angeles using Botox injections to smooth wrinkled skin. If this was not part of Simon's "wild life" series, I supposed it might have been, given the particular species of woman he was tracking.

Crisscrossing Perth in the overbearingly hot days that followed, I visited and talked to others resident in the tiny but scattered diaspora of laryngeal dystonia. By now my head cold had worsened.

Something sad about every story I heard travelling, from those who had lost their voices and then voyaged years in the vocal wilderness searching for a reason, made me wonder if part of this sadness was my own nostalgia for the vocal wholeness I'd surrendered at puberty when my voice, so I believed, betrayed itself for no other reason than a loss of nerve.

Yet mine was only an exaggerated case of what anybody with a voice underwent. Loss of the unbroken sound of innocence, I supposed, belonged to the biblical sadness over voice depicted by the myth of Babel. The ambition of humanity to build a city and tower to reach heaven had resulted in the CEO's decision to "confound their language, that they may not understand one another's speech" (Genesis, 11:7). And so henceforth were we scattered abroad, no longer able to speak in one voice, or even to remember what it sounded like.

I was still hoping to find and claim a glasshouse, wherein voice and structure seemed in puissant balance. I imagined a myriad of voices, coexisting peacefully in a kind of wacky wonder, an illusory oasis, some harmonious Eden. Stories, including my own, varied in the degree to which the voices telling them had become flexible and useable again, before paralysis wore off and our voice boxes needed to be reinjected. The day would come, I was pretty sure, when surgery and even gene therapy would eliminate the need for recurrent bouts of a paralytic drug.

Back at Royal Perth Hospital, I met Terence Stendage and his wife Sheila. Terence had travelled up from Rockingham for an appointment with Helen Sjardin. Had the severity of Terence's voice ever caused him to avoid people? "Not really," he said. Sheila would carry on talking for him. "I always talked a lot anyway," said Sheila, "so this was no great burden." Immigrants from England, they both spoke with friendly Cockney sounds. Terence seemed like a jolly man, balding and trim, dressed in a cream-coloured shirt and slacks. But he had suffered and continued to suffer much pain from a neck injury, sustained thirteen years ago, when "a piece of steel came down and hit me in the back of the neck, while I was carrying a heavy load." Since then, much of his concern had focused on his neck.

Neck injuries had continued to interest me among people I was talking to about damaged voices. I remembered my own case of whiplash. Robyn Mundy, a graphic designer from Leederville, told me that around the time she developed dysphonia, she had been sitting in a car when someone grabbed her head from behind and twisted it painfully. Earle Reeve had mentioned that in 1967, at a holiday resort down the coast, he had been doing somersaults for his children in the ocean, when he smashed his head against the bottom and severely bent his neck. "I saw stars." Five years later, close to the onset of his SD, he woke up one night with an excruciating pain in his arm, the worst pain he ever experienced. He needed morphine. He decided it was a pinched nerve, related to his original neck injury. Its legacy had remained a numb thumb, said Earle, along with a grinding sound in the head.

(Later, when I found out my teen idol Jimmie Rodgers had developed SD, I recalled old news that he had mysteriously lost his voice some time after a twenty-three-square-inch steel plate had been implanted in his skull following an unprovoked beating by police one night on the San Diego Freeway.)

In Terence's case, his neck injury had been so severe as to force him into retirement at forty-three. He then became suicidal. The Workers' Compensation Board, hoping to discover whether his injury was "real" or not, began hounding him and his friends in its "inquiries." "It was most unpleasant. There was all sorts of snooping."

His dysphonia developed ten years later. "My voice would break down in the middle of a sentence. My vowels would go." (Not only had his voice deteriorated; so had his hand, further evidence of dystonia. He had trouble controlling a pen and brush. Terence was an amateur watercolourist who had once taught art.) Following diagnosis, he received his first and last toxin a year ago.

Although his voice had improved after a fortnight, Terence had a problem with needles. Therapy for his original neck injury had been needles through the neck, so when he saw the needle used to inject him with botulin, "I almost freaked out." Since then he had investigated alternative therapies including reiki.

Terence and Sheila were both convinced this weekly laying-on of hands had helped him. "People are usually drawn to my neck," said Terence. "I can use their energy to help my voice. It's not religious, reiki. Everyone has it." The universal life energy, he meant. "It's a matter of not getting involved in the lunatic fringe. The more I do it the more I have to believe there's something there. Last night . . . it was such a strange sensation, when I touched someone. It was like my hand was welded to her body."

But recently the benefits of reiki had begun "to peter out." Self-hypnosis, visualization, crystal therapy were now favoured. Terence was even planning on a second injection. He thought the relaxation he had since learned would help him get over his fear of needles in his neck.

Robert Edwards talked about his neck, too, but that was another day.

Back in my motel room I called Elizabeth Jolley. She was sorry not to have got back to me. She said she had been busy, tied up with grandchildren. But I knew her ear for troublesome voices had put her decidedly off mine. I let go then, relieved.

───────────

Other voices I recalled from Perth, the night I flew to Africa:

The flat insistent voice of a cripple in Hay Street Mall, mournfully singing the anthem, "Me and Bobby McGee," every time I passed him belted into his wheelchair, rocking back and forth over an imaginary guitar atop his stomach.

The Australian drawl of a secretary in the extension department of the university, returning my call with the number of someone I had wanted to talk to. "Thry – it – two . . ." Sorry? "Thry – it – two – one – two – it – non – non."

An isolated man's piping question, "Wedjacumfrum?"

This last one on a torrid day near Daglish Station, after dragging myself toward the promised oasis of a deli along Hamersley Road. The temperature outside was 38c. Inside, a heaving air-conditioner made this store with its depleted shelves bearable.

I ordered a chicken sandwich. A man disappeared through a door and reappeared to say the chicken was "finished." I envisioned this chicken dead from heat stroke, with a past-due date branded into its feathers, beyond which salmonella was now a distinct threat. I then asked for toasted ham and he disappeared to check on the pig. Silence. Except for a fly and the air conditioner. Then something hit the glass case like an olive pit, and the buzzing stopped.

As far as I could tell, no other customer had been in today. I looked out to the sidewalk. Dead, a potted pine had lurched slightly skyward and turned over on its root.

My sandwich, when it appeared, was wrapped in a cellophane body bag, untoasted. I ordered a milk shake to go with it. The proprietor's curiosity got the better of him. "Wedjacumfrum?" His accent nearly impenetrable.

He himself, it turned out, had come recently from Melbourne. How did he like Perth? He said nothing, as his arm scooped ice cream from a shallow bucket. I worried he might not have understood my accent. When he finally answered, "Aintryllybinow," I had to rerun his voice through my decoder, to understand what he was saying.

"Ain't really been out."

I still didn't understand.

"It's like I don't have time, with the deli like. I'm here seven days a week, twelve ticks a day." His voice, high and compressed, sounded tight from isolation, a sparse clientele, the heaving air conditioner.

"Perth's isolated. Compared to Melbourne. A thousand dollars to fly anywhere." Innywear. He meant to Melbourne. I began to wonder if he had even been to Perth, since arriving last year at the airport.

On the day I was to leave for Africa, Helen Sjardin picked me up in the morning and drove us down the coast to her favourite beach. She was dressed in shorts, enjoying her weekend.

Helen's interest in voice was broader than one might have expected of a professional committed to the rigours of speciality. She was open to workshops on philophonetics, attentive to alternative therapies such as reiki, and responsive to choirs. Earlier that week, in response to my wondering about the possible effects of monasteries and convents on the human voice, she had passed along a recent issue of the newsletter she coordinated for the Australian Voice Association. In it was her report on an Australian radio program, about a French otolaryngologist-philosopher, whose study of monks in one Benedictine monastery told of their having done away with chanting, only to become torpid and unfocused. When the Gregorian chant was reinstated, the monks in this and other monasteries were gradually rehabilitated.

"This was used," wrote Helen, "to demonstrate the value of voice and sound in stimulating the brain."

She now told me of her own experience at a nine-day Buddhist retreat, where the emphasis had been on silent meditation. "In the process, I found I was able to control my energy level." She had learned through silence and thoughtfulness how to cut in half her medication for an overactive thyroid. She had learned how to ration what she wanted to say, and to whom she wanted to say it, upon her return to the everyday world. She had become much more selective among those she wanted to see. "Once outside again, your thoughts quickly scattered, so you had to remember what you learned in contemplation."

We talked as we drove past the University of Western Australia, which reminded me of Stanford, and we talked our way over the hill at Cottesloe, where we burst into view of the blue Indian Ocean. We talked our way down the coast to Fremantle, where Helen was taking me to meet one of her patients for breakfast.

I'd mentioned how I had been unable to "hear" the voices of abstract Aborigine painters in galleries in Sydney and Perth. Typically, she found this worth pursuing and had brought along some highlighted pages about Aborigine creation myths. The Creator had used his voice, rather than his hands, to mould the first man out of mud. His power resided in his voice. Pictures of the mouthless Wandjina-figure, a man-shape assumed by the Creator Wallanganda, were new to me. I now read how the Wandjina's mouth was considered sacred, beyond our understanding, and therefore unpaintable.

Perhaps my "ear" hadn't been so deaf after all.

Our discussion of the mouthless Wandjina led Helen to mention she had once taken a four-day trek with Aborigines into the outback. She said one night under the stars and a full moon, alone, she heard sounds coming from inside herself. The landscape had given her voice, she believed.

Arriving at the beach, we went inside the canvas-and-glass Beach Club cafeteria to continue our conversation. But her patient, Robert Edwards, had arrived early and rose to greet us, a handsome tan man of forty. A car broker.

He blossomed right away into a monologue about the tightness in his neck, pains in his hands and feet, the exercises he performed to relax the different regions of his anatomy. I glanced at Helen, who remained focused and sympathetic. I was puzzled as to why Robert was reluctant to admit a connection between tightness in his speaking muscles, and that in the rest of his body. I wondered why he was reluctant to admit he had dystonia.

His friendly, choppy voice somehow lacked the conviction of its expression. Yet it grew on me.

Beyond us lay the sun-bleached sand. Helen left to go for a swim in the creamy, turquoise surf. This was the stretch of coast where the America's Cup yacht races had recently taken place. Parachuters were falling into the sea. I was puzzled. No one seemed to care that these blossoming Icaruses were disappearing into the waves. Robert told me they were jumping into water, rather than onto land, because it was less risky for training novices. A practice begun during the war.

I was not entirely surprised to learn Robert was a pilot. Tonight, he and his lady friend would be flying off on a double date for dinner. Robert said he would probably fly his friend's plane home, because his friend liked to drink.

We got up and ordered coffee.

I began to understand Robert's take on his voice. In relating its long, unconfident history, during which time he had left a position in home finance, where he used to arrange loans for people, he said: "I realized I was in a stressful situation. I didn't think it was a chemical complaint. Primarily, I thought it was an emotional problem. I had to come to grips with my state in life and my emotions. I still have grave doubts that this is a neurological complaint. I feel it is a psychological condition. Because it comes and goes, depending on how I feel, how loose I am. I tend to feel I'm controlling it. To me it's not a chemical malfunction. It's a thing being influenced by emotions and thoughts. It's kind of like a child, who gets emotionally upset. I think it's the emotions that control your voice. Your emotions affect your whole metabolism."

I began to wonder if I had been presumptuous. Obviously, not everyone who was stricken with this disorder was overjoyed to be told their condition was neurological and incurable, rather than psychological and manageable. As with Maria Gerakiteys in Sydney, Robert seemed to think he might fix the way he sounded by working on the psychological condition that produced it.

I had begun to wonder if there was something Robert wasn't mentioning, besides dystonia. Worried about losing his job two years ago, he had gone to an ENT, and then to another specialist who diagnosed his disorder. Robert had had his first and only injection of botulinum toxin between leaving home finance and going back to selling cars.

"It was pretty unpleasant," he confessed. He meant the injection. In fact, he'd found the wires attached to him and the needles going in traumatic. He had not gone back for another needle.

I felt closer to understanding Robert's voice now, more sympathetic. If he could convince himself that his dystonia was psychological and not neurological—in other words, up to him to control—then he wouldn't have to bother with any more needles. It made perfect sense, in a perverse sort of way. There seemed to exist this contradiction between what Robert believed and what he wanted to believe.

"As time progresses, I'm getting better and better. And when the time comes, when I can't cope, then I'll go back. That might be the answer."

Helen returned looking very relaxed in her towel and wet bathing suit. She seemed like a kind of earth mother embracing sea life. I noticed she was reading the children's stories of Roald Dahl. Typically, she was curious to learn about a recent biography of Dahl evidently portraying him as a shit. "That's very interesting," she said, in her restful voice, "because I had already said to myself, 'I don't think I like this writer.'"

We said goodbye and Robert drove me back to Perth. I had come to admire his determination to change his life and thereby his voice. He had already come to Perth from Melbourne, looking for new opportunity. He liked it here. The weather, the dry heat. He was a genuinely friendly man, someone meant to serve the public if only he himself weren't disserved by a voice he took so much responsibility for.

He dropped me at Kings Park, overlooking the Swan and downtown Perth, where I was glad to be back in the Botanic Gardens after a decade. I had forgotten the vista of coast that could be seen from the State War Memorial, sweeping from the Indian Ocean to the Darling Scarp. It was my last day in Australia, and this seemed a fitting place to look back.

For some reason, a coda failed me.

I walked on through the fierce midday heat. The Mediterranean fragrance of pines made me think of Spain. The display glasshouses, set down in arid bush and dry, cicada-pulsing heat, were an unexpected treat—low rectangular houses devoted to native and South African plants from desert to tropical. I tramped the brick pathways of the Dry Inland house, revived by fragrant arid plants in red soil.

I was convinced I could smell the blue tubular flowers of the *Eremophila mackinlayi*, with its round grey leaves. Then I was taken in by a namesake of sorts, the *Eremophila cuneifolia x fraseri*, apparently a cross between turpentine bush and royal poverty bush, found around the Gascoyne area. This plant sounded suitably suggestive for someone interested in vocal cross-dressing—*pale lilac flower with a finely spotted throat*, I read, *carrying a very large cream-coloured calyx, which enlarges and persists, providing a prolonged display after the flower falls.* Sounded to me like a fancy metaphor for the pollinating effects of botulinum toxin, on an impoverished voice exactly like mine.

The scent of *x fraseri* buried itself deep in my lungs, affording a kind of relaxation and summing up of my semi-anonymous voice. This scent seemed to lift me from a too narrow and restricted striving. I supposed every sense produced codas. Hearing had its codas of symphony and opera, seeing of painting and architecture. In the voicey coda of a novel, such as *Invisible Man*, ears and eyes came together:

"Ah," I can hear you say, "so it was all a build-up to bore us with his buggy jiving. He only wanted us to listen to him rave!" But only partially true: Being invisible and without substance, a disembodied voice, as it were, what else could I do? What else but try to tell you what was really happening when your eyes were looking through? And it is this which frightens me:

Who knows but that, on the lower frequencies, I speak for you?

Adieu. A novelist writing for his life will write as though his latest performance could be his last. In Ralph Ellison's case, it more or less was. The imagination like the voice was a perishable plant, and glasshouses kept reminding me of this. Mine was a hothouse voice used to cultivating its dreams inside an artificial structure.

Years earlier I had found myself expanding as my throat filled with the air of a glasshouse. Alongside that frozen river, I sensed the plants inside were as necessary to the health of my voice as I to their own survival. Gases in, gases out.

And it was still nature of a sort, reciprocating nature of a sort. Toxin, these days, giving voice to a hothouse junkie.

6

The President's Voice

THREE OR FOUR YEARS after I flew from Perth to South Africa, I noticed a picture in a Canadian newspaper of Sidney Poitier in a brick-walled back alley pointing his pistol at a young black man on his knees. I assumed it was a publicity shot lifted from a film under review. In fact, it was a news photo of an off-duty police reservist, dressed in shirt and tie, screaming at a thief who had tried to steal his cell phone in the inner-city Johannesburg suburb of Hillbrow, a neighbourhood under growing siege since the end of apartheid.

I recalled my own week of having to hang around Hillbrow, in the year following the country's first democratic national election, when crime had increased in previously safe areas such as this one.

I was waiting for a phone call that never came.

When I landed, news of the city's increasing violence had not yet penetrated my guidebook, nor had it reached the international press the way it soon would, where stories of Johannesburg's murders, carjackings, burglaries, muggings and white flight became commonplace. I got interested in how the fear of violence affected voices.

I noticed how my own voice turned breathy and shallow after I was mugged on the Sunday morning I arrived. This effect of my own fear was understandable. But was it possible to generalize about an entire country? I would listen to Nelson Mandela's voice on TV. At times it sounded to me slurred and impenetrable. I would later ask one or two speech pathologists I met in South Africa to describe how he spoke. They seemed not to have thought much about the voice of the President, although it was now the most widely heard voice in South Africa. One woman in Cape Town mentioned that when you got older your muscles weakened and something happened to your vocal cords.

And yet Mandela had had the same high pitch in his one TV interview from the early 1960s, before imprisonment. The voice was just smoother then and better lubricated. Even today it was not a voice affected by fear, except perhaps indirectly, over a lifetime of violence done him. But it did sound like a fearful voice, if you thought about how fear dries up and pitches the voice higher. On the other hand, according to Anne Burgi, the therapist from South Africa who had helped to diagnose me in Vancouver and whom I later met in London, Zulu and Xhosa men tended to have more breathy voices.

Here was a man whose native language was Xhosa. He had learned English young and trained as a lawyer. He had become a militant in the African National Congress, gone into hiding, before being imprisoned for life by the apartheid regime. He had sat in a cell for twenty-seven years, most of them on Robben Island. It was conceivable his voice had simply rusted there, sometimes in solitary confinement. It sounded like an unused voice, pressed back into service of the nation, missing the lubricating habits of an uninterrupted lifetime of normal human conversation. However tight, breathy and effortful, it now possessed the most recognizable timbre of any political voice in the world. The sound and quality of the voice had everything and nothing to do with its inevitable eloquence. An unfortunate history had guaranteed its integrity.

Mandela's voice had never been heard widely in public before he was released from prison in 1990. A dead, already legendary man had come back to life. His was the unheard, unspoken voice of the past, promising to become the benevolent voice of the future.

The actual sound of it had almost no bearing on its appeal; the appeal of it was immediately determined by the fact it made any sound at all.

President Mandela was the first modern politician to bring a private voice so successfully into the public arena. Its very frailty ensured its honour. His voice—because of, but also in spite of, its weakness—helped him to become a statesman before he was elected a politician. Raspy, weak, poorly produced, the sound was also wise, tolerant, self-deprecating, witty, trustful, and flecked with iron fibre.

I had been thinking about the new president's voice before I landed in Johannesburg. Then, on a deserted bus ride in from the airport, I saw a billboard advertising something called the Voice Clinic. I now began to think of the country as a huge voice clinic governed by Nelson Mandela, trying to find its way to rehabilitation and assertiveness, discipline and resonance. Notwithstanding its bravery under oppression, I was still unable to hear Mandela's voice as one entirely separable from the fear and despair he must have experienced when he was incarcerated. There were now so many languages desperately competing for attention in South Africa—Xhosa, Sesotho, Siswati, Zulu, Afrikaans, English—that finding a unifying voice for such a divided nation had turned the country into the kind of clinic I imagined.

In Johannesburg, I tried calling the Voice Clinic and repeatedly heard a scream, which in my ignorance I did not recognize as a fax signal. I never did get through to the clinic in Johannesburg, although I would pay a visit to its headquarters in Cape Town and talk to its founder's father. Not surprising, it seemed to have found its niche among a largely white corporate clientele. Yet my image of it persisted as some sort of national experimental metaphor, even after my leaving the country.

I had wandered downtown to Joubert Park, from the Ridge Hotel in Hillbrow. It was a pretty park with an energetic fountain and very green lawns, acacia trees, and litter everywhere, in spite of a parade of trash cans along its paths. Unemployed men lay under trees, sprawled on benches, sat in desultory conference on the grass. Benches enshrouded in laundry belonged to people who slept in the park and washed their clothes in the fountain. Earlier, on my taxi ride up the hill from the bus compound, I had spotted a glasshouse. So I headed for it now, lightly conscious of the many eyes following my leather shoulder bag. I was being careful with it, but not in any more tense a way than in Lima, where the bag had come from some years before. I was trustful of this crowded Sunday morning. Not even four disenfranchised young men, who sullenly vanished as I entered the glasshouse, concerned me, although later I thought what a ripe target I would have made in here among the concealing plants.

Rather airily, I was thinking of Babel. I recognized that an interest in voice meant I would need to be aware of all languages in this multilingual country—not that I spoke any of them but my own. In a country such as this, most of the voices would be inaccessible to me. On the other hand, in South Africa as in the even more linguistically diverse India, one could still travel and communicate with a range of citizens by using the lingua franca. And one could do this—oddly perhaps—without necessarily feeling limited to one language. For the voice of English was no longer the British voice, and probably hadn't been since around the era of the Crystal Palace.

I was coming to think, incidentally, of glasshouses as another version of Babel, scattered attempts to put us in touch with the sunlight above, wherein a place in Eden might be reclaimed among the orchids down here. Adelaide's Bicentennial Conservatory had been only the latest example of hubris on the grand scale. Among those glasshouses I would never see was Joseph Paxton's immense Crystal Palace in Hyde Park, which in the second part of the nineteenth century, when it hosted the Great Exhibition of All Nations in 1851, had started a craze for glasshouses throughout the world. The largest building on earth, covering eighteen acres and extending a third of a mile, it was torn down the following year, and parts of it were relocated to Sydenham, where it was rebuilt at half again its size and double the glass. Courts from the ancient architectural past, including Assyrian, Byzantine and Chinese, were filled with fountains and fauna, heated by fifty miles of pipes and fitted out with a towering organ and tiered concert platform for four thousand massed voices. Opened by Queen Victoria in 1854, this glasshouse was destroyed by fire in 1936.

Somehow, my paper memory of the Crystal Palace had encouraged in me the mythical notion that the British Empire had reached its zenith there, where it spoke for the last time to the world in one assured, English voice. An imperceptible decline into disparate dialects had begun, until the colonial ascent of mutually incomprehensible languages led to its eventual fragmentation.

The voices of English were now various around the world, ethnically charged and culturally evolved. In Delhi, I was not hearing the same language as in Nashville, Durban or Dublin. In this way, it pleased me a little to think of myself as the linguist I wasn't. Unlike a Swiss or a Dane, that consummate linguist, an English Canadian could talk to other nationalities in his own language and be understood. Better yet, I could understand other voices and not feel excluded in the same way I did travelling through South America, say, where Spanish was the lingua franca outside of Brazil.

This glasshouse was actually four small houses. The one you entered surprised with its lily pond, and led into a somewhat taller palm house, off which stood two modest houses to either side. Each was cooler than outdoors, except for one house growing cacti. Any glass panes not broken had been painted white to filter sunlight. I was struck with a subtle yearning by the Victorian ironwork, repainted often, and by brick pathways and house cats. I had travelled through the Antipodes with a similar nostalgia franca, for an Ur-glasshouse I longed someday to reach. An air of disuse had not kept someone from watering the coleus, pothos and ferns. But there were no voices, no caretakers—no benches even—and no visitors but myself to talk to. I was reluctant to speak loudly, for fear of bringing back the four sullen young men.

"'And the whole earth was of one language, and of one speech....'"

It occurred to me the myth of Babel had got it fundamentally wrong. So had scholars, who'd never suggested (so far as I knew) that this mythical model of a single language from which all others had descended—and to which, ever since, they had found themselves yearning nostalgically back through such myths as the Bible's—was precisely the wrong model for what must have happened, when man first acquired the cognitive capacity to turn his voice into words. My layman's anthropological sense told me *many* languages had evolved from many disparate communities of caves, burrows, hollow logs—once human grunting began to take on shape and oral architecture, making life easier to share, survive, even plan for, through spoken nouns and (eventually) verbs.

One's voice had become another limb, another tool. But it had also become an instrument to tinker over, experiment and play with. Vocabularies had accreted slowly, entirely different in different communities, the private languages of tribes and families.

Over millennia, I imagined, as these communities encountered one another tentatively or violently, local languages were tested for their efficiency, euphony and resilience. Words, phrases, linguistic structures had partially and entirely replaced those whose appeal was lost in the hearing of either a more dominant and imposing culture, or simply a more pleasing way of using the voice to communicate the quotidian. Influential languages had expanded in hybrid forms, as they encountered rival tongues and insinuated themselves. At the same time, an unimaginable number of languages had thus slowly eroded over aeons, until relatively fewer and fewer of them were "needed" in a world growing perceptibly closer, a process continuing unabated today, among still thousands of spoken languages.

In South Africa, for instance, where its eleven official languages are in daily juxtaposition, the so-called purity of each language evolves through dilution and compromise. Apparently, the hybrids spoken in a vast South African migratory township such as Soweto are mixtures of Xhosa and Zulu and Sesotho. I concluded that as any new language builds, it leaves behind its predecessors—

either to wither in place, or to lose the influence they once enjoyed among speakers where it originated.

This had happened with Dutch. Whereas imperial English survived and flourished in a broader, mutually comprehensible form around the world, Dutch lost the influence it once enjoyed abroad, including in South Africa. Afrikaans, eventually spoken by most coloureds as well as Boers, evolved from High Dutch of three hundred years ago, as it jettisoned the difficult grammar and embraced words of other imperial languages, along with those of local African and Asian languages. A college course in Boer history, and my prejudice against the Afrikaans accent when hearing it in English, had inclined me away from any notion that it was a sensitive or attractive language. But I was told, by enlightened young and older Afrikaners, that their native language was beautiful, shaded in degrees, and they loved to speak it. Pride of idiom seemed just as brisk as pride of place.

I was easily persuaded human beings had never begun with one lost language, one primal voice at all, before the biblically imagined fragmentation supposedly occurred, and ten thousand tongues arose in the linguistic chaos following. I suspected, rather, we began with a thousand, a hundred thousand, tongues—something too complex for the simplicity of our first urban myth to accommodate in Babel, founded as it was on the attractive metaphor of a hubristic tower, and the abiding image of some previously harmonious time of human perfection, before it all fractured and fell away.

Still, once fired by this image of a pre-Babel state of vocal harmony, I was either culturally or congenitally unable to let go of it. I was looking at a worn Victorian screw handle, attached to a section of window above where I was standing, breathing in the faint, energizing scent of half-watered soil. I decided that in a remarkable reversal of the myth of Babel, the English language was now itself threatening to set up as a Tower, as a tongue all those millions of years and countless languages were coming down to, in the unspoken yearning of each of them to become universally understood. The nature of any language—expansive if possible, protective when necessary—suggested something organic and even aggressive about spoken language. About voice. Perhaps voice itself was the common language I yearned for. How, I wondered, to make of voice an art?

English had already commandeered the control tower of international air travel, had become the lingua franca of the heavens. It had also become nothing less than the default language of international commerce, science and politics. Its centre now, insofar as it could be said to have a centre, with any defining myth, was the Big Apple in New York. The UN Tower in particular. Such a linguistic capital, I thought, as evidenced by the once futuristic Crystal Palace in London (or, by the later futuristic model, London's new Millennium Dome), promoted a homogenizing model of the future, not unlike the metaphor of Babel. "And they said, Go to, let us build us a city and a tower, whose top may reach unto heaven; and let us make us a name, lest we be scattered abroad upon the face of the whole earth." (Genesis 11:4) English, I sensed, would seem to be the linguistic architecture of the foreseeable future, among leaders such as Nelson Mandela, who courted national unity, international influence and local wealth for their countries of historically scattered voices.

In this small glasshouse, I was beset again by the acute loneliness I had experienced on landing in Perth. I began to wonder if this always happened to me at those times when the immediate future seemed vague, uncertain, without prospect. *When I had no one to talk to.* Travel for the sake of travel was harder than it seemed, when my purpose (and speaking voice) needed reestablishing in every city and country reached, since I had neither schedule nor contacts. I began to wonder why I had come to Johannesburg, where voices did not appear to be mine for the listening. No one spoke to me, as they did in Bombay or Bangkok, to ask where I was coming from, where I was going, in the usual English argot of the streets. I felt that I was being watched, subtly tolerated. As the ANC T-shirt read—worn by a slender young delegate to a shop stewards' conference in my modest hotel—I AM BOSS NOW IN THE NEW SA. I was just another white man, who had come from yet another country that local white men soon hoped to emigrate to.

I now toured the Johannesburg Art Gallery, itself as utterly empty of visitors as the glasshouse had been, and without the slightest interest to Joubert Park's black population in such institutions constructed by Afrikaners for themselves. In fairness, it was an uninteresting gallery, with its fading European and colonial landscapes, except for some contemporary South African art in the basement. The bunker-like building resembled a monument to the rigidity of apartheid. I left the gallery after half an hour, to wander farther into the city, past the railway and minibus termini, crowded even on a Sunday.

I was about to cross the street into a bazaar when a young man stepped in front of me. His voice addressed me in English. "Hey, where do you come from?" It was an aggressive voice, not the usual voice of a young man practising his English, and in cutting me off its owner seemed indifferent to an answer. "Canada," I muttered, stepping the other way. I then felt him tugging on my shoulder strap, and a second person's hand in my right pant pocket.

After this second man had ripped open the pocket, his hand emerging with a piece of Kleenex, he too grabbed and tore at my bag.

I had never experienced fear so acutely before. My fear was not for my life, since no knife or revolver appeared, but for the ruin of my journey through the sudden loss of cash, travellers' cheques, passport, credit card, notebooks. Identity, mobility, freedom. Desperately, I fought back, managing to keep hold of my bag as the strap ripped away from its studs, shouting at my attackers, in front of many indifferent witnesses. Without my Botox-assisted voice, what would I have sounded like? Would spasms, guttural heavings, choking desperation not have encouraged them to detect weakness in their foundering prey, and so continue the attack in likelihood of this victim's imminent nervous collapse?

My predators abruptly sauntered off. The nature of their gait suggested they might just as easily reverse direction, should I provoke them further, and saunter my way again. No one threatened them. Pedestrians looked wary, if not indifferent. In poor shape to repulse them a second time, I would certainly have no chance at all, confronted with a weapon. Heart whacking, breath shallow, I made my escape clutching torn pant leg and mauled bag.

But something had been stolen from me. Appalled and flustered, I was now no longer free to explore the City, a right I seemed to have carried for decades, through Islamic holy cities and even Phnom Penh under siege. Here I was, like a defeated agnostic, seeking sanctuary in St. Mary's Anglican Cathedral, as its Sunday morning congregation raised their voices in a tranquil hymn of communal praise.

I had never entered a church so willingly. I sat down along a crowded stone ledge in back, self-consciously holding the leg of my pants together, bag tight against any further attempt by my muggers to burst in and tear it from me. I badly needed to plot a return route through these streets to avoid any more attempts on the fat target I carried. I needed to look strong and in charge, striding back up to Hillbrow, which might be difficult with a floppy pant leg. I tried to remember if I had seen any more taxis of the kind I had hired at the bus compound upon my arrival, two or three hours earlier. I hadn't.

The priest or vicar was climbing into the pulpit to make some last-minute announcements, in an English accent, to his mostly black congregation. He congratulated a new warden at the back of the church. The congregation turned in my direction to applaud a grey-haired black man in a charcoal suit, standing beside me, who looked as startled as I did by the unwelcome attention.

". . . A man must be faithful and meek and obedient, and he must obey the laws, whatever the laws may be. It is true that the Church speaks with a fine voice, and that the Bishops speak against the laws. But this they have been doing for fifty years, and things get worse, not better."

Thus the brother of the Zulu pastor, Stephen Kumalo, who has just arrived in Johannesburg for the first time, and already a victim of crime not far from this church where I now found myself. I was thinking of Alan Paton's novel, *Cry, The Beloved Country* (1948), which I had begun last night flying the long voyage across the South Indian Ocean, to Zimbabwe and then South Africa. It bore rereading for its historical perspective, I'd discovered, especially on fear and the human voice.

As the pews began to empty, I followed the congregation out, wrapping myself in the solace of relaxed Christian voices. I remained among them as far as I could, beyond where the narrow streets ran off from the cathedral's square. Then they began to fragment and call out goodbyes. I was on my own again. I had just been mugged and there was no one to tell. Would anyone care? I was safe, wasn't I, intact but for the pants? I must have still believed I could use my new voice to accomplish anything, even to assuage injustice.

I began to understand, for the first time in my life, exactly how fear of violence could abruptly change self-image and voice. I could see myself through the eyes watching my retreat back up the hill—and, because I saw a man ignorant and ready for plucking, I could also see how those eyes might belong to potential muggers. All these unemployed men lying around Joubert Park became suspicious to me. They became suspicious *black* men, and I hated myself for the way I had fallen so swiftly into the stereotypical attitude of pessimism and racism.

I seemed to have tumbled Alice-like through the history of apartheid and been brought up to speed within a couple of hours of arrival in the country. I was wary for my safety. I feared strangers. I was already plotting how to get out of Johannesburg.

I decided to refuse any taxi I might encounter and force myself to walk back the way I had come. I stared with some empathy at the piles of caged prostrate hens for sale outside Hillbrow Hospital, where I stepped inside, out of a traveller's habit, to see if there might be a speech pathology department. It was a shabby institution, no more capable of pursuing ailments of voice among poor blacks than those of ruptured breast implants among rich Afrikaner matrons from Rosebank.

I had to remind myself the fear I now felt for my safety was nothing new in Jo'burg. Paton had been writing of muggings here, house break-ins and murders, half a century ago. Fear among white and black alike was still dishearteningly topical. I began to learn that week just *how* topical, from talking to citizens, as well as from watching the glut of TV documentaries about violence. "The most violent society in the world," said one program. I heard this from a woman whose mother had been murdered a month before, after deciding to come back from England to live in Cape Province. Her murderer was now out on bail and free to murder again. Another documentary told of the widespread Soweto violence last year between Inkatha interlopers and ANC residents.

I began to appreciate on a small scale how much a daily awareness of violence could erode the sense of individual freedom that I, living in safe cities, took for granted. I had always assumed freedom was a political condition, rather than a state of confident being. Political freedom now existed in South Africa, and yet everywhere—in this city, anyway—people seemed in chains. Maybe this was why the president's voice sounded to me the way it did, a candidate for rehabilitation.

That afternoon, following my arrival in the second safe haven I could find to sit down in, one of the young waiters in the Three Sisters café on Pretoria told me: "You're lucky you still have your bag. Everybody in the city downtown is moving north. The businesses are moving north."

So I bought a baguette on the way back to my hotel, and for the rest of the week, whenever I went into the streets, left my leather bag behind and carried this loaf around in a white plastic shopping bag. The baguette was meant to give me the air of a local, out for a shop, carrying nothing more of value than my daily ration of subsistence. I carried it north one day, to the white suburbs, and I took it with me to Soweto. After a week my loaf of bread was hard enough to have used as a club to defend myself against a whole gang of malevolents.

I came every day and evening to the Three Sisters, listening to the caffeinated voices of whites, blacks and occasionally foreigners speaking French, Afrikaans, English and what I assumed was Xhosa. "Molo." The music could be loud in here and it was hard to over-hear conversations. I actually thought two black businessmen in suits, packing cell phones, were discussing an arms deal one after-noon, until I concluded they were likely lawyers who had just come from the opening ceremonies of the Constitutional Court.

On my Walkman, I had been listening to Nelson Mandela's speech to the court, an eloquent address, delivered in a much clearer voice than I had previously heard from him. It was as if all those impassioned years as an imprisoned lawyer had allowed him to deliver one of his great speeches, in this case, to remind the new Constitutional Court of its role in acting as a "watchdog" for the bill of human rights. This was a speech to eleven judges, who were to oversee with independence and creativity, in Mandela's words, the rights of all: black and white, rich and poor, male and female. The rights of the driver of an expensive car, as well as those of the barefoot prisoner in his cell. I sensed, as I listened to his words, the president's voice had momentarily refound the strength it once possessed, but which had only ever been heard in dramatizations since his famous trial for treason in 1964.

"The last time I faced a court," he eloquently told these eleven judges, "I was sentenced to death."

That the court would soon make a remarkable decision on the principle of capital punishment, in these early months of political change, attested to the persuasive power of Nelson Mandela's voice.

Another voice I heard at the Three Sisters was a sweet singing one at a table behind mine. I had noticed a perfumed black woman arrive on her own and sit down. We fell into conversation. She claimed to be studying voice, examining a score. What a coinci-dence, I thought casually. I tried to think where I might have seen her before. She wanted to know if Canada was near New York.

Was London nice? Durban, where I hoped to head next, was apparently safer than here. "There are fewer black people in the streets," she said. She seemed to know Cape Town as well. Only when she told me she had recently been staying at the Holiday Inn downtown, did I think she probably wasn't a music student. Then I remembered seeing her, or someone much like her, eating dinner alone at a table in the restaurant of my hotel, eyeing a tableful of shop stewards. Could Eunice have informed her of my interest in voice? I will come to Eunice in a moment.

This beautiful young woman, I concluded, was probably a hooker. I envied her the three languages she said she spoke.

After turning back to my newspaper, I could hear her trying to re-interest me in her sweet untrained soprano, by singing something scribbled down on a well-worn page of treble clefs. I was touched by her prop.

I had seen so few white and coloured faces in Hillbrow, since my arrival in this once segregated neighbourhood, that I could only assume the exciting cosmopolitan blend of races promised by my two-year-old guidebook as the future in this neighbourhood, and throughout South Africa, had moved farther north in the city. I began to wonder if it existed there either. The cultural gap, the divide between races, seemed like a moving line, and any blending of races along it, apart from here at the Three Sisters, was probably mythical—unless you counted the airwaves, a kind of abstract space of discussion and hope whose cultural voice was an odd mix of Afrikaans, South African English, English English and different black tongues, depending on the station selected.

I carried whatever valuables I required under my belt, more or less inside my underpants, which made it hot to walk, and I would only remove passport or traveller's cheques after I'd been buzzed through three different bulletproof doors at the money exchange place I found on the second morning of walking my baguette. I made a note to find myself a money belt. I carried a few small bills in my shirt pocket.

In any case, as I had hoped, all eyes went to my plastic bread bag. My leather bag had become a burden, a sign around my neck spelled "prey." I had left it at a shoe repair to have restudded for further travels. I had given my torn pair of pants to one of the cleaning ladies at the hotel. Her soft African voice made no promises. "Maybe we could stitch it along the seam. We have no sewing machine. It wouldn't be good, maybe." I could sense her doubt that this undistinguished pair of pants was worth mending at all.

On the morning of my second day, I had a long conversation with Eunice, the English hotel manager. Eunice agreed to lock up in her filing cabinet my valuables and to bolt the door of her office whenever she went out. Eunice lived in the hotel. Whenever I needed my wallet back, she told me to press her button. "Go north," she meanwhile urged. Her own daughter lived in Sandton, a northern suburb. Within Johannesburg, I sensed, had recently grown up this strong mythical imperative, equivalent to that of the Old West. "Go north, young man." And presumably, if that failed to work out once you reached northern limits, you were expected to migrate to another country.

Eunice talked non-stop in the bed-and-breakfast voice of an extremely competent, if slightly blow-dried manager in, say, London's Mecklenburg Square. No, a brunette version of the managerial wife in *Fawlty Towers*. She was telling me the story of a young female guest who had lost everything last year at knifepoint. Three knifepoints, actually. "She was hysterical." Eunice helped contact her London bank to put a stop on her traveller's cheques, and to get a hold of herself. The girl had her passport back in five days. Eunice rummaged round in her filing cabinet for a letter from one Linda Parry, which commended the owners of the hotel and Eunice in particular, for unfailing assistance during her ordeal.

Eunice was jolly. In a later year, when the English film *Little Voice* came out, my recollection of her changed from a bed-and-breakfast baroness, even from John Cleese's foil in a Devon hotel, to this film's slatternish mother with a fishmonger's tone and a daughter who mimics famous musical voices.

A photograph of Eunice's own daughter was stuck to her bulletin board. She was twenty-nine and resembled a glamorous, wind-whipped starlet. Eunice herself had black bountiful hair—it looked very much like a wig. She wore earrings half the length of a rosary, and a necklace twice as long. Her ring sported a stone the size of a translucent walnut. Eunice said she took her jewellery off whenever she went outside. Outside, I could see, was just beyond her unbarred window here on the ground floor along bosky Abel Street. I wondered, in the absence of bars, how safe my valuables would be in Eunice's filing cabinet.

"'Hi, Eunice!' is what everybody calls when I go out shopping." No fear in this voice. "Late afternoon is the worst time for thieves. They sleep in the streets and are just waking up."

She was from London. Stoutish now, softened by a ruffled blouse and a munificent cleavage, she had once worked in the fashion business. She had left her husband to run off with another man. And although she'd been back to England four times, having lived all over the world, she had come to Johannesburg twenty years ago and now called it home. "Everybody's so grey back there. I think it has to do with the drizzly weather."

That morning, I wandered off in the direction of Wits University, trying to look like a man who knew where he was going on his way home from the bakery. Under a blazing sun I wore a black shirt and no sunglasses, in a vain attempt to attract less attention than as a shaded visitor in pastel. Along the way I met the occasional white man, who seemed eager to compare notes on the drama underlying a whole new experience of democracy in South Africa. These conversations enabled me to flex my own voice and to sound in control. They helped me to feel less lonely, and I encouraged them.

Richard Widmark, as I thought of him in his thinning slicked-back hair, wore long blue knee socks into which he slid the few rand he needed on daily walks, and pastel walking shorts in which he kept his watch in a back pocket. "It's asking for it, to carry a wallet or wear a watch." Although his accent was Afrikaans, he had lived in England for the last twenty-three years and was now back visiting his daughter in Hillbrow. He was extremely sympathetic to the brief tale of my mugging, indeed delighted the thieves hadn't got a thing from me. "I wish I'd been there." His boxer's voice had the pitch of a bandsaw, just after it shut off but was still ringing in your ear.

His advice to me, if confronted again, was to crouch. "Like this." He dropped down, leant backwards, and feinted with his hands. It was a defensive posture. "Of course, someone your size, who stands up to them"—he said this admiringly—"they'll probably kill you." Richard Widmark was a veteran of Africa and had lived all across the continent. "It's bad all over. I couldn't live here any more. It's got really bad the last three years." Back when he and his wife divorced in England, she had returned with the children to South Africa. Now he was home for a couple of months, reconciling with his daughter. "Go north, I keep telling her."

Obviously indifferent to camouflage, in a strolling get-up that also included a striped dress shirt, my acquaintance felt he avoided attracting attention to himself by following one simple rule. "The best way to go into the city is down the sides. That way you avoid the middle." I noticed he often glanced side to side, warily. When two well-dressed blacks in ties and white shirts passed us on the sidewalk, he said, "They're even doing it to their own middle class. The older ones aren't bad, it's the fast young ones." And here he indicated with his eyes a potential fast one, strolling past us on Koetze.

I had found myself well beyond the commercial part of Hillbrow, heading vaguely in the direction of the Civic Centre. Following this man's instructions, I continued on in what I hoped was the direction of Wits. Along the way I met another white man who turned out to be the mirror opposite of Widmark. Don Brackle was from Canada, and had come to live in Johannesburg at precisely the time Richard had left it, twenty-three years earlier.

His Canadian voice sounded alien to my ears, less guarded than the Afrikaner's. He was slim and bespectacled, carrying a sports bag, and wondering what country he and his wife should retire to.

They were considering Gibraltar, because it was closer to the centres of civilization, especially ancient civilizations. Archaeology fascinated Don. Besides, Gibraltar had the blue skies he was used to here. He said the sky here hadn't changed colour since he arrived from Montreal, where he had studied engineering at McGill. Don wore a blue sport shirt and grey slacks, their crisp creases complementing his lean physique. Standing beside me in the hot sun, with cars sweeping up the hill and around us in a circle, he told me he was coming from a workout at nearby "Cardiac House." This grand-looking building was where he'd been coming to the gym every day since his heart attack, five years ago.

His voice smiled gently. It betrayed none of the stress of recent changes in Johannesburg—or in Hillbrow, where he had lived after emigrating to South Africa. He told me a lot had changed in Hill-brow over the last three years. It had got bad when the pass laws were lifted. "Previously, you had to have a job to come into the city. The trouble is there are no jobs for them." By "them" he meant blacks, using the pronoun-vernacular familiar to local whites. He objected to the fact he now had to carry his driver's licence, which he pulled from his back pocket to show me. "Used to be you had two weeks to present it. Now I worry it could be stolen with my blue identity book, and sold for two or three thousand rand on the black market."

So Don was being careful on different fronts. He was on the lookout for a recurrence of heart disease, although his ninety-plus father was still alive, and he was keeping a wary eye out for mug-gers. "I was mugged around the corner here, two, no, three months ago. They were trying to get my arms out of a leather jacket." He said he didn't know of anyone who didn't have a mugging tale to tell. But he suggested I not judge Johannesburg by what I had seen so far.

"Go north, to the prettier suburbs."

Don had a parochial air about him, even though he'd lived in several countries around the world, planned on moving to another one soon, and got off on other civilizations (preferably dead, of course). The native population didn't attract him. "How many Canadians have visited an Eskimo village or an Indian reservation?" Not Don, who had grown up near an Indian reserve outside of Montreal. He was distinctly unsympathetic to tourists who wanted to visit a local township.

"By the way, bet you didn't know they play ice hockey in South Africa."

I admitted surprise. He went on to tell me about the Carlton Sky Rink downtown, on top of a parking garage. "It's one of four rinks around the city. Season goes from April to November. Teams like Israel and Greece and Australia come to play. It's about the lowest rung that exists in international hockey. I went to a game once, and the score was twenty to one." He added, "But I think it's doomed. Anything downtown."

He was right. I would subsequently read of how guests came to be offered armed escorts by the Carlton Hotel, when they went shopping in the in-house arcade, and eventually of how this posh hotel, where Mick Jagger would stay the following week, had since closed down because of extreme violence in the inner city.

As for his retirement, Don thought Crete was another possibility, and he was looking forward to making up his mind before too much longer.

A blond girl I struck up a conversation with, outside the University of Witwatersrand, was wearing a T-shirt that said San Francisco. A year earlier she had headed west and finished her high school education in Wyoming. Her voice had all the brightness of this intense Johannesburg morning and, still lonely, I encouraged it. Her Afrikaans accent was sometimes hard to grasp, but not the story of her eighteen-year-old life.

Today, the first day of classes, she was enrolled in a BSc program with a view to medical school. The trouble was her biology class had hundreds in it and she disliked crowds. She always tried to avoid them for the same reason she avoided campus politics, and not just for security reasons. You lost something of yourself, getting mixed up in crowds. Her pink nose was peeling and looked as vulnerable in the intense sun as her scalp of thin yellow hair.

After ten minutes of listening, I heard a woman's voice calling "Karen." It was Karen's mother, come to pick her up after a short first day. So Karen reshouldered her packsack and was off, presumably north, with a wave and "Ciao."

Off Smuts Avenue, where we had been talking in the street, I made my way up the steps and onto campus. There, as I later learned, a faculty meeting was in progress, responding to the militant student organization, SASCO, which had been "trashing" the campus as part of its "free speech" mandate to get what it wanted—free tuition. I hung around the speech pathology and audiology department, hoping someone might return and agree to talk to me about voice. I later concluded I ought not to have bothered, yet at noon I was warmly welcomed into Claire Penn's office, and she soon called in the woman who oversaw the kind of speech patient I was particularly interested in.

Claire, whose specialty was bio-medical ethics, was appalled to learn where I was staying and offered to put me up in her home in a northern suburb. But she never returned to the subject. Heila Jordaan promised to set up interviews with some of her spasmodic dysphonia patients, but I waited the rest of the week for her to call. I tried calling her. She equivocated, blustered and bluffed. I would eventually thank her, politely, relieved finally to be catching a bus for Durban, after sitting around Johannesburg fruitlessly expecting her to get back to me promptly as she had promised.

I was surprised to learn that the use of Botox had reached South Africa. I had been unsure if laryngeal dystonia would even be a familiar disease. Perhaps not surprising, the knowledge of these speech specialists about it was sketchy, and neither pathologist seemed keen on using the drug for what they apparently felt was an often misdiagnosed disorder. A skeptic from the UK had passed through last year on the lecture circuit and impressed them.

They were also suspicious about the imposition on a Third World country of what they implied was a Western solution. Their current objections to the drug sounded misplaced and defensive. And they professed to have no concerns about its use for other forms of dystonia.

Heila thought SD had become "a waste-basket term" for other pathologies, such as unilateral vocal cord paralysis, stuttering, aphonia, tumour. And she was "not delighted" with the results of injections she had observed in her somewhat arm's-length relationship with fewer than half a dozen patients diagnosed with the disease. When I asked how large or small a dosage her patients were receiving, she confessed she didn't know. She was present at injections, but didn't pay attention to what the neurologist was injecting. I suggested the mixed results could also have had something to do with the skill of the practitioner.

This disorder that interested me—and I mentioned suffering from it—was a small sideshow in the department at Wits. I was received with kindness and soon forgotten. Or perhaps the unsmiling Heila was confused, because at one point she wondered what angle my novel on this voice disorder would take. On the bus to Durban, I could only conclude that since she felt spasmodic dysphonia was a waste-basket term, that is, something of a fiction, the fancifulness of my interest was not worth her time bothering over.

I listened to other voices, white and black, during my idle days in Johannesburg. Later that week, walking back from purchasing a one-way Greyhound ticket, I spoke to a shirt-and-tie employee outside one of the railroad office towers. He was a beefy young man who had worked here for seven years, after quitting his policeman's job, which hadn't paid him enough. He told me he'd been talking to his boss just yesterday about which parts of Canada were supposed to be "good" ones. These included "Vancouver, Ontario, and somewhere else, I don't know."

His accent was heavily Afrikaans, and so, it seemed, were his attitudes. "It's getting worse. The streets around here now are full." In the absence of the shorthand pronoun, I thought he meant full of litter. He didn't say anything when I mentioned litter. Litter, yes, he was thinking. He meant of course "them." He lived in the western suburb of Roodepoort, a fifty-minute train ride away, for which undoubtedly he had a pass. He wore a security badge as his ticket into these several safe towers. Apparently, the railroad had decided to keep its headquarters downtown here, where the main station was, and I was reminded of what Don Brackle had called this "world within a world" of office towers, to which his son also came every day from a suburb "up north."

I supposed this Afrikaner was just one of many white-collar colleagues giving up on South Africa. Don Brackle's engineering daughter was heading to Sydney. I had not been surprised when Claire Penn, a member of the speech pathology department for twenty years, told me that nowadays most of the undergraduates they trained went abroad to better opportunities. I was reminded of young Indian-trained doctors I'd once met at a party in South India, all planning to emigrate as soon as they could get admission to the UK. In Britain, meanwhile, where I was living at the time, many of the English doctors were emigrating to Texas.

Eunice must have thought I was a doctor or specialist of some sort, because one afternoon she asked me whether there might be some link between her three-year-old granddaughter's shorter leg and her delayed speech. I told her I thought not. And retired to my room on the ninth floor, with its view of water towers and apartment balconies in nearby streets, festooned with laundry, out of which arose poignantly the American soul voice of Percy Sledge, singing *When a m-a-a-n loves a woma-a-n* . . . Inside my room, temporary refuge from urban fear, I could hear the melodious, melodramatic baritone of Jeremy Brett in an old Sherlock Holmes rerun about a racehorse.

"Go north," he seemed to be telling me, as I waited for Heila Jordaan to call.

So the next morning I did. Seen off at the door by Eunice, who had telephoned for a reliable taxi and suggested I head for Sandton, "safer" than Rosebank, I watched as my driver curled through the streets of Berea and Yeoville, travelling along Victoria Street and through Rosebank, with its large houses of razor-wired walls. But the later sight of Sandton, with its expanses of looming hotels and office towers, was enough for me to ask the driver immediately to safari us all the way back to Rosebank, where I might venture out on my own to inspect white suburban life inside the defined boundaries of a large mall.

Marble floors, floating escalators, glass walls, antique shops, cinemas and a carpark full of German cars: it seemed as foreign to me now as home. A similar apartheid existed in Canada, if you thought about it, not only in the gulf between rich and poor citizens, but also in the gulf between rich and poor countries—Canada and this one, for example. To my eager-voiced driver, Rosebank's glitter must have seemed as remote as Canada's moon dust. He had been telling me of life in Hillbrow over the last four years, after his abandonment of Soweto when people there were being murdered "for nothing."

In the mall, among finely dressed matrons and corporate yuppies, I felt as safe as I had in Perth. I was privileged and the boss again. At an Italian bistro run by an Afrikaner, I was served by blacks in dark pants and green aprons. I had the lunch special—minestrone, white wine, three kinds of pasta on the same plate—for the equivalent of Cdn$6.50. No wonder the locals were reluctant to see any encroachment upon their pampered lives. "We shall be careful, and knock this off our lives, and knock that off our lives, and hedge ourselves about with safety and precaution. And our lives will shrink, but they shall be the lives of superior beings; and we shall live with fear, but at least it will not be a fear of the unknown." Thus my lunchtime reading of Alan Paton.

On the way back to Hillbrow, my second taxi driver was sullen, until we got closer to payment time when he asked, in a voice as utilitarian as tar, where I came from. He pondered my answer, then asked if I thought there was any improvement here. I didn't know, I admitted. What did *he* think? "No. Apartheid is still here. Everyone has moved to Rosebank." By which he seemed to imply that the people who could make any difference were white, unlike him, and they had let Hillbrow become another ghetto by leaving it.

Far from giving up on inner Johannesburg, one well-dressed, gold-necklaced young black man struck me as someone very conscious of putting in time here among the grassroots. He was trying to persuade four or five idle employees of a Kentucky Fried Chicken outlet to register with him for next October's municipal election. I had read in the news about apathy throughout the country toward municipal elections, partly because voters had regarded last year's national election (the first truly democratic election) as the crucial one. But many citizens were simply reluctant to give their names and addresses for fear of having to pay water and power rates, which they were not paying now.

With no customers except me, the young employees of Colonel Sanders had nothing better to do than listen to him and be persuaded. He was pitching them in English. Listening, I finished my drumsticks and coleslaw. One by one, the employees slowly produced for him their blue identity books in order to be painstakingly registered over the next hour. He even offered me a form, perhaps to make up for any racist tinge to his remarks that I might have overheard regarding the white-dominated council in Johannesburg he was hoping to vote out of office. His educated voice was eloquent and determined, as must have been his dedication to the cause, to spend so long over a mere handful of votes. Possibly, he was on commission. I noticed a place for his own signature, as registrar, at the bottom of every form.

He lived in Hillbrow, he told me. "I'm trying to take responsibility to the people here. If we become lazy, we might as well go back to the drawing board. You could say this is the drawing board, at the grassroots. The movement has many, many obstacles on the road to real democracy, and travelling down it by vehicle won't get myself far. That is why I go by foot, store to store, house to house, talking to them."

That pronoun-vernacular again, this time spoken by a black man, to denote the majority of the population he wished could see the reasonableness of his own thinking. "If we don't do it ourselves, to take control, we are lost to the past. I can see it is up to myself to take them the message."

I couldn't help but admire his voice's mixture of political acumen and evangelism. He was hustling himself, but in service to a larger cause with the potential to benefit many. He had the patience I was trying to practise myself these days, waiting for the put-upon Heila to phone. Listening to his remorseless pitch, I admired his faith in the outcome of his efforts. There was something in his tone that reminded me of the young Nelson Mandela, who had set up the first black lawyer's office in Johannesburg.

From my hangout at the Three Sisters, I would often listen to uniformed schoolchildren walking home through the streets of Hillbrow, bantering among themselves. In the evenings, I liked to watch a woman in a great blue smock and colourful bandana selling corn on the cob from half an oil drum full of hot coals on the corner. I would listen to the way her voice, when she sold a cob, broke abruptly into chatter, as if in his parting with a rand every customer somehow expected reassurance about the delectability of her kernels. Her toothless husband would sometimes relieve her on the box, a man staring at a river of people rolling past, but I never saw him sell anything. I thought his own voice would probably have resembled a fisherman's, had he suddenly and unexpectedly got a bite.

I was reading a copy of *The Sowetan* whose vernacular disappointed me for its lack of township news. It seemed to take its tone from larger newspapers in Johannesburg, about what a black hole Soweto was, by keeping any discussion of it to a minimum. Editorially, it was anti-Winnie and pro-O.J. Simpson.

One day I went to Soweto, with Jimmy's Face to Face Tours. Our small van carried six Germans and Kratzie, the black driver from Soweto, who wore a white shirt and black knit tie. "Soweto is very large," he told us on the way. "Soon you will be in Soweto, and it will stretch as far as you can see. Three millions of people live there. They live up and down every hill you will see, over a hundred thirty square kilometres. You will see homes of the very wealthy and the very poor. I am going to show you the good, the bad and the ugly."

There was a large gap in Kratzie's front teeth, and stress lines under his eyes. His "tour" voice, very up, was also repetitive.

"Break my window, take me home . . . Break my window, take me home." He said this whenever a BMW passed us on the main highway to Soweto, or whenever we saw one of these cars in the township itself. "As I said . . . beat my wife, take me home." He sounded like a Baptist preacher, intolerant of silence and northern dourness. He got a chuckle from us the first time, and thereafter nothing.

These local catchphrases, so delightful to Kratzie, referred to the frequency with which BMWs were stolen in Johannesburg and driven back to Soweto. And indeed these luxury German cars were far more conspicuous in Soweto than I had expected, at least in "Zone One," where our driver pointed proudly to posh brick mansions surrounded by security walls, the homes of drug dealers, car thieves, and "mafia" in general. Even "Jimmy," who owned our tour van, lived in one of these garage-appointed houses.

We drove down a paved street to visit one house, an art gallery, but no one bought so much as a watercolour, to Kratzie's disappointment. The voice of the striking woman in native costume who owned the gallery was subtle and worldly. "Yes, this carving was done by Theodore. Marvellous, isn't it?" There was something *unworldly* about her prosperous presence in Soweto, if Zone One could be considered part of Soweto, and not a nefarious arrangement for redistribution of the wealth in Rosebank. The concept of the township was contradictory, as our guide had implied. It contained multitudes.

"Chris likes to talk."

Thus Kratzie warned us about Chris, a handsome young man with the eyes of a criminal, who guided us on foot through the maze of the Mandela squatter camp, an old and rather established slum of corrugated walls and wire enclosures, whose paths and tiny courtyards were neatly swept. Chris was trying to raise money for the completion of a primary school. Or we could choose to contribute to his football team. Evidently, some weeks before us, a Swiss woman had pledged money to buy short pants for the entire team, and Chris held up a pair that looked several years old. They now needed jackets.

He would take questions. Perhaps he also took Mastercard and Visa. He made us stand in the hot sun of his school's foundation and think about our moral position—apparently built on sand. He claimed to speak nine languages, and to judge by the dexterity of his voice in English he probably did. Our having to listen to Chris was the price of admission for slumming it. He seemed to enjoy condescending to us from the unassailable position of moral authority granted him by the surrounding poverty he surveyed. Notwithstanding the pledges he reported receiving from foreign visitors such as ourselves, we could tell by looking at the school's foundation not a concrete block had been added to it in years.

Still, two young German women on our tour agreed to sign his guest book, unable to resist Chris's invitation to participate in the "Soweto solution."

Their husbands were still muttering as Kratzie reloaded us into the minivan on the other side of the squatter camp, slid shut the lock on all the doors, and drove off to Winnie Mandela's palatial mansion with its wall-mounted security cameras. Widespread reports of Winnie's corruption seemed to have made her part of Soweto's problem. You could stand on a rocky outcrop and stare down into her compound. Her house was in another world, compared to her husband's small house where she used to live, not far away, as a young woman. We drove by it, and other brick bungalows built between 1930 and 1952 here in Orlando. Schools, a huge stadium, houses of famous leaders ("Bishop Tutu is in"), sites of uprisings. Then past wire-protected hostels for foreign migrants—the Inkatha sympathizers Kratzie said were responsible for the slaughter of many blacks on trains, a couple of years earlier, and armed by militant whites. Down the highway we travelled, past the largest hospital in the southern hemisphere, Vista University, and a mammoth power station.

"All Soweto, as far as you can see. Break my window, beat my wife, take me home. Thank you. You're welcome. Thank you."

I was the last passenger Kratzie dropped off in Johannesburg. Alone, his voice was suddenly softer, quieter. Off stage, he dropped the rhetorical tone and told me he was paying school fees for his three children. He had been driving for Jimmy's for the last ten years. While we were sitting in traffic on Pretoria, waiting for an ANC protest march to proceed down the hill, he locked all the van's doors again. He told me no one had jobs. From Soweto, where he lived, he travelled into the city every day to work—by train, because minivans were too dangerous now that a murderous turf war was going on between two rival companies.

"I am very pessimistic," he said softly.

I thought if this was how fear changed the voice of a man with a good job, I could not begin to imagine what it did to the voice of an unemployed and hopeless one.

It was possible such a man had no voice at all. He might even commit murder, as the urban-transplanted son of the Zulu clergyman-protagonist does in Alan Paton's novel. What exists of young Absalom's voice is laconic. The novel's public voice belongs to his uncle, John Kumalo, a union organizer.

I was thinking of these fictional voices over the following days, as I travelled by bus to Durban, Grahamstown, Port Elizabeth and Cape Town. In hindsight it seemed ironic to me that the black voice of political consciousness in South Africa had turned out to be Nelson Mandela's weak one, rather than an equivalent of the fictional John Kumalo's "great bull voice":

> There are those who can be moved by the sound of the voice
> alone. There are those who remember the first day they heard

it as if it were today, who remember their excitement, and the queer sensations of their bodies as though electricity were passing through them. For the voice has magic in it, and it has threatening in it, and it is as though Africa itself were in it. A lion growls in it, and thunder echoes in it over black mountains.

But, of course, this might describe Mandela's voice as well. Mandela understood the moral authority, even of his own voice, to move a population. He, like this character, understood the importance of restraint and a moderate tone:

> The crowd stirs as though a great wind were blowing through it. Here is the moment, John Kumalo, for the great voice to reach even to the gates of Heaven. Here is the moment for words of passion, for wild indiscriminate words that can waken and madden and unleash. But he knows. He knows the great power that he has, the power of which he is afraid. And the voice dies away, as thunder dies away over mountains, and echoes and re-echoes more and more faintly.

Not that the Afrikaner woman travelling beside me in the bus to Durban would have acknowledged such a voice as speaking for the Africa *she* knew, from her lifetime of farming in Rhodesia. The blacks, she believed, had had the "same opportunity" as her family to make lives for themselves, and done nothing. What they had done, on her recent visit back to Zimbabwe, was to relieve her of her purse with the equivalent of eight thousand dollars in rand and jewellery. Mrs. Applegarth had suddenly found herself contributing to the anthology of stories of violence committed against whites, and was insistent that I publish my own (in the newspaper at home) "so people will know what it's like here. People in Australia wouldn't believe me."

Her gentle, seventy-six-year-old voice, with its precise consonants, reminded me of the novelist Doris Lessing's. An attractive voice, softened by a sense of wonder for the natural world of

Rhodesia. But also a rumbustious voice, full of life, hooting as my maternal grandmother's used to, when tickled by unexpected events, especially those she could invest with trust against the rainy day of retirement. She was resigned to whatever happened to her, believing there was a reason for everything, including the amazing trouble it had taken to replace her passport and ticket in time to return to Jo'burg, where she'd just spent a few recuperative days with her sister. White-haired and wrinkled, she was far from the dour person I imagined when she took her seat beside mine. Taking off her sweater, after "getting settled," she unveiled a bright personality along with gold rings and necklaces. By covering these up, along with her brilliant blue dress, she had outfoxed at least the local thieves in vicinity of the bus station.

On our seven-hour bus ride through vast maize farms of Transvaal, the dry veld of Orange Free State, and Natal's green Drakensberg mountains, we talked. I learned of her husband's death twenty years ago, from a blood clot originating in a damaged toe, of her despair over his death, and her eventual resurrection. Born in South Africa, she had loved farm life in Rhodesia and delighted in the beautiful landscapes there. "Do you have wind in Canada?" When that life was over, she'd learned to take pleasure in "keeping busy"—knitting, travelling, volunteering. Gardening, too. She was holding a potted orchid on her lap, as though it were a baby.

Mrs. Applegarth's children lived all over now, including Brisbane, where she had recently lived for fourteen months with a son, and was now heading to live with another son and his family in Durban. In Durban, at the station, I heard "Donny" greet her in a marvellous baritone voice. "Mommy," he called her, as she stepped down into his arms, "we've been waiting for you all our lives, and I think it's time Jenna fed you her beef medallion. Robert's outgrown his diapers and asking for fith' and chip. Did we ever have fith' and chip on the farm?" He beamed as she handed him the orchid.

I took a room in a seedy hotel called Four Seasons, worn out by a year-round assault on its faucets and towels (leaky and threadbare), by guests attracted to this humid Brighton-cum-theme park of a city. A long wall of hotels faced the steaming ocean. My hotel was among those of the second or third wall, buried like an archaeological fossil of Afrikaner holiday-making in a street behind.

By Johannesburg standards, this was a relaxed city of endless diversity. Here along the Indian Ocean were aquariums and paddling pools and trampolines and amusement piers and water worlds and snake pits. And yet the "true" voice of this sybaritic life was possibly disguised behind a sign I saw on a van moving slowly along the promenade of the vast ocean front, where mist and mugginess rolled in off the breakers. "Recreation and Culture" it said. The vehicle was a paddy wagon.

Late that afternoon, I walked to Addington Hospital far down the point, and spoke to a beautiful Indian nurse in a crowded reception room. "We have no speech pathology at Addington." For some reason, this pleased me. "But there must be problems," I suggested. "There must be," she admitted, returning my smile as though we were conniving to ignore them. "What is your interest in voices?" she asked. It turned out, as we ignored the braying room, she had a familial interest in the subject.

A side story made brief: She invited me home that evening to meet her brother in Clare Hills, a neighbourhood of upscale houses and swimming pools. Nam, her equally beautiful younger brother, was suffering from an undiagnosed aphonia, and said nothing through dinner, which included Celia's two lively parents.

"It's from a bad birth," said her father, Amir, a successful magnate in merchant shipping. He sounded very pukka. "Forceps, you know, badly applied, shortly after we arrived in Durbs."

"No, no, no," answered Dali, the mother. "He has it all wrong, as usual. Nam's oxygen wasn't what it needed to be at his birth. This is causing severe problems for Nam his entire life. It was an unavoidable brain damage. Nam can't speak. And he has other difficulties. In general, he is Charlotte Eyre's secret in the attic."

Celia rolled her eyes in my direction. "Jane Eyre. If it matters."

Nam smiled. He understood he was being talked about.

Celia then asked, fetchingly, if I had any experience with voice-lessness. I was certainly willing to have had some experience with it, if only to keep her attentive, and to prolong this pleasant evening after my long journey from Johannesburg with Mrs. Applegarth.

All I could think of was the unlikely coincidence of having created a character who also couldn't speak. I alluded to this minor character in my imminent novel.

"So you have some knowledge of the problem," said Amir.

I dissembled. "The trauma, was it neurologically induced?" I asked.

"We don't know that," said Amir.

"Oh, daddy," said Celia, "we do know that."

"The forceps are just your dreary concoction," scolded Dali. To me, she said, "It suits him to believe Nam's neck got twisted and his larynx damaged."

Celia asked again about my interest in voices.

This time I mentioned laryngeal dystonia. I told them a bit about the disorder, and about injections I and others received to help us use our voices more easily. I suddenly had an eager audience, wondering whether my mysterious toxin might help their son and brother.

With its air of cosmopolitan banter, this family was eager to know things they might have missed out on by not living in the West—whether about medical advances in speech-assistance, the Internet, or about an upcoming Rolling Stones concert in a Johannesburg park. Celia told me her father often visited other countries, sailing under the flag of many nations because he fancied himself au courant. "My dear," he told her gaily, "you should know I don't ape French fashion."

According to his wife, Amir's notion of forceps was an unfortunate atavism.

She gazed fondly across the lamb roast to her mute son.

I asked if they'd had Nam examined recently, and yes, they had taken him to London last year, but so far the problem had defeated "the Empire's best medical brains." They had not given up in the nineteen years since Nam should have first begun to speak, but they were now more accepting of his voiceless condition. Not that he didn't have a "voice." Nam could sign. They had all learned to "listen" to his sign language.

"His hearing seems fine," said Celia. "He can understand most of what is said to him, if you speak slowly. That – is – if – he – *wants* – to – hear – you. He – is – sometimes – *naughty*."

We all looked at Nam. The beautiful young man, his hair a little flat from a recent nap, remained entirely unresponsive, teasing his carrots with a spoon.

On the morning I left Durban, the Translux bus was full of students returning to Rhodes University in Grahamstown— twelve hours and a world away from the holiday frivolities of their sprawling coastal city. Sweeping down the freeway, along the Bay of Natal, I was thinking of Celia and Nam. Amir had breezily promised to take them to Clairwood, later that day when Celia got off from the hospital, and I was watching out for the racecourse.

Emerging from the city's port area a little earlier, I was struck by how the dawn's humid light struck the art deco-ish apartment buildings, the little yachts at anchor, the off-loading ships beyond. Amir had told me, in explaining his shipping interests, that this was the busiest harbour in Africa, among the top ten ports in the world. Vasco da Gama had sailed past five hundred years earlier, he said, and Indian labour was imported into Natal in the mid-nineteenth century. It was to the "top-top" of this latter "heap" of immigrants that Amir had risen.

For a province famous for its wars between Zulus and Europeans, Boers and British, its south coast was now a deceptive string of serene resorts, stretching nearly a hundred miles through tropical vegetation. At Port Shepstone the bus stopped for tea. I spoke to a friendly Indian student, who looked a little like Nam, and he told me what he was studying at Rhodes. "I wanted to study medicine, but my marks weren't the very top, and you need the top-top for medicine." So he had settled on pharmacy, following a year at college in Durbs. I remembered his extended family seeing him off, as though he embodied the hopes of two earlier generations, and, by the look of his pregnant sister, the one to come.

The bus turned inland and began the long trek across Transkei with its stunning valleys, worn-out soil, and white Xhosa villages of conical-thatched houses. Both the huge skies and the litter, washing up along wire fences, nagged at my heart, as I imagined my own son being raised among these impoverished rural children so far from hope. The dilemma here for young barefoot blacks, herding goats, remained largely as it had for at least half a century: stay and suffocate, or go to an urban shantytown and risk another sort of suffocation of the sort dramatized in *Cry, the Beloved Country.*

I spent all day gazing out the window at this neglected homeland. The students seemed oblivious. They watched videos on the screen above, listened to and whooped at Springbok scores on the radio, and sang "*Bridge Over Troubled Water*" off-key. A blond young man asked me, when we passed through the black capital Umtata, if I had ever seen such a hopeless city. It was all so "boring" to him he could hardly summon the voice to express contempt.

A young woman from Pietermaritzburg, a journalism student seated behind me, had been sensitive to my gazing at the passing Third World conditions. She would occasionally try to mute my imagined criticism of South Africa (of her), by mentioning over the top of my seat that the Transkei was suffering a drought, or was simply over-grazed. Her goal was to become a journalist for *National Geographic*. She hoped to teach English in Japan next year, before graduation, to help pay off student loans she had accumulated.

As we neared Grahamstown from East London, late that afternoon, I was appalled by black slums sheltering thousands on the outskirts of town. My friend behind, noticing the direction of my gaze, tapped me vigorously on the shoulder, pointing straight ahead to Rhodes shining in the sun. "Look!"

Her excited young voice saddened me more than any other in South Africa.

For I somehow *expected* to hear the schizophrenic voice of the Cathcart Arms' manager, who warmly welcomed me into the oldest hotel in South Africa, a modest structure dating from 1825, in this tomb-quiet town of past British imperialism. *His* voice, gentle and accommodating, I later heard shrilling at a filthy black man who had ventured in out of the night. *". . . And don't ever come in here again!"* It was the Afrikaner voice, more or less trooping the colours.

The next morning I myself was at the receiving end of the equally indignant voice of his wife. *"We're not a bus station!"* she exploded, her voice rising in a way I thought her black staff would be used to. *"He told you no such thing!"*

It was this defensiveness that defined for me the Afrikaner voice at its worst, trying to bluff through the fear of having made a mistake. (She was covering up for her husband's error, the night before, in giving me the wrong time for the morning bus to Port Elizabeth. He'd also promised to arrange an early breakfast and then forgotten.) With her pinched vowels and explosive consonants, she sounded like aggression personified.

Having to wait around all day for the late bus, I explored the hot empty town and small university, trying again to locate an old friend who had come to teach at Rhodes, after graduating from the University of London twenty years earlier. I'd found no listings for him the night before. A British-sounding woman in the linguistics department remembered him leaving Rhodes, about twelve years earlier, to return to England, and she was kind enough to ring a mutual friend who passed on my friend's daughter's number in Cape Town.

Later that week, when I called her in Cape Town, the now grown-up Lisa told me her parents had left Grahamstown and South Africa around the time the black activist movement began to build. In London, where I finally met up again with her father in a Hampstead pub, Con Baxter told me in the same reedy voice I had found attractive twenty years earlier when we were students together, how he and Vanessa used to have blacks and students to their home here in Grahamstown, to the chagrin of authorities who parked undercover men outside their house.

Standing by a map of Grahamstown, outside the closed Information Office, I was disturbed by the large map's euphemism for the blank area I knew to be the vast black shantytown I'd observed on the town's perimeter: Grahamstown Commonage East. To the west curled detailed suburban avenues of Somerset Heights, West Hill, Oatlands, Mayfield: all shady, tree-lined streets, I was sure.

As safe as this provincial town apparently was—safe to stroll around in, as the manager had insisted last night—I noticed a gun shop and its telling name just off the cathedral square: A. N. White Arms & Ammunition. There were other signs in shops and on houses: Hi Tech Security / Armed Response. Defensive postures seemed the national mode, and I soon overheard it in another snappy voice back at the Cathcart Arms. *"Thankyouverymuch."* This Afrikaner guest was accepting a tea tray from one of the black servants, at the same time closing her door on him smartly, in the Sunday afternoon heat. She had no intention of acknowledging one iota of dependence on a black man.

I was getting spoiled myself.

Another historic hotel, the Edward in Port Elizabeth, made for an even more pampered stay. Although the mahogany lift was "Out of order because of the weather" (whatever this meant) there was a grand staircase, wide corridors, a palm court and formal dining room. Located across from the spacious lawn of the Donkin, with its old lighthouse above the harbour, the Edward was hosting a "success" convention, as well as a convention devoted to hairdressers. I could hear a vigorous mix of black and white voices floating down corridors, calling out "Dear" and "Ranald, sweetheart, power to the *man*," and was amused to bide my time assigning these voices to either one convention or the other, depending on my whimsicality of the moment as I soaked in a clawfoot tub blowing soap bubbles.

The driver of the hotel's minivan would not have approved of any such idle game. On the morning I left, he drove me down the hill to the bus station, going out of his way to point out Port

Elizabeth's original fortifications. He was ex-army, retired, of British pukka accent until he spoke of black Africans, when his voice slipped into a somewhat strident Afrikaans accent: "People from where you're from call it ignorance" (this by way of our apparently excusing blacks who committed violence). "They call these street boys uneducated. *I* call them bush monkeys!" Then back to pukka voice: "Those are the original guns, they've never fired a shot. You couldn't attack this position from below. The view was perfect."

Polite, white-haired and weather-faced, he had spent twenty years in the army, including seven on the Namibian border. "Did you shoot anybody?" I asked him. "I did my duty." He had also been stationed in Grahamstown. "Nice little town." Said he loved to read about Canada, especially the Mounted Police. About the architecture here in Port Elizabeth, his British voice reeled off the facts and nothing but the facts. Pulling up at Norwich House, he took my bag and proceeded to introduce me to my bus drivers, as though as guest of his hotel I required his personal protection and Edwardian hospitality from stoop to stoop. I couldn't begin to imagine what he made of the hairdressers' convention, and its vocal participants, back at the farm.

I began this last leg through South Africa thinking voice was one of the commoner ways we had of breaking the habit of self. We welcomed new voices and listened avidly to their otherness. And yet often the choice of listening was no choice at all. On the road to Mussell Bay and beyond, along the Garden Route to the Cape, through farms and mountainous landscapes—instead of just letting some of the most beautiful scenery in the world silently lift passengers from their habits of domestic selves—the Translux bus chose to screen a surfing movie, whose voices of American adolescent characters blared tinnily from the speaker above our heads. How often, I thought, we were subjected to voices when we neither needed nor wanted them. And why were these the voices of American popular culture, or of British popular culture, in hotel rooms where the voices of CNN and SkyTV came with the wallpaper?

I supposed this was the price to be paid for the new Tower of Babel and the global culture to follow.

In Cape Town, where every hotel room in the city was booked because Parliament and other sporting events were in session, I was reluctant to take any room lower than the Edwardian standard to which I was now accustomed. I spent two hours at the Tourist Office, resisting the one available place I could afford and whose sink-in-the-room, toilet-down-the-hall recalled starkly those years of student travel and peeing in the sink. It cost sixty rand a night. The only other available room in town was going for eleven hundred. I eventually settled for the temptations of the sink.

Yet I found the voice of Travellers Inn distinctly less seedy than that of the B&Bs I was convinced I had risen above. For one thing, with the TV located in the breakfast room on the first floor, a kind of communal voice emerged day and night from this historic building on Long Street, owing to the mix of black and white guests bantering over televised boxing matches and black rock videos. At night, on the long lacy-iron porch, surrounded by scruffy potted palms and woodsmoke from the brazier, we would sit at picnic tables talking, while staring together up at the stars, or up to the purple shadows of Table Mountain, floodlit from two thousand feet below. Below us, in the street, petty criminals would come out to roam. Our resident hookers, just arisen, would stretch their ebony tattooed arms out of white singlets and smile. "Good evening." They were also part of the family, paying less for rent by the month, so long as they didn't bring business home.

Here you could just as easily listen to a Frenchwoman, boring you to sleep about the correct mixture of nitrogen and oxygen in your diving tank to stop the bends, as to the distinctly paralyzed-sounding voice of the inn's owner, a generous and personable man of forty, who spoke as though he had *had* the bends and managed to survive them.

He now spoke with the high-pitched voice of a lazy, but not unattractive castrato chewing peppermints. He would sweep straight back, with one hand, winsome blond hair, just starting to grey, while drawling on in a hesitant, but oddly fetching manner, stealing amused glances at his interlocutor to gauge the effect of whatever he was telling you about his hotel or voice.

Jeremy Harris had developed Guillain-Barré syndrome when he was fifteen. It took them a week to diagnose this neurological and viral disorder, he said, after he fell down some stairs and couldn't get back up. "I spoke like this . . ." He mimicked a barely audible cleft palate. But he doubted that Guillain-Barré had caused his current vocal sound, since he had never much liked his voice anyway, after a teacher had played a tape of it back to him at the age of seven or eight. Even at that age, his parents had wanted him to take speech therapy, as they felt he spoke too quickly and indistinctly.

He confessed to listening the other evening in the breakfast room to the way an English guest was talking. "He sounded so effortless, I envied him. I think I could do with voice lessons."

Jeremy enjoyed listening to his guests and was patient to a fault in attending to his staff. But his own speech didn't float, and his conversations with guests and staff reminded him daily of the effort it took for him to speak clearly. This seemed to have made him more tolerant of others, and perhaps of himself. I found it difficult to resist Jeremy's charm, and was never certain whether its source was his strained voice—as sometimes happened with stammerers—or his willingness to care about others and be entirely honest about himself.

Two years earlier, he had considered leaving South Africa for 100 Mile House, British Columbia, where he had friends. But instead of emigrating, he decided to buy this run-down building and do it up, sanding and varnishing the plank floors, painting and redecorating bare rooms by concentrating on simple fabrics and Mediterranean colours. There were feather duvets and pretty lampshades. Everything, including the long bright windows in my room, was spotless. Jeremy had a five-to-ten-year commitment to the hotel, which would see him through to whatever summer games had been scheduled in Cape Town. Recently, to the relief of staff at Travellers Inn, he had bought out his abusive dope-smoking partner. The help much preferred this skinny-chested man, in the blue shirt, tan trousers and red sockless loafers.

"Yaw," he would say, in response to questions from guests at the front desk—a throwback to the Afrikaans he spoke, although English was the language he had inherited from pukka parents. I learned his wife and he had separated one Christmas Eve, five years ago, and that he was now living with a woman interested in "holotropic breath work"—evidently a marriage of breath and music, as a consciousness-releasing tool.

Jeremy was attentive to personal makeovers, and he still hoped one of these might strengthen the way he used his voice. When I returned one day from visiting the Voice Clinic, in Park Road, he decided to clarify what he meant earlier about hoping to take voice lessons, and confessed he'd once gone there himself for training. That he now sounded ambivalent about the results was understandable; despite liking his tutor, he'd failed to complete the course.

He remembered to bring me a sheet of tongue twisters, from a source that interested him more than the Voice Clinic and its "corporate" approach to voice. "Big brown bumblebees, bumbling and buzzing by. . . ." Jeremy was quite taken by what he called the Waldorf School, based on Rudolf Steiner's teachings, and its interest in awakening one's awareness of the dormant life force in all matter. Its vocal mantras challenged one to become physically lighter, more integrated with the universe, less corporeal: "My fingers are flames of fiery red, fling fire, flame fire, with air am I fed."

I spent my days in Cape Town carrying on a running conversation with Jeremy, something I looked forward to, and exploring the city. I wandered to the seventeenth-century Castle; I visited Falcon Arms, a shooting range downtown where you could also rent or store arms; I toured the Botanic Gardens and its surrounding museums more than once. I also ascended to the top of Table Mountain, the cable car a mere white speck from a café on Kloof, and I walked miles down the mountain to Camps Bay. I toured the seal-littered harbour with an Afrikaner oceanography student.

And I visited the university where, had I not felt like such a tourist, I might have summoned the courage to knock on the office door of J.M. Coetzee, who four years earlier had kindly allowed me to reprint an excerpt from one of his novels, gratis to CIVA, for my anthology of bad trips.

At night, I stayed close to the Travellers Inn with its community of black and white voices, reluctant to venture into the largely empty streets for fear of muggers. I came to understand what women elsewhere had voiced about their desire "to take back the night." To accomplish this, the classified section of *The Argus* bluntly offered weapons: 357 Magnums ("as new") for sale, army issue Colt 45s, a BERSA pistol including holster and cleaning accessories. The Protection Shop at Parkade Mall was offering free delivery and a money-back guarantee on electronic stun guns.

Mornings were safest, when the hot and humid city was thronged with people. In St. George's Mall I spotted Joe Clark, former prime minister of Canada, striding anonymously forward with a well-known Canadian bureaucrat, both of them no doubt on junkets here to advise the new government in South Africa. Clark's baritone voice had always interested me, as though at a young age he had learned to step on it with his shoe, to keep it lower and more authoritative than was natural, thereby developing his trademark and intermittent "Ahh. . . ," as a kind of tonal primer and home note, a vocal trait among Canadian Conservative PMs from John Diefenbaker to Brian Mulroney.

Perhaps he was here to advise Mandela on vocal exercises.

I preferred the piping voice of an elderly fare collector in the "black" minivan I caught back from Camps Bay, through Clifton and Sea Point, who was saying ironically: "Oh, Winnie's in hot water again! Poor Winnie! She's a royal!" That day, she had flown off to a West African country against the wishes of her President-husband. It was her fourth or fifth transgression in the last two weeks.

The day I found my way to the Voice Clinic off Kloof, the founder and owner was in Johannesburg attending to her branch office there. I interviewed her father, who told me he'd sold his chemical business to become her business manager. I assumed this title was an acknowledgement of his investment in his daughter's company, which she'd started in 1988. The walnut doors, polished mahogany desks and smoky glass partitions were calculated to appeal to a business clientele. Joel Riessen, I supposed, was meant in his laconic man-of-the-world style to soothe away any anxiety over parting with two thousand rand per corporate client for an eight-week session of vocal workouts, certain to enhance one's confidence, spontaneity, self-image and (it went without saying) bottom line.

Sales directors and secretaries, bankers and executives, media types and marketing managers had all apparently benefited. I found Mr. Riessen's oral reading, from the long list of benefits included in the corporate folder, rather uninspiring, and presumed that his daughter Monique, a speech-and-drama graduate from the University of Cape Town, was the crackerjack. Assertiveness, dynamism, creativity and clarity in public were promised, as one's new voice emerged from a previous swamp of tense insecurity and wretched indecisiveness. Jeremy Harris notwithstanding, remarkable results were more or less promised, cheered on by a remark from Benjamin Disraeli: "There is no index of character so sure as the *voice*."

Behind the tapes, notes, personal videos, power speaking kits, and graduate certificates to be earned at the Voice Clinic lay the usual fundamentals of relaxation and breath control in support of good vocal production. Included in the package to potential customers was a copy of a five-year-old article, "Teaching SA to Speak," about Monique Riessen and the origins of her idea. "It was a hot windy Cape summer's day. Driving home from a day's teaching it occurred to Monique that no matter how much time and money people spent on improving their outward appearance the facet of themselves which could do the most for them—their voice—was often totally ignored."

Numerous testimonials to her success were enclosed in the package. From a television presenter for SABC: "Monique adapted the training to suit my professional needs and was interested enough to ask about progress. I love playing with my voice now . . . Professionally I feel more confident to take more risks on camera." And from a writer for the *Sunday Times*: "What interested me was that I was being offered an opportunity to work with something that was within my control . . . There's no describing that first moment when you know you're going to stand up and speak. When you know that even if the words don't come out right, you're going to sound absolutely wonderful saying them."

Amidst such satisfied customers, it was no wonder the owner of Travellers Inn had been reluctant to admit he had once been a client at the Voice Clinic. Not that his guests were complaining or his hospitality business suffering. Dennis, the night porter, a former brother in a monastery, was happy to be employed by Jeremy. I talked to him late one sultry night when I couldn't sleep, partly because Evangeline and Carla had brought back customers to the hotel and were bouncing noisily somewhere above my head on the third floor.

Remembering Melva McIlroy in Christchurch, I asked Dennis about silence in his old Benedictine monastery in Kwazulu Natal. His voice took on a slightly resentful tone. The black brothers, he said, had refused to observe periods of silence. But his resentment was directed more at the German abbots, who always seemed to want to appease and take their side. Dennis, who had been the monastery's jack-of-all-trades, didn't believe this political correctness was the way to true equality. So he had forsaken the stressful existence of brotherhood for urban life in Cape Town, where he looked after the books in a welfare mission by day, and at night let in whores with their johns to the Travellers Inn.

Not even a loud car crash, outside in Long Street as we spoke, bothered him. City life compared to that of the monastery seemed to breed in Dennis nothing but calm.

His English voice was light, precise, Afrikaans in accent— and snappish, I could imagine, if pushed to impatience by political correctness. The monastery, where supposedly silence was good because it created reflection and purpose in individuals, had made him impatient when it turned out less cooperative than he felt it should be. He was hoping to fictionalize his monastic life, by writing a volume of stories based on four of his notebooks. But nothing snappish, it seemed. The last thing he wanted was a dour or humourless voice, as seemed fashionable in the book of a hundred South African stories he had recently read in preparation for authorship. He wanted to show the humorous side of monastery life. And he hoped to flesh it out in a vernacular voice.

The Afrikaans voice, speaking English, was so commonplace in South Africa as to make English seem to a visitor the tongue of choice among Afrikaners. Yet the same student who had driven me in her rikki taxi up to the cable car terminus said, on the day she took me to Groote Schuur Hospital, how much she loved speaking Afrikaans. My destination was the large Afrikaner hospital now under budgetary assault by the new ANC government. Here I spent unexpected hours, talking to the clinical head of the speech pathology department. She, too, had grown up speaking idiomatic Afrikaans. "I feel pride in my Afrikaans," she said, in her Afrikaans accent. "I know exactly who I am." When her mother had forced her to go to an English-speaking school, she hadn't been allowed to speak her own tongue. So she'd honed her English-speaking voice till she was bilingual. "Being with English people doesn't bother me. I teach in English. When I speak English, I am not an Afrikaner. I become English. I still think my English is better than some native English-speakers, who haven't developed a pride in their language."

This linguistic and cultural awareness was now mirrored in her clinic, where they kept precise records of patients' skin colour, in the unspoken hope of looking more like an institutional Babel, representative of the polyglot population at large and therefore worthy of public funds. Hetta Pieterse claimed these statistics were necessary in order to look for diseases prevalent in particular groups. She was anxious for me to see the pages of these statistics, broken down month by month, over the last year. White, coloured, black—males, females, children. Clearly, the withdrawal of government money, especially for voice therapy, had increased the pressure to appear accountable, even here at the site of the world's first successful heart transplant, in 1967, by Dr. Barnard.

The hospital's statistics overwhelmingly favoured whites and coloureds. The fact was, as Hetta Pieterse acknowledged, the clinic saw mainly Afrikaans-speaking males and females. They accounted for 70 per cent of voice patients; 25 per cent of the rest spoke English. The remaining 5 per cent was black, speaking a mixture of Afrikaans and English.

Eighty per cent of all coloureds evidently spoke Afrikaans. They grew up speaking a very picturesque Afrikaans, but at school, unable to cope with the written language, chose to speak English instead. The result, according to her, was language development problems. "Even black children are put into English schools, when they don't speak English at all, and neither do the parents. It's a political issue."

My persistent image of the country as a huge voice clinic, vocalizing a way to communicate better with itself, seemed embodied rather poorly by Groote Schuur Hospital. The hospital was, as Hetta Pieterse averred, a political problem proving susceptible to punishment by the new government in power. Whenever someone in her department left, money to fill the position disappeared, and the remaining staff took on more of the load. She told me her own appointment had been as an administrator. Now she saw as many patients as the rest of her staff, she administered, and she tutored in speech pathology and audiology.

What surprised me was how much time she had for a visiting writer, with barely an introduction. She would mention from time to time how busy she was, and yet thought nothing of talking on through the hours I spent with her, interrupted by no more than two calls, and without worry of neglecting either patients or appointments. It became increasingly apparent to me that she had none. She was lonely. She needed to talk. She wanted to be quoted and to make an impression. She went into a long, increasingly enmeshed discussion of her professional and private lives.

I did not discourage her. She had lots to say. I was travelling to listen to voices, even to those of the voice-fixers. My desire was to understand how hers, or a voice such as Jeremy Harris's, had come to be shaped. I gradually realized that along with her linguistic and cultural duality had come a gender preference, partly vocal in origin. Hetta Pieterse preferred the company of men to that of women. While she resented the paternalism and arrogance of most older Afrikaner males, she heartily disliked the affected, high-pitched voices of their wives, trained from girlhood to be feminine. She herself had felt more like a boy growing up. But wanting to be a doctor, she couldn't get a bursary, which always went to less qualified men. Studying speech therapy had become her way of postponing a choice between doing a BSc and a BA. Interested in drama, acting, languages, she was drawn increasingly to voice work. Perhaps it had satisfied a need for control and professional respect.

"I was always very aggressive."

I asked if she spoke in different voices, for different people.

"Very definitely. I will give you an example. I am an elder in the church, which is very male. But it's not the males there who discriminate against me, but the women. When I am with males I have a much more relaxed voice. I can be myself. In a meeting I am very authoritative. I lower my voice. People listen to me. I speak slowly and evenly. When I get with females, I tend to withhold a lot of emotion. I listen more and talk less. I'm almost smug. I don't know how to say this . . . I can't converse with women who put a little . . . what? . . . into their voices. But when I speak to women in a workshop, I can relax."

At first distant with me, she'd gradually warmed to our conversation, relaxing into an almost flirtatious tone. I learned of her leaving a weak husband, of her outside interests such as Toastmasters, her four grown children—one of whom was epileptic and another deaf—of suitors. She didn't care what a man looked like, so long as he was a friend. She would not be uninterested, she said casually, in an affair with a man who travelled the world, a journalist, a businessman, an artist, someone who would allow her space to be independent.

Her cheerful pleasure in using her voice as an instrument of seduction reminded me of Ford Madox Ford, a male novelist I felt Hetta Pieterse would have found sympathetic. I recalled a passage in Alan Judd's biography, where he recounts Ford's relationship with Elsie a hundred years earlier:

> . . . He stressed the importance of being able to talk to her, a theme that featured largely in all his relations with women and which no doubt was a substantial part of his own attractiveness. Nor was it simply that he had a quiet, reassuring voice and manner and was sensitive: talk was to him the final communion of souls. It was what it was all about.

Intelligent, forthright, and knowledgeable about vocal hygiene, resonating cavities, incorrect tongue postures, this tall woman in sandals and white smock, who acted with worldly assurance, was a passionate believer in the power of the spoken voice to govern a life. She was fascinated by the voice as an instrument to be played and kept in tune.

"As a child I was aware of how much emotion you could put into something you read. I used to read to other children. I could make a story sound, I don't know . . . When I read a story book, I almost got the same feeling of the people in the story. And now when I treat people for therapy, whether they are stutterers or singers or teachers, I teach them using your voice is an art. Your message is influenced by how well you use your voice. I will lower my pitch with someone who is depressed, I will relax my body posture, make my speech clearer . . . and the patient tends to adapt in the same way."

She loathed the way a politician like Pik Botha exploded his *p*'s and *t*'s, especially in Afrikaans. "He sounds awful. Aggressive and excited." On the other hand, she admired how Ronald Reagan had calmly delivered even the worst sort of news in a reassuring way. And here, in her Afrikaans accent, she began to deliver an un-Reagan-sounding speech, to "my fellow Americans," on the occasion of his invasion of . . . "Where was that place?" Grenada? I suggested. "No." Lebanon? "No, no." I tried to remember where else the affable Reagan might have invaded. "Vietnam?" she asked, answering herself immediately. "No."

I did wonder afterwards how she might have treated Jeremy's high voice. She said she liked treating the unnaturally high voices of homosexuals—partly, I supposed, a little unkindly, because she believed they liked "the finer things" and did "their hair nicely." She had no problem with homosexuals, and held enlightened views on their genetic makeup. Freddie Mercury, from Queen, incidentally, had a nice tenor voice, which he had ruined by singing falsetto and developing nodules.

"I'm interested in the natural voice."

She enjoyed people who walked out of her office knowing how to cope better. I wondered if she might already be including me among these. A specialty of hers was inspirational aphonia, presenting as asthma. She took an interest in hysterical aphonia among women with abusive husbands. I should have asked her about Nam's voicelessness, in Durban. As for spasmodic dysphonia, she had heard of it, but someone else treated whatever cases they had of it here at Groote Schuur.

She picked up the phone and called Dr. Seppo Tuomi, head of the hospital's teaching wing. She then led me through corridors to his department, introduced us, and after two and a half hours of intense conversation promptly vanished.

Tuomi, a courteous bearded Finn, had come to South Africa fourteen years ago via the Universities of Chicago and Western Ontario. Three years ago, when he moved to Cape Town from Jo'burg, his marriage had collapsed. He loved Cape Town; the ocean reminded him of home. Nowadays, teaching as well as writing a report on government cutbacks to "primarily white" institutions, he rarely saw patients, and perhaps only a couple of cases of spasmodic dysphonia a year.

He confessed some ignorance about the disorder, although he tried to keep up on the research. In the absence of botulinum toxin treatments in Cape Town, he concentrated on treating its symptoms by reassuring patients their problem wasn't psychological. He would encourage either a whispery or else a high-pitched voice to relieve the strained and chopped-up articulation. He mentioned two cases he was acquainted with: the mother of a secretary here at the hospital; and a "beautiful" gym instructor in her early twenties, whose voice was "literally severe, literally every word"—and here he broke into a wood-chopping sound to illustrate the way she spoke. Both women had been in car accidents (as I had), shortly before developing the disorder.

He kindly walked me back out the maze of corridors, to the palm trees in front of this huge hospital, pointing out Tygerburg Hospital in the distance (originally for blacks?), and telling me how to catch the train back into town. Instead, I caught a "black" minivan on the highway, eventually making my way to the Yellow Pepper in Long Street, where I resumed the novel I was still reading, over a late afternoon meal.

I thought: this is the saddest story. Ford Madox Ford's line now occurred to me in context of Alan Paton's often melodramatic, pseudo-poetic, exceptionally moving story. A son is soon to be hanged for murder. I thought of my own son, of how achingly one loved one's offspring especially when something went wrong in his life. Seppo Tuomi had been telling me of travelling to fetch home his anorexic daughter from a private girls' school in Grahamstown. I was still vaguely concerned over passing on my vocal dystonia.

My spasms had begun to recur. Nothing as yet unmanageable, although I had begun to notice myself starting to reach out, holding on vocally, as it were, to prevent a spasm, to prevent the disorder from spreading through my syntax. The Botox had begun to wear off. I noticed an *effort* to speak, not present in New Zealand and Australia in the preceding two months. I found myself a touch less confident on the phone, or explaining in person to a British Airways representative the kind of worldly ticket I held. Mine was no longer quite a floating voice, insofar as the draught of it had sunk lower, forcing me to concentrate a little more on steering than on where I was going.

It was as though my present travels with a voice were to encompass one complete cycle of the toxin in my vocal cords. I was on the downside now. I found myself subtly forcing conversations into slightly jollier modes than required, in order to relax. Seppo Tuomi had noticed a catch in my voice, though he congratulated me on sounding as smooth as I did. A month earlier, his noticing a hitch would not have bothered me at all; it would have been no more than an aberrant wrinkle in a sea of calm. Now I recognized it as a foreshadowing of vocal choppiness, of loneliness, of failure to connect with others on the island where I was headed. For in the lowly spasm, to anyone afflicted with laryngeal dystonia, lay the social death rattle.

Why anyone should be so *ashamed* of a vocal spasm as to hear in it death seemed to me the sad story I was tracking. There were so few of us who had felt this inexpressible fear of vocal unpredictability that I despaired of making appreciable such private disorder. Far more measurable was the fear of public disorder, say, inside South Africa. "Cry, the beloved country, for the unborn child that is the inheritor of our fear. Let him not love the earth too deeply . . . Let him not be too moved when the birds of his land are singing, nor give too much of his heart to a mountain or a valley. For fear will rob him of all if he gives too much." Pessimism, whether over one's small disorder or over a disordered nation, was clearly a temptation.

Several months after my visit, the voice of the South African Supreme Court was heard on the death penalty. It reasoned that in spite of the astronomical rate of murder in South Africa, no evidence existed to suggest state execution deterred homicide and therefore the death penalty was abolished. In this decision was a cause for optimism, as it was usually the violent countries, such as the United States and China, that punished by violent means. So at least something had improved since Paton's novel. And yet, some years after my visit, by the time of the second national election in South Africa, it was revealed that in the same block where the minister of safety and security lived, fully a third of the homes had been broken into. It sounded worse than what Paton had portrayed.

I ordered another glass of Chardonnay, brought in from the local Cape vineyards, and for dinner the chicken poached in pear juice and sauvignon blanc. I loved Cape Town. But I intended to be home, at the Travellers Inn, before dusk, when talking on the veranda with Evangeline and Jeremy and the others would commence. I would be safe among voices.

7

Not I, Not Me

ON SUNDAY, unable to buy a ticket to that morning's sold-out concert at Wigmore Hall, I continued on to Speakers' Corner in Hyde Park. Coming from South Africa I felt safe to walk whatever street in London caught my whim. Inside the long subway at Marble Arch, siren voices, enhanced by tile acoustics and acoustic guitars, pleaded with pedestrians to leave behind spare sterling. I could hear voices on pedestals, as I re-emerged into the cool spring sunlight, entreating me to leave behind spare convictions.

"Banish your patronage of so-called fine restaurants," implored one speaker, in a damaged voice of Etonian regret, as though impersonating Eric Blair. Cried another, Cockney to the core and anti-vivisection by persuasion: "Gi' me your minds and I'll put a luv of sheep in your 'earts. Cats, mice, f'rsaken monkeys." The mongoose on her shoulder did not flinch as she touched a hanky to her nose.

Voices harsh, mellifluous, occasionally close to breaking down when supplicating (say) for "HIV compassion": public voices (or rather voices in public) soliciting acquiescence, funds, discernment. A kind of Babel of inexorable yet witty speech, atop soapboxes that had punctuated this crowded corner for the last century and a half. Four years after the Exhibition of All Nations at nearby Crystal Palace, a large demonstration at this site, protesting the

Sunday Trading Bill, launched the association of Hyde Park with free speech. "Free speech" was a term I had come to associate over the years more with its literal than its figurative meaning. You couldn't have the political concept of free speech without first having the ability to speak.

Speakers' Corner fascinated me. It was a place I used to visit as a student in London twenty-five years before, walking up from Tachbrook Street in Pimlico. The current speakers seemed not to have changed out of their frayed tweed coats, woollen berets, baggy-legged corduroys and army surplus jackets over cotton dresses. The place was a living museum of wear and worn opinions, often of socialist bent, but also of bizarre and radical ideas on everything from St. Augustine to zoos, expressed in a panoply of pungent voices.

Since hearing him once tell the story of his own voice, on the Alan Parkinson show, I'd long thought of Marble Arch and its chattering corner in connection with the English neurologist and theatre director Jonathan Miller. I remembered him sinuously entwined in a studio chair, hands on head, a man ready to doze off as he drifted in his punt down a verbal river (the Cam, say, flowing into the Ouse). In fact he deployed this body language to ward off suspicion of his spoken language, for, as he casually confessed, he'd suffered since childhood from a speech impediment.

Him?

My ears retuned themselves to our rented TV. This corduroyed interviewee was spilling the beans in public about a stutter, yet managing at the same time to put on a deft exhibition of avoiding any stutter at all. He was even willing to demonstrate how he conducted these successful and not infrequent avoidances of time-bombed consonants. As a schoolboy, for instance, he recalled preparing to ask a bus conductor for a fare to Marble Arch, profoundly aware as the conductor approached him that he was about to vocally founder over the momentous *M* in the name of his destination. By a quick portage, Boy Jonathan contrived to get round the approaching rapids by suddenly requesting a ticket ". . . to the, um—" hesitating here no more than a distracted don, before jumping back into his punt—"you know, to that Arch known as Marble."

If someone like Miller had entwined his body, tendril-like, to give the impression of utter relaxation, I was soon to look more like a lying politician made uncomfortable by exposure. This happened not many months after I left London to return to Canada, when the first inexplicable spasms started up and I developed any number of physical mannerisms intended to ward off suspicions concerning the failure of nerves (and nerve). In fact, many years later when a syndicated newspaper article revealed how to tell when a politician was lying in public, I recognized the hapless mannerisms of the person with laryngeal dystonia. A flattening of voice in order to take control of an uncontrollable situation; a lot of lip-licking as well as mouth-covering; throw in nose-rubbing, ear-tugging, shallow breathing; so that unnatural pauses, or speech breaks, were merely the final giveaway. No wonder, I thought, the person with SD appeared to be covering up some essential truth about himself. Because he was.

He could no longer count on free speech to avoid the truth.

Using a distorted voice required courage. In the debilitating (inescapable) act of trying to avoid spasms, it seemed nearly impossible to sound sympathetic or believable. It was difficult to digest the awful feeling of dismissal in another person's eyes, when your voice seized up and you caught a whiff of your own dissolution. Who could bear to look straight into another's eyes, without glancing guiltily away? Once in a while I was able to emulate Miller and get on a roll, discover some improbable balance of deeper breathing and functional head voice, which permitted a rill of eloquence to allay the spasms and slay the doubters. But this was rare.

Miller understood well how to control his stutter, so he was not disembowelled by it in public. After that BBC interview, in later years, I would occasionally hear him interviewed and listen to how his incipient stutter seemed to govern not only how he spoke but also what he said. Wherein exactly his winsome talk? One was alert to how often he rerouted spoken sentences in order to avoid or overcome identifiable consonants threatening blockage before words. But what mattered, and gave his sentences charm, was how this need of circumlocutions seemed to make his brain work harder than it might have, searching for smooth neural channels, until he managed by dint of small but clever portages to change the direction of his verbal river—never less than naturally, it sounded, and to arrive in an even smarter punt (cushions and a picnic basket, with crystal goblets for the bottle of German Riesling) than the boat in which he had started out to answer the original question, say, about directing *Così fan tutte*. This seemed to account for his rich and playful vocabulary. With one channel blocked, he imperceptibly devised another, producing in the end perhaps a more interesting conversational cruise than if he had suffered no speech impediment whatever.

But was there another explanation, other than his brain needing to parade itself in this fluent way, to account for his avoiding a stutter? If in the Beginning was the Word, then was Creation not woven from the Voice? The voice, in other words, on a self-perpetuating roll, where words seemed to precede thought and pull it like silk from a hat? How *did* you separate the dancer from the dance?

Coming back to loquacious London always felt like returning to the capital of voice. It still intimidated someone with my vocal background—not least on this current trip, of which the primary purpose was to talk to people about their voices, with my own now on the downturn of its Botox cycle. I felt less confident of its reliability than when crossing the Pacific to New Zealand two months earlier. Unless I received another injection before too long, the nerve endings in my vocal muscles, previously knocked out by toxin, would soon be up to their old unpredictable backflips.

Asking for a program at the Olivier Theatre one night, I knew I sounded spasmodic. The theatre would restore me. I sat in the lobby, listening to a piano and flute duet, to the chattering English around me, marvelling at a culture so secure in its rule of law that coming to the theatre at night wasn't only safe but a right. I took my seat, glad to be out of South Africa. Waiting for the house lights to go down always made me feel as though I were on the edge of a renewable world—vocally as well as visually. In that moment of darkness, between lights down and lights up, existed an immeasurable period in which the voice (my voice) might be recreated.

Not that I'd had any luck in persuading the influential voice teacher Christina Shewell to talk to me the day before. She had been recommended by the therapist Jan Hooper, in Adelaide, as someone once associated with the Royal Shakespeare Company, and I called her up with trepidation, after standing in Dillon's reading her contribution on public speaking to a book on the Alexander technique of relaxation.

"A small child utilises all the energy and spaces of his body to empower and amplify his voice," she had written. "But as we grow older, our holdings, clenchings, slumpings and imbalances restrict the strength and distort the quality of our voices, and this is usually worse when we are nervous."

I sounded nervous and probably put her off, as someone not in touch with his body. She explained how she was only in London one day a week and therefore very busy. I studied the photo of a smiling, pretty woman in a page-boy haircut and dotted dress. I felt like a vocally tremulous teenager again, phoning (unsuccessfully) for a date.

"As Alexander himself discovered, the voice cannot flow freely unless there is musculo-skeletal balance within the body, for the body is the housing for the whole vocal instrument."

Feeling misaligned, I caught a number 24 bus on Gower, riding its top front seat through Westminster, down Victoria and eventually to St. George's Square, near where I used to live. This journey was unexpectedly therapeutic. It was like a movie played of time past, before my voice crossed the divide from which it never came back. I used to catch this bus every afternoon after sitting all day in the glass rotunda of the British Museum. Staring out its windows at sunlight on buildings, at people on congested sidewalks, would stir in me a sense of present time as if I were seeing it from the future. This was exhilaratingly odd. And now here I was, *in* the future, as though nothing had changed and my voice had remained undivided. In Pimlico, I wandered across Vauxhall Bridge Road and along Islip to the Tate. The late afternoon light, the sometimes blue March sky, seemed so complex and mysterious, so *vivid*, I felt as though the Alexander technique knew nothing of true relaxation. The smell of freshly showered pavement in London was like no other.

An evening later, walking the Embankment in cool darkness, I sensed relaxation giving way to implacable nostalgia. If Vancouver was the city I loved as I loved myself, then London was the city I loved as I did my wife. This same nostalgia had been a recurrent feature of past visits alone here in the two decades since we'd lived in London. Such homesickness, for this place I was actually *in*, had overwhelmed me on a visit four years earlier. From France, I'd come here during the hottest May on record, which contributed to such a suicidal feeling of lost time, and of having let down others because of my voice, including friends here in London, that it forced me to cancel the rest of my stay and fly home.

The thought now of Lorraine losing any more bits of memory and thus our past, as she'd begun to do since her seizure, compounded my nostalgia for London. This city, like her, had been a watershed and over time and successive visits had grown more mysterious, complex. I watched the Thames' light-absorbing eddies and concentric current. Should she happen to die before me, I couldn't bear to visit London alone again, though the city would keep on implacably without either of us. Almost three years later, walking together along this same South Bank one afternoon, after a visit to the Voice Box at Royal Festival Hall, she and I would call in at the reconstructed Globe, and then continue downriver to Southwark Cathedral, happening upon such resonant family voices after a graduation ceremony of dentists that we longed for our son, before crossing London Bridge by foot and ending up at a

Barbican production of *Hamlet*. Shakespeare's was the voice we always seemed to find here in the end, whether spoken by Glenda Jackson or Susannah York, Alan Howard or Alex Jennings. Friends of ours, a renowned British dentist and wife, had once treated us to an RSC performance of *Antony and Cleopatra*. And I remembered one stormy night, on an even earlier return visit, arriving overland by bus from Athens, and sleepless after three days, we'd gone immediately to see Donald Sinden at the Aldwych in *Lear*. "Howl, howl, howl! O, you are men of stones! / Had I your tongues and eyes, I'ld use them so / That heaven's vault should crack." London continued to play me with its concentric voices.

When the stage lights in the Olivier came up on *The Merry Wives of Windsor*, I saw Terry Hands's production as a wild orchestration of voices. I heard squeaking and bellowing, mincing and croaking, knightly rage and children's songs, grunting and flirtations, a range and rage of accents. The highlight, for me the evening's transforming moment, occurred when all actors on stage disappeared from view into the home of Sir John Falstaff's hoped-for conquest. Then all proceeded to talk at once, making a marvellous beehive of *indecipherable* voices, thereby demonstrating (for me) how the visual stage depends on the aural stage for us to see anything.

I was sitting in the very middle of the Olivier stalls, mellow in my cut-price seat, alert to the effortless floating out and up of voices from servants, principals, townspeople, children. Eye followed ear up long shafts of light, into the concrete balcony, back down into the soft colours of a seasonal production (ripe wheat, tavern beams, fallen leaves, earth-coloured costumes). An autumnal staging from a veteran director. And it starred the veteran Dennis Quilley as Falstaff, an actor I could remember from as far back as the Old Vic's production of *The Front Page* in the early seventies; also opposite Laurence Olivier in *Long Day's Journey into Night*. I could still see Olivier, from the second row in the Duke of York's, hopping atop a table as he made verbal business of an allusion to Prospero, throwing away his lines in a little vocal riff that electrified the house. "'We are such stuff as dreams are made on, and our little life is rounded with a sleep.'" (I did not remember him so vocally indelible, on the other hand, from Jonathan Miller's so-so Old Vic production of *The Merchant of Venice*, for which he fashioned his infamous nose.)

Another SD might have forgiven my vocal hall-of-faming. Reconstituting highlight reels of the theatrical soundscape seemed unavoidable for anyone haunted by voice. If Shakespeare had helped make London the capital of voice, then the National Theatre (like the Barbican) was its boisterous cathedral—where citizens came not to reverence speech, but to reinvigorate their voices by listening to actors play artfully with theirs. Without art we might as well be in camera, in a class, a board meeting, listening to voices drone, lecture, pontificate. The fullest experience of voice was what theatre offered. Absence of theatre—its replacement by seductive cinema in North America—had led to my own avocal culture.

Perhaps the crack in this culture was nowhere better heard than in Marlon Brando's leaving theatre for films. So disconnected had his voice become from Stanley Kowalski's diaphragm in Tennessee Williams' *Streetcar* (from the character he was supposed to be, rather than his own mumbling self), that after Bertolucci's film *Last Tango in Paris* we found out his actor's eyes kept straying sideways and down, in intimate scenes, because he could no longer remember his lines and was reading cue cards.

Et tu, Antony?

I began to feel like an amateur acoustician on the muddy banks of the Thames. At intermission, I stood overlooking the city's skyline across the river. The oral landscape of Elizabethan London expanded before me. I wondered if some day we might not find a way to uncover the DNA of sound in order to rehear voices from the distant past.

I noticed in the *Merry Wives* program that "Company Voice Work" was credited to Patsy Rodenburg. After the play, standing on an Underground platform at Waterloo and listening to the faint cyclone of a train gathering down the tunnel, I imagined this woman as the high priestess of voice at the National—and by extension wherever voices performed in the English-speaking world. The thought of calling her up to talk, despite Christina Shewell's refusal, did not occur to me till morning, walking up Broad Walk in Regent's Park, Constable sky scudding and daffodils bouncing in the cold wind. I bent down to snuff up their scent like a dog addicted to perfume. Then I found a callbox and left my number at the National Theatre. I was uncertain about talking to an influential woman whose *raison d'être* was making sure professional actors' voices floated like pipe organs and rang like bells.

Meanwhile, I was locating strangers with my own disorder through the local coordinator of the Dystonia Society, who suffered from writer's cramp and who'd once lost her secretarial job (ironically) at the National Hospital for Neurology. Margaret Jones estimated there were fifty people in London with laryngeal dystonia.

I called Alwyn Knight. Because my first conversation with Alwyn was by phone, I didn't know what he looked like until visiting the National Hospital the following week to view its video on SD. Some days later he came to see me at my hotel, where we sat under the lobby's glass roof and drank tea. It felt as though we were sitting in a glasshouse whose plants were standup ashtrays. Alwyn's hair in the video was browner.

Now forty-four, he'd been a theatre manager for a local council at the time his normally powerful voice changed, seven years ago. Two years into his job, he awoke one morning with what he thought was laryngitis. It got worse. Two months later a doctor prescribed a muscle relaxant, which did nothing to relax his voice. It had fallen apart. A speech therapist agreed with Alwyn that his predicament must be stress-induced, as did an ENT specialist, who proceeded to traumatize him further with a fibre-optic laryngoscopy.

Both Alwyn's parents had died the previous year; he himself had been involved in a car accident; the family had been moving house, over a protracted period; and his wife had had another baby. Moreover, hoping to complete a postgraduate diploma in management, but without benefit of an academic degree, he'd sounded strangled, unable to swallow, prone to panic attacks. A hypnotist, alarmed at such tension in his handshake, taught Alwyn to relax. This helped everything except his voice.

In the video made of him before his first botulin needle, Alwyn speaks in a lost, squeaky voice: "You name it, I've tried it." After treatment, several months later, it's a much deeper, more characteristic voice: "Everybody I speak to on the phone can't believe it's me."

When his theatre later closed down because of the poll tax threat, Alwyn was appointed deputy manager of a public swimming pool. His earlier job, to negotiate with agents and to book comedians, vocalists and mimes, had lasted five years. This new job lasted just one, before he was fired. The reason? His voice—although smooth after Botox—was unable to *shout* in case of emergency in the pool.

Alwyn, who lived in Borehamwood, now had three young daughters and was volunteering as a social worker at rest homes and private residences. He talked of his trouble regarding sickness and work benefits, and of his not very good chances for future employment. For the last two years, he had begun to put out issues of a self-help newsletter called *Vocalis*, for those with spasmodic dysphonia. He was keen to spread the word that those of us with this affliction weren't mad.

He spoke matter-of-factly. His answer to a question about how he actually felt on getting his voice back therefore surprised me. "Euphoric!" That moment of unmitigated bliss, in those of us treated successfully with the drug, was often tempered in later years by the flattening knowledge of recurrent decline.

Ivy Black remembered her first injection with an equivalent wonder. She was the first patient treated with botulin for laryngeal dystonia in the UK and became a modestly celebrated case in newspapers, magazines and on radio. Shortly before Christmas in 1988, she awoke the morning after anaesthetic surgery to the voice of a nurse: "Anyone for tea?" Ivy, without realizing she could now speak, responded: "Good morning. Yes, please." This recovered voice astonished her. She'd been through five years of agony without it: strangled, confounded, hardly able to whisper.

Ivy had invited me to visit her in Reigate, Surrey, but when Renata Whurr thought to ask me along to visit Dr. Gerald Brookes's clinic one afternoon, and to look at a film she and he had made on SD, it was decided I could meet and talk to Ivy at the National Hospital in Queen Square. So we met one dark sleety afternoon in the bowels of the Powis Wing, where I observed a succession of voice patients receiving laryngeal injections through the neck. A light-bulb had burned out in the windowless clinic. A visiting doctor from Bombay was loading glass syringes. Whereas Ivy had once spent three days in hospital for her first injection, these patients were in and out like clockwork. Dr. Brookes had nothing to say to any of them, having sympathetically interviewed each beforehand.

Ivy had had some forty injections by now, one every six weeks, with varying degrees of success. Lately the frequency had changed. Her last, the previous December, had given her her best voice of all, although it had reaped five weeks of breathiness. She did not complain; she was grateful for any voice. In her late sixties now, she was fifty-seven when her voice disintegrated over a period of four months, forcing her to retire from secretarial work with a metallizing firm. During the next five years, not only was Ivy prevented from reading to her grandchildren, she couldn't babysit them since they couldn't hear her. She could barely make a sound. Taking a bus and shopping for groceries were excruciating chores. Speech therapists, neurologists (four) and acupuncturists had all failed to diagnose her disorder or to help.

"Those years were terrible. I could only speak in a strangulated whisper. It took all my energy to produce any sound at all."

As Ivy talked I observed her soft white hair and smooth face. For the clinic today she was wearing a black, embroidered sweater, black corduroys, and pearl-inlay earrings.

It was the *fifth* neurologist she saw who thought she might have dystonia. And so, diagnosed with a rare incurable disease, this intelligent woman was finally relieved to learn she had something

238 The Voice Gallery

to explain the way she talked. But the good news did not stop there. Her diagnosis coincided with the pioneering use of Botox in America for the same disorder. And so the National Hospital offered Ivy the chance to test the drug in Britain.

Speechless, she wondered what she had to lose.

Afterwards, astounded by the result, she ran up phone bills calling her son in the Middle East and her brother in Australia, neither of whom could understand how her voice had been resurrected. Best of all, she could talk and read to her grandchildren. The treatment had brought her back from a nightmare of loneliness and isolation. One granddaughter, as if carried away by a fairy tale she could actually believe in, told her she'd never heard Ivy's "real" voice before.

Losing her voice seemed to have uncovered in Ivy a generosity of spirit previously fettered. "Losing my voice has been my claim to fame," she told me. "I used to be very shy, even before I lost my voice." Since then she had worked as a volunteer for the Dystonia Society, helping to raise money and national awareness. Today, as on other clinic days, she had travelled into London to chat with patients who felt uncomfortable about impending treatment.

Afterwards, sitting in Le Piaf in Southampton Row, I thought of how much use novelists make of characters who are spiritually deficient. We believe such characters offer the most interesting possibilities for dramatic narrative. For the purpose of painting an interior life, an apparently good character offers less allure. The nearer the fictional pendulum swings toward moral conflict, the more likely a "story" is to show up. Yet apparently good people, like many I'd met and talked to about their unusual disease over the last months, could be just as conflicted as characters I might make up. "Good" was not less interesting than "evil" for being normal. No one (or did I mean everyone?) was normal.

I polished off my pear mousse. Who would have bothered making up a truly good character such as Ivy Black? Katherine Mansfield, possibly, who knew something of incurable illness and of epiphanies tinged with ecstasy, as she explored the darker side of experience at the same time. Maybe Ethel Wilson. A chance to be meeting people like Ivy Black made me glad to have dystonia. I was hearing how their stories could be as illuminating as those of imagined characters.

Once upon a time (1969), Ivy had left her husband to raise a son and daughter on her own. When her voice fell apart she lost job, self-respect, the understanding of grandchildren. Then a miracle happened and she blossomed into life. But she worried about her son, watching the erosion of his self-confidence after losing a job in the Middle East, where he'd had an illicit affair with a married woman. Unable to find work, he was back living with his mother now and possibly undergoing a breakdown.

Such characters were teaching me compassion.

She had brought along a pair of educational videos on dystonia, so we went to the audio-visual lab and watched ten-year-old Clare, who with generalized, progressive dystonia was unable to walk except on the tops of her feet. The child spent most of her time crawling or in a wheelchair. The other video, narrated by William Conrad, was about a young American who, realizing he would never play basketball because of his worsening pigeon toes, became a coach.

If doctors ever saw a case of dystonia, they tended to misdiagnose it. This tended to increase a patient's isolation and suffering, particularly in the case of laryngeal dystonia, when the basal ganglia origin was passed off as psychiatric. Ivy herself made a brief appearance in the British video, before treatment. Professor David Marsden, a neurologist and leading authority on dystonia in the UK, talked calmly about the disease and predicted a breakthrough for its genetic treatment in the next ten years. Three years after my visit, I learned of his unexpected death at the age of sixty.

Earlier the same day, his colleague Renata Whurr had shown me the video she and Gerald Brookes had put together on spasmodic dysphonia, its clinical features and treatments. "The term *spastic* should not be used, as there is no evidence of spasticity," narrates Whurr in a careful voice. Alwyn Knight and a variety of patients are featured, speaking mournfully and with great difficulty—and then, after injections, with quicker lighter voices. Renata confessed to me her embarrassment at a European conference, when this good-news film had followed the screening of a Greek documentary about a single SD patient treated unsuccessfully with speech therapy.

So far she had helped diagnose two hundred voice patients, referring them to Gerald Brookes for treatment. Of these, 150 came from the UK and fifty from European countries. Dr. Brookes had a private clinic as well, and for patients not on National Health he charged £500 for an injection. No wonder the corporate competition was keen in Europe for the botulinum toxin market, between the American Allergan and English Porton Down. Big money drove the drug market and Renata, as senior research fellow, was not above making her pitch for it.

Blond, smartly dressed in a navy blazer and red skirt, she must have been a powerhouse at conferences and on committees. She enjoyed talking about her research and about applying for grants. We had spoken the day before in her office at the National Hospital's College of Speech Sciences, in Wakefield Street, where I learned that this daughter of Czech parents had been head of the speech department for ten years. I asked why she had gone into speech therapy.

"I never really knew," she confessed. "I don't think I chose speech therapy. I think it was a process of elimination." Voice was her secondary interest, after the brain. Her early work on aphasia had become a standard text and was widely translated. Her current interests included linguistic differences in the conduct of left and right hands. In her high-ceilinged, double-desked office, with its Indian prints on the wall, she pulled out a prosthesis for an arm to show me her interest in helping amputees learn to write again. There was a hole in the hand, to cradle a pen.

I later visited the Royal National Ear, Nose and Throat Hospital in Gray's Inn Road, the site of Renata's first appointment many years earlier. I had an appointment to see the speech therapist who had helped diagnose me in Vancouver. Anne Burgi (now Pijper) had recently married and moved to London with her physician husband, finding this job in the trenches, as it were, working with stroke and post-op patients on swallowing and elementary speech. She greeted me in her soft-spoken way, wearing a well-cut maroon blazer, and guided me up and down old staircases to the speech department, where we talked for an hour in the fading light of a low-windowed office.

A listener by nature, Anne confessed she liked music and did not particularly enjoy asserting her own voice. "I find it easy to listen to people's voices." A recent respiratory infection, however, had left her aware of the importance of providing a good voice model for her patients, especially when she tended to be retiring and shy anyway.

She described her therapy for patients without tongues and voice boxes. This included pre-op consultations with cancer victims soon to experience a permanent loss of voice, when they would be breathing through throat holes. She counselled them on the insertion of electrolarynxes. Or else, if they did not need their voices right away, on esophageal speech: how to make the segment of tissue between esophagus and vocal cavities vibrate. Anne taught them how to burp—how to prolong the burp—then how to articulate on top of the burp in order to diminish the amount of unnecessary sound in the airway during inhalation. She taught them how to slow their speech, to make it audible.

Her tactical reports of these extreme battles for voice made me thankful for my comparatively small border skirmish with dystonia. Those of us with spasmodic voices had larynxes. It must have taken great empathy to work with those who had none. I could not imagine a more sympathetic therapist than Anne. Her study of voice at Wits University in Johannesburg had inspired her. She talked about a documentary film on the Kalahari bushmen and the wondrous clicking sounds these people made with their voices.

When I asked her about Nelson Mandela's voice, she spoke thoughtfully of his intonations, pace and breathing patterns. I trusted her ear. As someone who spoke Afrikaans, she also spoke English like a native.

Later, taxis and bus traffic splashed by outside, rush-hour hordes hurrying voiceless past me to King's Cross, mute as the flowing crowd in Eliot's "unreal city." I walked back to Russell Square in the falling rain and darkness. A cold, miserable night for someone still in summer clothes carrying a cheap pop-up umbrella.

Landing in London from Johannesburg, following a circuitous two-day debacle from Cape Town, I had ridden into town at dawn with a twenty-year-old soprano from Sydney. "Everything feels so strange," Rachel Kavanaugh was saying of the cool abstract light, after her abrupt dislocation from the southern hemisphere. I felt it too. Two years ago, she had come to London for eighteen months, and was now returning to study voice over the next four years. A renowned voice teacher had accepted her after a brief audition in Sydney. The resemblance of this aspiring Australian soprano to Joan Sutherland was ghostly.

"Yes, my friends say I have her chin."

I thought she had her brow. I supposed everyone who listened to Rachel was also hoping she had the diva's voice. This must have added to the pressure and expectation on her to succeed. Two nights earlier, unable to board a chronically overbooked BA flight to London, I'd driven back into Cape Town with a Dutch filmmaker and his wife, a stunning woman whose mother, she told me, had been an opera singer. And what a *difficult* world it had been for her mother to break into. Rachel Kavanaugh agreed the risk she had embarked on was high and odds of success long. Her own mother was a musician in Sydney. Rachel herself played piano and violin. She spoke precisely but quietly, as though her musician's ear were so acute she did not think to take into consideration that of a travelling companion in a rumbling bus. I wondered about that.

Kensington Gardens and then Hyde Park slid into view along Bayswater Road, as she talked about her plans.

She would be looking for a house to share while staying with friends in Black Heath. Sanguine, idealistic, she seemed determined to learn as much as she could about voice, and about using her own over the coming years. I found it nearly impossible to imagine in myself such vocal self-possession at her age. Before she disappeared with an outsize suitcase into Euston Station, we agreed to meet and talk more about voice. I never heard from her again. And yet I still expect to, listening to a Met broadcast some Saturday afternoon in the foreseeable future, when she debuts as Butterfly to standing cheers.

Countless voice students such as Rachel must arrive in London full of hope, never to emerge as quite the bel canto promised by their talent. For every Kiri Te Kanawa from Auckland, a steady supply of trained voices must return home to Houston, Swansea and Sydney for local opera choruses and community choirs.

Strolling one day through Covent Garden market, I overheard two young sopranos, one a mezzo, singing the Barcarolle from *Hoffman*, accompanied by a tape deck they had set up in the trendy café below. As with the Underground folksingers at Marble Arch, they were using the vibrato effect of walls, as well as the glass roof above, to give their semi-trained voices a flattering boost. When the mezzo struck up an aria from *Carmen*, her peasant-dressed companion bobbed among coffee drinkers with a bowler hat, ascending the staircase to solicit donations from the rest of us listening above.

I assumed they were voice students. I did not make the same assumption of the bleach-haired punk rocker, singing with his band outside the market, rabid in the ruination of his voice. Ruination seemed his self-mutilating message: How can I sing about extreme feelings without deploying this iconoclastic voice? I was moved, in an unwilling way, by the extremity of his voice and by its pounding rejection of any pretence of artistic control, charm or lucidity. It was everything a listener with spasmodic dysphonia should have found abhorrent. I didn't.

How else, I supposed, except by some such extreme could you render the spasmodic voice in art? I myself had tried to find metaphors for it in stories of characters with different afflictions and shame-causing conditions. I had never written of dystonia directly.

Then one evening, sitting in the Coliseum at the English National Opera's production of Leoš Janáček's fantasy opera *The Cunning Little Vixen*, I was struck forcefully by an idea for a libretto on the theme of the dystonia voice. (If you could impersonate a fox and badger, why not a feral-voiced human?) It occurred to me the quest for a reliable voice, originating in the mysterious demise of a voice, could make for an organic and even chimerical opera of discordant passion and appeal—especially if some magic elixir were to transform this instrument of broken pitch and strangulation into a voice capable again of harmony.

It seemed that such a libretto of ruination and recovery, odd loss and tentative restoration, could, with the help of an adroit composer, become an operatic quest worthy of the glass slipper. The fragility of the human voice was something forgotten in opera houses of powerful, cosmopolitan voices—robust survivors of academies and vocal competitions. Yet a flawed voice's breakdown might be a theme at least as compelling as the rupture of tragic love (say). I thought again of Maria Callas's career. She was a diva who had made a sometimes unbeautiful voice not only unique but uncomfortably haunting, as in Lucia's mad scene in *Lucia di Lammermoor*. I remembered Marie Allison in New Zealand, singing for me on tape with her own soprano voice in decline, and how much this had touched me. I then decided that a painting I had viewed a year or two earlier in Vancouver, *Diva in Extremis* by Kathryn Jacobi, could grace the cover of my opera's program.

Watching the choreography in this *Vixen* production, I grandly broadened my idea to embody generalized dystonia. Indeed, an opera-cum-ballet to complete the theatrical dictum I had once established for myself, while writing plays: to hear what I saw on stage, and, at the same time, to see what I heard. Dystonia offered the complete package, among neurological disorders, and it was time someone more enterprising than I saw its artistic potential for the stage. Muscular contractions leading to involuntary movements of larynx, and also limbs.

Next day, signing traveller's cheques at an American Express office in Haymarket, I was ruefully amused trying to sign my name. Was I simply worn out by too much travel, my sense of identity taking a beating? Or was it my old failure in the face of expectation to perform on demand? My hand seemed not to move in quite the way I wished it to. The written stroke failed to exactly match the letter of intention. I worried my lower signature would not enough resemble my upper one, penned months earlier, to convince the teller I was not an impostor. It was as if part of my muscle memory had disappeared. My hand clenched, touched with writer's cramp. Lately, I had noticed this same clenching while writing in my notebook, just enough muscle contraction to remind me of how dystonia shadowed other parts of my body outside the larynx, causing other involuntary movements of head as well as eyelid. These were no more likely to progress than my splay foot had when I was a sprinting boy. But they helped to consolidate my conviction that an opera devoted to the theme of dystonia would interest at least its librettist.

Later, when I read the memoir by Julie Sheldon, *Dancer Off Her Feet*, given to me by Ivy Black, I saw where my theatrical idea might find its text for the choreography. Sheldon had been a young British dancer, gradually cut down by dystonia, until paralyzed and near death she experienced a "miraculous" recovery that helped her walk, run, even dance again. In the diaspora, we all dreamed of such a spontaneous remission.

Up the street at the Haymarket Theatre, on the strength of loot extracted from American Express by my imposture, I attended a National Theatre production of Tom Stoppard's *Arcadia*, directed by Trevor Nunn. I seemed to recall this theatre was where George

Woodcock, for sixpence, saw Charles Laughton act in Chekhov's *Cherry Orchard* in the 1930s. For that price George got to sit in the gods, which, for considerably more, is where I found myself with squished knees, imagining Laughton's voice carrying better than those of some of these modern actors to the upper circle. I leaned down towards the stage.

Voices then and now, past and future, were a theme in *Arcadia*, with its Derbyshire setting of a country house shared alternately by characters from different centuries, occupying the same grand room on stage. Bernard Nightingale, the modern and misguided don, says at one point of Lord Byron: "There is a platonic letter which confirms everything—lost but ineradicable, like radio voices rippling through the universe for all eternity."

Paul Shelley's voluble, virtuoso role as this swaggering researcher reminded me of dons I had heard in the 1970s, in *The Philanthropist* by Christopher Hampton at the Royal Court and in *Butley* by Simon Gray at the Criterion. Their voices still rippled in my oral universe: without static, speaking with élan and bathos. The voices required by actors such as Alec McCowen, Dinsdale Landen and Alan Bates for these audience-pleasing roles had been immeasurably nimble and unforgettable.

In the same vein, the pair of actors I would see three years from now playing A.E. Housman, as old don and young scholar in *The Invention of Love* by Tom Stoppard—John Wood and Paul Rhys— were equally required to talk through hoops and did. Lorraine and I would stand for three hours in the sold-out Cottesloe, held by Richard Eyre's excellent vocal production, with its nice distinction between the lighter and heavier voices of the two Housmans. Company voice work here at the National was credited, as usual, to Patsy Rodenburg.

I was still waiting for Rodenburg to call back. It seemed unlikely she would, yet this did not stop me from wondering how deeply vocal coaches went into roles such as Paul Shelley's in *Arcadia*. Responsibility for the wit and timing, tone and phrasing, the *flexibility* of voice required in roles bearing the influences of Congreve,

Wilde, Coward—possibly even the influence of a recent, loquacious don like Isaiah Berlin—could not reside entirely with actor and director. Whatever "voice work" entailed, I supposed in the case of a playwright like Stoppard it required an awareness that parody was important. Even so, what counted most in theatre was the simple enactment of voice, through effective speech. Illusion depended on making us see through the ears.

I supposed this was a test of the telephone voice too. It sometimes disappointed me that I could not meet, face to face, a particular person who was otherwise willing to talk to me about his or her vocal disorder. Thus I needed to imagine Liz Taylor in Purley, Surrey, somewhere in the stockbroker belt south of London, looking a little like the novelist Anita Brookner, sounding impossibly calm considering she (evidently) suffered from a fractured voice. This voice helped me to *see* her (a bank "researcher") as a precise, professional woman sitting at home in a French provincial chair wearing Calvin Klein jeans.

Her soft-spokenness and middle-class life reminded me a little of another attractive woman, Ginny Collinge, in New Zealand. Now forty-four, Liz Taylor had developed spasmodic dysphonia at twenty-nine, following a stressful house move. "At its worst I was out of breath. I couldn't breathe." Misdiagnoses followed, although a speech therapist suspected SD and referred her to a neurologist, who chose to prescribe anti-Parkinson's drugs. Liz took these for a while and tried hypnosis once. Then, in 1982, she and her husband went on holidays to Crete.

When they returned, she noticed her speech growing dramatically easier.

A remission of eight years followed, with no severe spasms or broken words, until her voice again deteriorated. Her doctor prescribed beta blockers for hypertension, and Liz was still on these now after five years. She calmly credited them for her current remission. She had never been tempted by botulinum toxin.

I admired her honesty in helping me see beyond her calmness, especially to her frustrations in the early years of affliction.

Whereas her husband had resented the psychological explanations for her voicelessness—and was relieved to hear her problem was neurological in origin—Liz herself (like Robert Edwards in Perth) actually preferred the psychological explanation, and had never objected to talking to a psychiatrist, which she'd done. We talked a little about this. Perhaps by believing she was the source of her own difficulty, Liz could also take credit for her remissions. There was something irresistible, I thought appreciatively, in controlling your own destiny.

Sometimes it was a relief for me to see old friends in London and not to have to take notes. I travelled north for miles on the Metropolitan Line one cold Saturday evening, to Croxley, dusted in snow, to visit Lily Cloote whose husband had died unexpectedly a year or two earlier. Lily, turned out in raven hair and a generous red blouse, picked me up at the station in her new white Ford. "It's my turn now," she said. Her voice was a robust instrument, a bit drillish perhaps, well forward in the mask of a middle-class woman, who now spoke RP (Received Pronunciation, Standard English), having emigrated from South Africa in her early twenties to work as a secretary before falling in love with an overbearing military man.

Lily, my wife and another girl, Jenny Smallwood, had all worked in a small office in Bury Street for the World Energy Conference. Their boss was a man they loved to mimic, answering the phone with imagined potatoes in their mouths: "RRRRR—UTT—LY HE—AHH . . ." They made him sound even more vocally defiled than the usual public school product of his age and pedigree. I could recall their stories of Mrs. Pridham, a pukka-voiced closet drinker, who kept the office books and complained, every morning she was late, that her train from Tunbridge Wells had had to contend with another "shhuicide on the line."

Lily treated me to a Chinese meal in Moor Park, and mentioned the loosening in her life of purse strings, knotted spirits, and the discipline of her sons since Michael's sudden coronary. I marvelled at the way her voice assumed the unselfconscious right to an extended space in public, even when this space was a small restaurant.

"I'm fat," she said, picking up another spring roll. It was a voice hard not to prize.

Also from South Africa was Con Baxter, the old friend I'd tried to find in Grahamstown, and whose daughter in Cape Town had given me his number in London. Con and I had been English literature students at the University of London, eventually living near one another in North London. I remembered a leaving-London party Lorraine and I had given for ourselves, at which an independent-minded American woman, married to a rich prospective candidate for the Conservative Party, had turned to Con and said, "I like your voice."

I was reminded of it again, listening to him talk at the Flask, in Hampstead, where we met for a pint along with his pretty Belgian girl friend, Thérèse. I had not seen Con in twenty-two years. He now had pouches under his eyes and had lost some of his still-dark hair, but with his patrician nose he continued to remind me of Robert Graves, a poet he had written a thesis on before turning his interest to Malcolm Lowry. Con's voice was clear, lightish, and a mild reediness lent it colour. I could faintly hear the South African precision in his consonants, as he told me what had happened to him and Vanessa, on their return to South Africa to teach under apartheid in the mid-seventies.

"We were stupid. Naïve." He was describing their messy involvement with undergraduates at Rhodes, trying to encourage in them liberal ideas by socializing with blacks, and passing around marijuana at parties. The police would later accost these students, promising not to arrest them in exchange for names of other guests at the Baxters' house.

"It got to the point where blacks were showing up in the middle of the night and asking for rides back to the townships."

Eventually, with the arrest and murder of Steve Biko, Con had had enough of his native country and attention from the Special Branch. He'd been stopped and searched in the same roadblock Biko was arrested in, before Biko's transfer to a Johannesburg jail. So Con decided to return with his family to the UK.

Still a political animal, since divorced, he was now a union organizer at a small North London college where he taught, having experienced downward mobility since his heady days at Rhodes. His politics, as he talked about them, seemed personally and professionally entwined. He wistfully described attacks on his person and car by a jealous, psychotic colleague whom he used to court. He and Thérèse, a fellow teacher, were forced to keep their affair a secret for fear of persecution and reprisals by this crazed woman. Something Lucky Jim–ish about their college made it sound fetchingly farcical.

A gregarious, patient man, Con struck me as the kind of careerless academic who appealed to students (and old friends) more than to deans who awarded tenure. He had been back to South Africa only once, twelve years ago, and was thinking of returning again should he be fired because of academic cutbacks or his union organizing. His daughter Lisa was studying at his old university, in Cape Town, and wanted to be a political journalist. Con thought he could probably get a job in the new South Africa.

I admired his abiding idealism. In an open-collared green shirt, jeans, black sports jacket with a pen clipped to the front pocket, he seemed a throwback to the sixties with his un-uptight values of the young activist. He had recently applied for a mortgage to buy a flat in Finchley, not far from where we used to smoke pot in his rented Meadway flat with Vanessa and their sleeping infant daughter. Con sounded a little forlorn, or perhaps shabbily proud, that all his possessions would now fit into three boxes.

I was uncomfortable waiting at the stage door of the National Theatre for Patsy Rodenburg. With Botox effects wearing thin, my voice rang flat. I sounded breathless, evasive of spasms, unsociable. Anticipating our meeting, I felt neither relaxed nor natural. A day earlier I had been reading one of her books when the high priestess herself phoned to set up an interview. Concerned, I now ran through vocal and relaxation exercises advocated in her pages.

Her writing seemed its own answer to anything I might think to ask about her life in voice.

From Peter Straus's book-choked office off Fulham Road, I had thought to wrest a copy of *Worst Journeys* to offer in exchange for signing her own work. Straus, a laconic yet devoted publisher, recognized Rodenburg's name when I mentioned it. "The voice person," he said, preoccupied himself with travel and fiction people. And so it was on a sunny day in March I walked across Waterloo Bridge and waited for the voice person to be paged.

I already sensed she would not fit my high-priestess image of someone who administered exclusively to plummy voices at a theatrical temple. From the opening sentence in her first book, *The Right to Speak*, I realized her interests were broader than liturgical. "The right to breathe, the right to be physically unashamed, to fully vocalise, to need, choose and make contact with a word, to release a word into space—the right to speak . . ." She was fascinated as much by the use of voice in society as in theatre, understood the fear of one's own voice, and appeared still to have a sense of wonder at vocal expression uncommon among professionals. "My job, as a voice teacher, is to remove that dreaded fear and to hand back to any speaker the fun, joy and ultimately the liberating power that speaking well and forcefully can engender . . ."

Patsy Rodenburg greeted me dressed casually in jeans and a bulky sky-blue sweater. She suggested we go round to the Lyttleton buffet for a sandwich. I seemed to tower over her short, unpretentious figure, and felt even more awkward trying not to sound awkward. I bought coffee while she found us a quiet table off the upper circle. She then removed her wristwatch and placed it on the table. She'd agreed to talk for fifty minutes, before her rehearsal. Her enthusiasm in person was as forthcoming as on the page. After fifty minutes, she waved off her departure, picked up her watch and refastened it to her wrist.

In the end, we talked for two and a half hours.

I wanted to know what she made of vows of silence. Of deliberately repressing the voice in convents and monasteries, of postulants such as Melva McIlroy, sixty years earlier in Sydney, who denied their voices for some supposed spiritual benefit. I wondered if a vocal coach might have something to say about the *absence* of voice.

"I go into silent retreat for about five days a year," she said immediately. "You suddenly realize a lot of communication is with the inner voice." For someone who had devoted her life to the appreciation and workings of the outer voice, this was revealing.

"I remember, after a lecture I gave at Oxford, some Buddhist monks in the audience came up to say how after a year of silence, when they began to talk again, they started to speak in the voices of their childhood." With simplicity and clarity, she meant. "I teach in prisons. Prisoners know they have lost their voices. In the case of monks . . ."

She brushed a hand through her short blond hair and carried on in a voice I found curiously ordinary. Around theatre lobbies, including this one, you were used to hearing middle-class voices insisting on their territory. Educated voices, drawing attention to themselves, as part of a public game in which cheeks were bussed and insider news tossed off like confetti. Patsy's voice, which I would have expected to command attention, did, but in the space between the pair of us and not beyond. She was talking to *me*. She had something to *say*. Her modulated voice was suited simply to this communication. It resembled her body: round but not plump, wholesome without being fashionable. I had expected posh, fearing plummy. Her voice had its own style, self-contained and befitting the occasion. It was really no style at all.

I later found my notes about her monks incomplete. My stiff hand was not keeping up with my ear. Or perhaps my ear had gone into digressive-surveillance mode. I wasn't proud of this habit, forced on me at a young age, of hearing delivery over message. Too often for someone like me, delivery *was* the message. I think Patsy went on to say that since the loss of a monk's voice in silent retreat was a voluntary loss, this served to enlarge the speaking voice by connecting it to a quiet, inner reality. Ian McKellen, in his foreword to *The Right to Speak*, writes: "She'd be the first to agree that in the end what matters is what we say rather than how we say it. Her revelation is that, at best, the sounds, like the sense, can respond to the heart of our inner selves."

Patsy now sipped her latte. Weak sunlight over the Thames lit up the large streaked window beside us.

I asked if she liked her own voice. A pause. "It doesn't let me down. If I give a master voice class in the Olivier Theatre, I can stand and teach for two hours." Used properly, in other words, her voice was a reliable enough instrument. She felt no need to push it. The voice in service to a text, in the case of actors, would always quash temptations to empty flourish and hollow sound.

"On one level, my work is just getting actors to commit to texts, to read a text, where the jewels wait to be uncovered."

I could see how her time at the Royal Shakespeare Company could only have enhanced her reverence for "the text." And yet her love of poetry and written language went back to girlhood. There had been no books at home, so she discovered poetry at school, in particular Coleridge's. "I remember discovering the power of words." But school had been difficult at first, because of a speech impediment.

"Really? Tell me more."

"Initially, I didn't like my voice. I found speaking very difficult when young. Certain sounds. I couldn't do a *d* and an *r* together. Or a *b* and an *r* . . ." She also had trouble with *th* in "father." To this day, said Patsy, her father still spoke with a Dutch accent, her mother a Cumberland accent. At public school, she discovered the emphasis placed on having a proper sound meant she was criticized for her accent, as well for her "hesitant and incoherent" voice (what one teacher called "ugly"). I pictured young Patsy as shy, short and apple-cheeked. I learned she was sent to speech lessons to rout her trepidation and impediment.

Not until age fourteen did she speak with any confidence to strangers. Yet she considered this a dubious achievement. "I was trained to think of speech before breath and voice." She disapproved of this old-fashioned method of putting sound before meaning. Of placing bones in mouths to enhance articulation, before instilling knowledge of basic mechanics.

Patsy began acting at school, then carried on with theatre by training as a teacher at London's Central School of Speech and Drama. She discovered in herself a passion for teaching—but not the "cruel" kind that counted on fear to break down a speaker just to build him up again. "I would never think of telling anyone they had a bad voice." She didn't believe there was such a thing.

"If I hear a voice fail, it's because of breath."

I understood this better than others. I also knew the failure of a voice like mine went back to the brain stem. I didn't breathe right when signals from my basal ganglia triggered vocal-fold closures. So poor breath control was sometimes a symptom rather than a cause.

But the vocal aberrations of dystonia seemed remote just now. I was temporarily in another world, a theatrical world going back centuries, on this south bank of the Thames. Its vocal history came down to an intelligent woman telling me about breath. Through her teaching and writing, enthusiasm and hard-won knowledge, she was helping as much as any actor or director to make an art of voice. The wonder she felt at the tradition of the stage disguised the work she did behind it.

"You *have* to work," said Patsy, "at producing and maintaining a trained voice. I stand for hours a week. My students work at it two hours every morning, four times a week. Like a ballet dancer, you have to stand at the bar and exercise your muscle."

She worked fifty to seventy hours a week. If her reward had once been audience approval, it now lay elsewhere. In working with actors, for example, who might rediscover a lost power in their voices; or else in her working with "normal" people at speech work-shops, who learned of the voice's power to tell them truths about themselves. She related the "moving" example of an anorexic girl, who knew immediately she was in trouble while standing with thirty-five other students and trying to breathe from her diaphragm. The girl sought medical help.

Patsy liked teaching first-year students best of all. She spent part of her time at the Guildhall School of Music and Drama. Aside from private coaching, and travelling abroad to give workshops, she devoted her time to the National. Five years ago, at the invitation of Richard Eyre, she'd left the RSC after working with Cicely Berry for nine years, to set up the Voice Clinic here. She was now forty-one. "I can work with any star I want to," she said. Yet her real satisfaction came from working with young students.

"I love teaching people who don't know anything. If you do your job correctly, you can change actors now and for the future. I don't do the third-year students. I do the basics. I enjoy doing the basics. Most teachers find that boring. It's much easier teaching Ian McKellen."

She related how after twelve weeks her students would return from their first home holidays with more power and confidence. "I teach choice." Received Pronunciation, for example: a student could adopt it or not. An amused black student from Brixton told her that he had been stopped by the police, but when he spoke to them using RP they had let him go right away. He had learned to modulate his voice in Patsy's class.

She also taught singers. "Voice, not singing. A lot of them have never been taught to speak. I trouble-shoot."

I recalled Rachel Kavanaugh's very quiet voice. And later, reading further in Rodenburg's second book *The Need for Words*, I learned "devoicing" was sometimes used by reticent young women still learning to focus orally. Yet devoicing was also a notorious habit among quiet sorts of control freaks. It existed at the other end of the bluff scale (on which those wanting power spoke too loudly).

Her range of vocal insights was impressive. The theatrical world was simply a microcosm, a playful model of how the free voice, the voice free of fear, might exist in the larger world. Her interest in voice was encompassing: physical, social, moral. Presumably, anyone who thought deeply about voice, and worked on his or her own voice, could expect to be a better and more sympathetic person. You understood the world through voices. It was (like the theatre) as deceptively simple as that, and just as easy to take for granted.

"What always amazes me about voice is how extraordinary it is."

I asked her what she would include in a voice gallery.

"Breath," she said. "Breath. The sound of breath being released. The gabbling of breath."

I mentioned how a speech therapist I knew in South Africa thought breath in the production of voice was "overrated." Patsy was appalled.

About such speech therapists, she related an anecdote of an American voice coach "really setting the cat among the pigeons" at a conference in Banff, where, as Patsy recalled, she stood up and said: "I'm sick and tired of sending people to voice therapists, who come back sounding worse than when I sent them!" In other words, voice therapists did not necessarily understand how the voice needed to be exercised in order for it to work "naturally."

As she spoke about Canada, I seemed to recall hearing a woman interviewed on CBC radio during her stint at Stratford, Ontario. She'd had to put her interviewer at ease, which had spoken to me at the time of the discomfort her profession caused among professional voice users, especially in North America, who acknowledged their vocal inadequacies but did little to eliminate them. It had been Patsy Rodenburg.

"I owe Canada a lot," she said, as if the experience of other cultures, including those in South India and South Africa, where she'd also given workshops, was always an opportunity for her to appreciate anew the cultural context of voice. For her, locating true voice was never limited to actors, although actors required ongoing lessons in voice location. She remembered a Canadian actor at Stratford telling her he couldn't speak Shakespeare in a Canadian accent because it sounded "ignorant." The result, she said, was actors speaking Shakespeare in antiquated English accents.

"I mean Shakespeare is full of rural accents, from all over the country. No one spoke RP."

As we talked on through the afternoon, laughter would erupt from the matinee performance of a production of Joe Orton's *What the Butler Saw*, which I had seen the night of my arrival from South Africa. At intermission, people crowded the air around us with their mirthful voices.

Patsy had no strict preferences among the kinds of voices she coached. "I like any voice that hasn't come to the end of its power. I like any actor who owns every word." She mentioned one of her favourite actors, Judi Dench. "Hers is a voice that doesn't get in the way." She mentioned others she admired: Nigel Hawthorne, Tony Sher, Rosemary Harris, Claire Higgins. "I find it very moving when an actor just works and changes."

Her job as head of voice was to ensure actors' voices worked up to their potential at every performance. She or one of her assistants warmed up voices before each curtain, hoping to time this to the "half"(-hour) call when actors left for their dressing rooms prior to performance. In rehearsal, she helped voices decipher and animate texts, then to adjust and sustain themselves for an entire run of performances. At present she was rehearsing Fiona Shaw as Richard, in *Richard II*.

"I *never* give a line reading," said Patsy. "Some directors actually do." I could hear the incredulity in her voice.

She refused to acknowledge that her own role as a voice coach approached that of the director. Yet, as Antony Sher writes in the foreword to her second book: "What makes a great teacher? The qualities are similar to what I hope for in a director—enormous positive force, and enormous imagination—and indeed, when working on a classic role, the great voice coach can offer as many insights as the director."

But Patsy had no interest in directing, which sometimes people suggested she try. She enjoyed working with directors, rather than competing against them. Directors who never went to one another's productions, she told me, would ask her what working with so-and-so was like. I wondered about her role in Terry Hands's splendid production of *The Merry Wives*. She gave me to believe her own job had been piddling, because of the director's experience. "He's of the old school and knows exactly what he wants. Two things. Actors must speak loud and fast."

The fast bit reminded me of Billie Whitelaw's stunning performance in Samuel Beckett's *Not I*, the original Royal Court production in 1973. Whitelaw's logorrhea, as the non-stop "Mouth," had remained for me the most electrifying voice I had ever heard in theatre: An old Irishwoman's voice barking non-stop in the wilderness, her almost incomprehensible stream-of-consciousness monologue uttered at speed from a lit mouth eight feet above the stage and surrounded by darkness. ". . . and now this stream . . . not catching the half of it . . . not the quarter . . . no idea . . . what she was saying . . . imagine! . . . no idea what she was saying! . . . till she began trying to . . . delude herself . . . it was not hers at all . . . not her voice at all . . ." This coup de théâtre, lasting less than twenty minutes, was the kind of vocal performance (all about voice) no actor without consummate coaching could have attempted. Which was why the tiny Whitelaw had been drilled in the role, unremittingly, by Beckett himself.

I supposed he was of the old school, somewhat dictatorial in rehearsal, although Patsy mentioned working comfortably with him at a later date.

We began to gossip about playwrights.

She told me rehearsing with Tom Stoppard was a joy. He was evidently an accommodating writer who, unlike Pinter, say, would ask for advice and be willing to change a line to accommodate the speaking voice. Working with each of these playwrights, both of whom she got along with well, was not so much a difference in degree as in kind. I concluded Pinter was comfortable with his characters' voices; Stoppard with his own voice. It was perhaps a difference between private and public speech, pointing the contrast between this pair of seminal dramatists.

Talk of Pinter reminded me of my greatest theatrical experience, watching Ralph Richardson and John Gielgud in Peter Hall's original production of *No Man's Land*. Richardson's laconic, liquor-soaked voice gradually segueing into his ruminative, expansive voice of the second act; with Gielgud's infinitely flexible instrument giving way to self-doubt, and eventually to an aria of note-perfect pleading, in the wake of his antagonist's burst of lucidity.

Patsy had mentioned a video of hers, and on our way out through the Lyttleton lobby we stopped at the bookshop to find it beside her other works. "Some people actually go in and sign their books, so they can't be returned," she said innocently. "I'd be too embarrassed." I asked her to sign one now, and offered my travel anthology in return.

Unfortunately, back in Canada, her British video needed to be retaped to North American frequency, so it wasn't until later that year I watched Patsy giving voice lessons to students with untrained voices. One could see by her actual coaching, through exercises, digressions and good humour, why she had risen to the top of her profession. Enthusiasm, not limited to actors, conveyed her evangelical belief in "the right to speak" and "the need for words" in everyone with a voice. Who could remain mute in face of such coaching? Who could doubt her calming influence in Babel?

Not I.

On the afternoon I travelled to Kew Gardens by Underground, I thought of *Arcadia* again. Into the neo-classical paradise of the past, I recalled Stoppard introducing the vocal worm of Septimus Hodge, the tutor who has seduced poet Ezra Chater's wife in the gazebo. "I assure you," he dexterously tells the aggrieved husband: "Mrs. Chater is charming and spirited, with a pleasing voice and a dainty step, she is the epitome of all the qualities society applauds in her sex—and yet her chief renown is for a readiness that keeps her in a state of tropical humidity as would grow orchids in her drawers in January."

This ribald allusion to glasshouses reminded me of how devoted the English eighteenth century had become to improving

on nature (even on neo-classical language, in its irregular shift to
the Romantic). In the play, Lady Croom worries that her landscape gardener, loyal to the new Picturesque style and keen on
introducing wilderness and a hermitage into pastoral Sidley Park,
has replaced her Chinese bridge—"superior to the one at Kew"—
with a toppled obelisk suitably overgrown. Kew, Ur-model of
botanical gardens, was also the enduring prototype of botanical
glasshouses. I now found myself walking toward one of them,
through a blustery cold wind torturing the daffodils. A low afternoon light shone from a swirling Turneresque sky right through
the Palm House's approaching glass walls, against which I could
make out shapes and shadows of tropical exotics.

Inside, Arcadia.

I had been here in the past. Indeed, the past here seemed a
place of humid sun-held warmth as would grow voices in March,
or any other month, and I was ardent to listen to them, as if in
Mrs. Chater's state of tropical readiness. Inside this most beautifully designed and famous glasshouse in the world, I breathed
deeply. I could *breathe* again, as if this unnatural environment were
the most natural one for any voice that had begun to run down.
My throat opened like a tropical plant, its vocal folds now full
leaves. "'Let me not to the marriage of true minds / Admit impediments.'" I was quoting aloud in the bosky light, as though hon-
ouring Shakespeare's servant to the diaphragm, Patsy Rodenburg.

The idea of *not* being able to draw breath made me think of
curare, a lethal poison once arrow-dipped by Indians to asphyxiate
the invading Spanish in South American rain forests. Like the
Botox bacterium *Clostridium botulinum*, curare acted by paralyzing
muscles—in its case, the respiratory muscles—and predated botulinum toxin as a therapeutic poison, especially for muscular spasms
arising from anaesthetic surgery in the 1930s.

But I felt my soul expand in here, not just my lungs and throat.
It was as if I had just received a fresh injection of Botox at Vancouver Hospital and been released into the sunshine of a summer
afternoon to wander through art galleries on Granville Street

redolent of impasto. If only, I thought, a memoir constructed from voices about voice could find a repository as oasis-like as this structure to embody its theme.

Kew's Palm House enveloped me. If Rodenburg's contribution to my voice gallery had been breath, this glasshouse embodied breath. Its glazed skin, arching high above and enclosing the curvilinear ribs, appeared to breathe in tandem with the plants. You felt that when these palm trees grew higher, the glass-clad frame would expand with their height. Similarly, the structure seemed responsive to one's own breathing, expanding and contracting as necessary, welcoming my carbon dioxide exhaled in exchange for oxygen emitted by foliage.

I knew the miles of tubular intestines in such a historical conservatory, from which heat arose out of iron-grilled shafts in the floor, were hooked up to distant boilers whose coal smoke was once siphoned off to chimneys hidden outside in trees. The Palm House had twelve boilers and over five miles of concealed pipes to maintain its humidity and temperature. All this seemed vaguely analogous to the elegant regulation of a human body.

Listening, I wandered the steamy aisles crowded with plants. I heard the sound of a voice amplifier from the past, before recognizing the voice of my old friend, Sinclair Ross, in Vancouver, sitting among the ferns and attempting to read from *A Sentimental Journey* as he waited out the war. I could hear other voices, even choirs, as I climbed the spiralling staircase to the gallery with its aerial views of air and plants. You *expected* to hear disembodied voices in these public glasshouses of the nineteenth century. This building, designed by Decimus Burton and Richard Turner in the 1840s, though far more intimate than Joseph Paxton's Crystal Palace in Hyde Park, had still attracted over three hundred thousand people to Kew Gardens in 1851, the same year the Great Exhibition of All Nations drew six million to the Crystal Palace.

Vocal cornucopias both.

I now associated the mythical Crystal Palace, erected in just seven months by thousands of workmen, with choirs and conversations.

Not only had it attracted forty thousand visitors a day for five months—their Babylonish voices presumably echoing off its acres of glass roof and walls—but its later permanent home, after reconstruction in Sydenham, became a centre for the singing voice, with renowned opera soloists and huge choirs, led there by Sir Michael Costa of the Sacred Harmonic Society, contributing to the entire musical life of London well into the twentieth century. (Paxton, as if deciding his Crystal Palace needed echoes of Babel, had added not one but two water towers at either end of his reconfigured glasshouse at Sydenham, each 282 feet high. There was even a design to rebuild the Crystal Palace entirely, as a thousand-foot tower of glass.) Handel's oratorios were among the favourite choral works performed here, until a raging fire destroyed it all after eighty years.

I spent hours that afternoon wandering through Kew's major glasshouses. I was searching for a model to transport me into the next millennium—an oasis in the desert to float a traveller greenly through a moon-filled night, as he partied amidst plants from many countries, listening to divers voices and pitching his own invariably secure instrument. I did not think this dream any more discordant than a voice juiced up with poison to help it sound natural. Possibly, my fictitious structure arose from the same impulse to create fantastic enclosures of reassuring glass, as had arisen among early architect-engineers of winter gardens and crystal conservatories. I played with this. It seemed just as important for those craftsmen such as Turner, Paxton and Burton to have shared their aesthetic pleasure in design, as it was for them to advance botanical or scientific knowledge. I concluded this made the form and content of their works inseparable, roots, really, for private repose and social interaction.

Kew, as the grandest of all botanical gardens—repository of thousands of species extinct and threatened, local and exotic, rare and historical—seemed to me the great depot of dislocation and reunion.

I listened, I looked. Burton's Temperate House (1862) sat on an acropolis and, at twice the size of the Palm House, was among the largest in the world. I climbed its cascading, mahogany-railed staircase to the skywalk, for commanding views of the great span. The light was clear and effulgent. The cool clean scents of the building, less steamy than the Palm House, entered my lungs and animated my voice:

> *. . . Love is not love*
> *Which alters when it alteration finds,*
> *Or bends with the remover to remove.*
> *O no! it is an ever-fixed mark*
> *That looks on tempests and is never shaken. . . .*

In a place like this, I could believe these sentiments, memorized once in the same high-school class my voice first failed in. I could believe in my voice to proclaim them. I could equate its column of air and soft cords with the wrought-iron subtleties of pillar and bracket. In here, I could love my voice. Rectilinear, impressive in a way entirely unlike the curvilinear Palm House, it seemed less skin and more body. Yet everything in both houses, springing lightly to the sky, seemed resistant to gravity and decay. Peering down into the temperate jungle, I could hear murmured conversations among nomadic visitors like myself.

We were all in awe of citrus, palm and tea plants. These exotics, amazing to a Victorian public, amazed us too—not because modern film and travel had not jaded us (they had), but because our wonder for glass and iron cathedrals still managed to encourage a concurrent wonder for what they held.

I watched a gardener up a ladder, balancing in air—a woman who loved her job and would not fall. Her broad brow reminded me of Rachel Kavanaugh, the girl in the airport bus. I could hear her faint, squeezing spring of a pruning pole—and something else. She was singing an aria from *Madama Butterfly*—"Un bel dì vedremo"—in a sweet, swaying soprano. I thought of the old crone in Beckett's *Not I*, and wondered who would not be charmed to reverie by this young voice and the scent of lemon blossoms?

Well, I wasn't. Not me.

For, I am afraid, she was not singing. I made up this small white lie, training back to London in the Underground, watching the sun sink resplendently on the Thames. I was concocting a blend of event and yarn to recount to Telemachus upon my arrival home. I was already remembering some luminous fusion of Palm and Temperate Houses inside a place far from Kew. From the bridge, we then plunged underground to the dark city, and the car's dirty windows threw back only reflections. I almost froze in my dinky jacket, emerging from the deep lift shaft of the Piccadilly Line into Russell Square.

After my Kew junket in London, and a flight later that week to the venerable glasshouse range in Edinburgh's Botanic Garden, it seemed perfectly natural to encounter a gardening student from Switzerland standing in line at the Lyceum for a free but over-subscribed preview performance of *Waiting for Godot*.

It was my first evening in Edinburgh. Marie had an extra ticket and, overhearing my conversation with another ticketless couple, offered it to me. We then chatted, waiting to go into the theatre. Her non-Scottish voice had a stridency I put down to her pushing it over the noisy student crowd. I hoped to learn more of what she was finding out about landscape gardening here in Scotland. Instead, I learned she was working (for this year only) as a bus con-ductor. And then, because our seats were apart, I heard no more about gardens. I looked in vain for her at intermission through cigarette smoke.

When the curtain rose on act 2, I saw from her empty seat she'd abandoned the play. Perhaps Beckett's landscape had appeared un-salvageable to her, although by now his one sickly tree had grown several leaves overnight. This play in which, famously, "nothing happens, twice" spoke to me of the repetitive recurrence of voice as the only grace left. Lucky's extended speech of gibberish in the first act seemed to illustrate, as Mouth later did in *Not I*, that what voice came down to for Beckett was a "terrifying" exercise (as he indicated for Pozzo's voice), sometimes capable of pathetic dignity by dogged perseverance. By act 2, however, Lucky is dumb. The two tramps dumbfounded.

In the Lyceum production, directed by Kenny Ireland, there was such a theatrical, *un*trampish sound in the posh British accent of the actor playing Estragon that I sensed an intentional atonal orchestration in casting the working-class Scots of the other actor playing Vladimir.

Why?

By now I was blotting up voices. And using my own to run up large phone bills in conniving hotels. In Edinburgh, staying at the Clarendon on Grosvenor Street, I ran out of luck. For the first time in any city since Christmas, I failed to connect with someone who had dystonia, or who had anything to tell me about voice, including the director of *Godot*. I left messages, as requested by "voice messaging"—I misheard this as an ad for "voice massaging"—yet no one returned my calls. I recognized the hesitancies in my own voice as it deteriorated. Perhaps I would have better luck getting through in Glasgow and Dublin.

At breakfast a very fat woman, taking orders in the dining room, was a walking testimony to the munificence of the Scottish breakfast. I asked her in a pliant voice, closer to abject Vladimir's than imperious Pozzo's, for the continental. Then I walked to Haymarket Station and boarded the bullet train to Glasgow. The beautiful, bald Pentland Hills were painted with snow along the way. At the Glasgow station, I made two unsuccessful calls, then emerged into pouring rain and headed for Kibble Palace. I wanted to see where famous Victorian politicians and American evangelists had spoken to crowds of up to seven thousand, without amplification. I was surprised, on arriving at Kibble, by the glasshouse's domed modesty, compared to the scale at Kew.

In these Botanic Gardens, opposite fortress BBC and its Union Jack, I escaped from the rain into the circular palace. I decided this was how glasshouses in inclement climates wanted to be visited, by benumbed men in nylon jackets, carrying collapsible umbrellas costing a pound. Perhaps even by men running low in the tank on Botox, looking for another pit stop to recoup their vocal composure.

Past the sealed entrance wing of the tropicarium, with its fishpond and palms, a broad brick pathway carried me in a circle round wrought-iron pillars supporting the large central dome. Here in the temperate main zone were plants from Australia and Southern Africa, South America and the Canary Islands. A crimson bottlebrush from New Zealand reminded me of Faye Bergonzi's blooming garden in Auckland. Directly under the dome, where they used to lay the floor for concerts and speakers, was a stunning fern forest planted over a century ago. This had once been a pond and multijet fountain, underneath which John Kibble had built a pit for the orchestra to bounce music off the glass above during light and sound shows.

Kibble's Crystal Art Palace (1873) had begun life as a modest conservatory in Coulport, Loch Long. Kibble, a retired entrepreneur, then donated his glasshouse to the Glasgow Corporation on the condition that, once towed up the River Kelvin to be reassembled into a much larger house in Queen's Park, it would stay in his possession for twenty years, during which time he would be free to charge admission for shows, lectures and concerts. Here, six months after its completion, Benjamin Disraeli addressed four thousand people during his inauguration as Rector of the University of Glasgow. William Gladstone did the same six years later.

What I liked about Kibble (unlike the pinched Main Range Glasshouse nearby) were the benches, placed every twenty feet or so, where I could stretch out and smell the humus. This building, its ironwork painted bright silver, was slowly rusting. The glass above leaked in spots, and toads squatted on damp bricks amidst neo-classical statuary devoted to biblical figures, Sicilian kings and Nubian slaves. The curvilinear glass descended gracefully to ground level, but you could hear traffic behind, rumbling along Queen Margaret Road.

In my hand I held a night photo of Kibble, shedding its light into the surrounding darkness. I sat back, surrounded by miles of heating pipes, and reflected on night voices as they might have echoed in this dome once lit by six hundred gas jets. ("My fellow citizens, forgive me, I seem to have a frog lodged in my throat this evening. I am nevertheless delighted to discover myself in this beautiful palace, speaking to you as the new Lord Rector of your remarkable . . . Can you hear me in the back row? I promise not to read aloud from my novels, à la Dickens—so be warned sleeping among the orchids is not an option! An old Parliamentarian like me, an old novelist, expects and indeed tolerates a plethora of dissenting voices, yet I feel compelled to say, having overheard all of yours upon my entering this crystal structure, blending into the botanical constituent and enriching the green life herein, has not made me long for any quick return to London. I feel both educated and humbled tonight, by your turning out for my inauguration . . .")

Politicians, evangelists, lecturers, singers. And these days, strolling couples decoding life in susurrating voices over lunch hour. There was something paradoxical about human voices, I thought, wondering if I understood the paradox. What made every voice unique was the physical shape it retained of the body, once it left the mouth to float intangibly on air. Its traits lingered briefly before decaying forever. Only recently had we learned to preserve it on wax cylinder, vinyl record, eight-track tape, compact disc— convinced, we thought, through progressively better technology, of the unsurpassable "faithfulness" of this endeavour.

But with every generation of recordings we had come to understand how misplaced was the previous generation's faith. The voice "in person" remained different in kind, it seemed, rather than in degree. How much attention after all did real dogs pay to barking dogs on TV? And the enduring image of that cock-eared terrier on old RCA Victor labels, supposedly listening to "His Master's Voice," now seemed more like wishful thinking than actual heed to any "faithful" sound. Audio imaging and acoustical holographs notwithstanding, I wondered if the next generation's recorded voices weren't always the dogs of tomorrow.

Not necessarily. But live performance trumped electronic, any day.

In the fern forest in front of me, an aging businessman with a rolled umbrella had stopped before the naked Nubian slave, because a noise had gone off in his pocket. He disengaged his arm from a young woman's and took out his cell phone. I listened to how he used his voice. He spoke in a heightened, unnatural voice to an electronic ear considerably closer to his mouth than the ear of the person he was strolling with. These two had been conversing in voices I couldn't overhear. For some reason, he felt it necessary now to practically shout into his phone. It was a bit like overhearing one's grandfather on "the blower" forty years ago. What was it about technology that continued to distort voices?

Once he collapsed the antenna, his voice returned to the way nature intended its use in conversation between two people. I stood up and wandered closer, pretending to look at the prolific ferns, to see if I could hear what he was saying to the young woman who was admiring the marble slave in nubile repose.

"She makes me think of what I'd rather be doing with the rest of my day."

"Gardening?" The young woman was teasing him.

"I'm talking about *Mary*."

"I know you are, Duncan." She took his pinstriped arm again.

"Gardening, OK . . ." He got it now. "Yeah, my little thicket." He pronounced it ironically, emphasizing the second syllable to make it sound like "coquette." ". . . Yeah, my little thickette. I *would*."

What continued to beguile me about the human voice was what it retained of each body uttering it, to distinguish it from every other voice. Pitch, modulation, timbre, projection, and so on. A voiceprint was as unique as a fingerprint, its vibrations on air as precisely measurable as skin traces on a doorknob. It seemed amazing that something as common as a voice had so many variables shaping its sound: stomach action, expansion of lungs, the air vibrating against vocal folds, neurotransmitters governing movements of the larynx, relaxation (or not) of the throat, tongue placement, the spacing between teeth, size of nasal resonating capacity, social expectations . . . A voice was genetically determined and environmentally conditioned. And yet hearing it seemed more *immaterial* than if it were apprehended through any of the other senses such as taste or smell, sight or touch.

How was it possible, therefore, to describe a voice?

The voices of the past were gone. Yet weren't voices, even of the present, "gone" most of the time?

I listened to the lunchtime lovers, May and November, disappear around the brick pathway in Kibble Palace. A private detective, suddenly, I wondered how in the absence of electronic proof I was going to convince a divorce court to award Duncan's loyal wife, Mary, the settlement she would require to keep herself in the style to which she was accustomed (as well as to cover my fee). What remained, after all, of voices once uttered and diluted in air? It was a little like homoeopathy. Air must somehow retain the memory of a voice, yet the voice itself remained irrecoverable and beyond molecular trace. I supposed such memory affected belief in its mystery—of whether it remained part of the body once uttered—and depended, finally, on a belief in metaphor to define what otherwise was indescribable, evanescent.

Back in Edinburgh I remembered what a painter friend had observed a decade earlier in his (now published) diary, about his time in the Arctic, where historical voices had seemed entirely unlikely. Reflecting on a frozen landscape before him, and on numerous men who had hoped to find a shorter passage to the spices of China and India, Toni Onley had written: "If only a warm breeze would come now and unlock the voices frozen in this air, what a tale they could tell." On my last night in Scotland, I sat in a steaming bath listening to sleet drive like nails against the window, and felt myself inside a loquacious hothouse. The plants were talking to me. I was now as batty as the Prince of Wales.

I had begun my journey on an island in the South Pacific, and was about to end it on an island in the North Atlantic. Flying from Edinburgh to Dublin, I managed to relocate the diaspora of spasmodic speakers I'd last heard in London. The most compelling was a priest, a missionary to Nigeria, now retired in Ballyboden. Maria Hickey, who coordinated a network of dystonia sufferers in Ireland, had given me his number—warning me, at the same time, of muggers in the vicinity of my bed and breakfast in Gardiner Place. I thanked her for her concern, mentioning I was more worried about bandits robbing me of sleep, their resident voices besieging the wall between our rooms every night till 4 a.m.

Maybe it was this lack of sleep, but Dublin made me cranky. I wanted out of the stifling cigarette smoke of mobbed suburban pubs on Sunday afternoons, where children played at the feet of parents after mass, chewing their roast beef and watching shouted football matches on giant screens. The old Palm House in the "Bots" struck me as sad and inglorious. I disliked the whiff of coal smoke at night, the burned odour downtown, the rotten scent inside buses. Seething crowds in side streets and on bridges over the Liffey pressed in on me, as did skies, and the braying voices of women selling tobacco off O'Connell. In the pedestrian mall on Grafton, a banjo, guitar and bass, plonking out a voiceless "Tennessee Waltz," seemed emblematic of Ireland's stolen love, its sentimental passion. A single older man, leaning on a pub door, was tapping his foot to the ruinous tune.

But when the sun came out I warmed to Dublin. I was impressed by the new entrepreneurial spirit of a country embarked upon prosperity with the European Union. The young were no longer leaving, were in fact returning. They filled galleries and restaurants in the once seedy district of Temple Bar. In the Well Fed Café, a small vegetarian place in Crow Street, I struck up a conversation with a young woman looking for "production work" in "costuming." Filmmaking had evidently burgeoned with the international sanctioning of all themes Irish.

I listened to her voice. Perhaps it should have come as no surprise that Irish fashion had led inevitably to Irish accents among foreigners. As she relaxed, her lilt became more American in inflection, until she drifted vocally all the way back across the Atlantic. She had come originally from New Hampshire. She even knew Vancouver, where she'd gone "to check out Asian studies at UBC," before coming to Ireland three years ago. Her most recent job had been waiting tables in Galway.

Sitting later in St. Stephen's Green admiring the daffs, I could remember meeting an old man once in the Aran Islands, who recalled from boyhood seeing the visiting playwright John Synge. But the Irish literary renaissance meant nothing to the child. It had still meant little to the old man. All Martin Konneally knew, all his family had known, was that Ireland's future lay in America. His relatives all lived in Boston. I shouldn't have been startled to hear he had visited Boston more than once, but never Dublin. "No need." He was then eighty-seven.

It was his and other voices I now recalled. And soon added Maria Hickey to my gallery of hospitable Irish. She had no trouble talking, because her own dystonia resided outside her voice box. Her spasmodic torticollis had started ten years ago, following a car accident. The involuntary pull of muscles had dragged her head sideways. Ignorant about the disorder, a local doctor had suggested they drill into her head to straighten it with a brace, rod and screws. When Maria visited Professor Marsden in London, this specialist in movement disorders said the weight of her head alone would eventually have bent the rods.

Maria was now forty-two and in remission. The remission was fortunate, as she had developed antibodies to the Botox injections she used to receive in large doses. She now carried her head at a tilt—over her left shoulder—that was barely noticeable, except to the odd busybody who would come up on the bus to commiserate and press on her the name of a chiropractor. "You poor dear," they would say. She was not allowed to drive a car.

We had arranged to meet one Sunday evening for tea, in the elegant lobby of the Westbury Hotel. Gregarious and well-dressed, Maria introduced me to a speech and language therapist, Patricia Gillivan-Murphy, from Royal Victoria Eye and Ear Hospital, and to a young man with spasmodic dysphonia, David McNamara.

We poured tea and talked over the white noise of the lobby. Patricia told me there were only 160 speech therapists in this country of four and a half million. Poorly paid, many left Ireland to practise abroad. I pondered this. It was as if a nation that prided itself on the gift of the gab could hardly bring itself to value those who treated people claiming to have trouble with their voices. Patricia had five patients with laryngeal dystonia, but knew this figure wasn't representative of the national population. Around Ireland, she did her best to publicize the disorder in seminars. She'd been responsible for encouraging an ENT from her own hospital to learn how to inject botulinum toxin, and so save local patients expensive trips to London.

In her assured, soft-spoken way, Patricia embodied a kind of noblesse oblige, as a graduate of Trinity College and daughter of professional parents. A shy young man like David McNamara felt entirely comfortable with her. Arriving late, he glanced often for reassurance from Patricia, with her long flaxen hair, pearls and matching sweater set.

At twenty-one, David was the youngest person I had ever met with spasmodic dysphonia. Moreover, he had developed the disorder at fifteen—which fascinated me, as someone whose own dystonic tremor, though not spasms, had originated at the same age. I felt as though I were talking to the self whose worst neural degeneration had not been delayed till the age of twenty-eight.

David had first noticed "a catch" in his voice, and then it got worse. He told me his mum had a catch in her voice too. His doctor sent him to a psychologist, who told David his problem was "a lot of nonsense." The psychologist in turn referred him to a psychiatrist, who pushed for tranquillizers. The young man refused.

"I wasn't happy . . . Wasn't functioning . . . Took a year off . . . Sort of couldn't get a job . . . Read a lot . . . It was my voice, the way I talked . . . I went to interviews . . . Wasn't tuned in at all . . ."

David had difficulty carrying on a conversation but I was unable to tell whether his halting manner was related to sₚ. Supposedly, over the last two years, he'd received a half dozen successful injections, the earliest of them in London. Perhaps he was just inarticulate, at loose ends after leaving school, and unable to find a job. His neat slacks and polished shoes, on the other hand, suggested a willing job applicant. So I was inclined to put his frail conversation down to shyness and immaturity.

I was astonished to learn David was in his third year of medical studies, at University College Dublin. He was obviously a gifted student, in spite of how he sounded. Had I fallen into the conventional trap of making wrong assumptions about a faulty voice? I wondered how he had passed the entrance interview, as he would have been admitted even before his injections began. Had spasmodic dysphonia worked to his advantage? You heard of quota systems working in favour of other disabilities, but never a disabled voice.

David revealed his first injection had left him unsatisfied, the second happier. "I started getting into . . . you know . . . going out." I asked what his friends had thought of his new voice. "What friends?" He chuckled self-consciously, glancing to Patricia for support, then drinking again from the glass of water he'd ordered in place of tea.

Lately, he was feeling more relaxed. "I'm learning to do the little things." He was using the telephone, making the odd friend, giving oral reports at school.

If David lacked the sort of perspective on voice I was used to hearing, he had read more than others, including Patricia, about the neurological implications of his condition. He felt remission wasn't out of the question. He hadn't had an injection in over six months. Unable to imagine a family doctor, I thought of him as a future neurologist, specializing in dystonia. His future seemed open to remission, genetic discovery, the transposition of the clefts in his speech into verbal music the rest of us might eventually acquire.

Father John Gough's future, on the other hand, was near an end. Not that it hadn't been near an end twenty years ago, when he flew home from Nigeria after twenty-four years, not expected to live. An operation to have his spleen removed was performed in Dublin. For five preceding years, in the 1970s, Father Gough had suffered intermittently from malaria. Six months later, another operation, to remove his gall bladder and treat his pancreas, had ended his missionary work in the tropics. He never returned to Nigeria.

I arrived at St. Augustine's late one afternoon after a long bus ride through endless southern suburbs of brick rowhouses. An occasional passing yard would boast a small palm, or a barely flowering cherry tree. Overcast, chilly, this was weather Father Gough would have found unfamiliar upon his return to Dublin. He'd first gone out to Nigeria in 1951. He was now sixty-nine. His wrinkled face and forehead attested to years of mapping the African sun.

He remembered blaming the deterioration of his voice on the harmattan, a wind blowing out of the Sahara from November to April every year, coating tables and lungs with the same fine sand. Home on holidays once, Father Gough consulted an ENT, who told him he had "preacher's throat." He was supposed to stop talking for six months.

He never bothered.

Then, following his permanent reassignment to Ireland in the mid-seventies, his voice suddenly got much worse. The "frog" in his throat had become a snake. He noticed his strangled speech more in preaching sermons (where he was forced to finish his sentences) than he did in private conversations, where he could disguise his impediment. His congregation thought he was just nervous.

"I wasn't nervous. But I thought I might have cancer."

One consultant told him to try a faith healer. Father Gough chuckled. Other doctors thought he was having a nervous break-down, not unrelated to the brutality of the civil war he'd lived through in Nigeria. So he tried relaxation therapy, which he enjoyed, but his voice remained forced, throttled, staccato. This went on for fifteen years.

"Some of the parishioners objected to my taking any public service. Whether they felt it was too much of a strain on them-selves trying to listen, or too much of a strain on myself trying to talk, I never discovered. I do think they felt sorry for me."

I was enjoying his company. We were at a table off the lobby, where glass cases bulged with anthropological souvenirs from African missions—baskets, hunting knives, black-and-white pho-tographs of skinny villagers, snakeskins, finely beaten necklaces. Compassionate and witty, a lover of talk, this priest struck me as a man of the people in his comfortable sweater and unfashionable glasses. As I listened, I concentrated on the carbuncle behind his left ear.

"I was told I couldn't preach any more, people thought it was too much for me. They couldn't understand me. So they gave me the red card."

Forced into semi-retirement, Father Gough took over parish finances and visiting old folks' homes. He was "OK, one-to-one." He had even built this large two-storey monastery, where we sat talking in Taylors Lane.

Following his demotion he was asked one day to say mass in a neighbouring parish. The woman who read the lesson introduced herself and told him his voice intrigued her. "I told her it intrigued me too." She told him to contact her if he wanted help. She thought he might have "spastic dysphonia."

This woman was Patricia Sheehan, a speech therapist who had taught Christy Brown, author of *My Left Foot*, to speak. She had also taught Daniel Day Lewis to speak like Christy Brown for the film adaption of the book. She put Father Gough in touch with

Professor Marsden, in London, who referred him to Gerald Brookes and Renata Whurr.

"I was delighted. I now had a name for what I had."

Father Gough was the first Irishman to receive an injection for his voice.

"I couldn't believe it. I could not believe it. Nobody could believe it. It was really wonderful."

The beneficial effects of the drug emboldened him. "I would even say a few words at mass. I didn't want to chance any more than that." Neither, evidently, did the other priests, as he remained officially out of the sermon business.

"Botox came too late to be of benefit in my work."

But he was not complaining. Tomorrow, it so happened, he was going for his fifteenth injection, his third in Dublin. He was now an authority on the difference between the kinds of botulin used by English and Irish doctors. Irish was stronger, closer to the American.

Father Gough told me of Patricia Sheehan's death in a car crash, two years earlier, at the age of fifty.

I thought again of her death, as I flew back to the United Kingdom in a small Aer Lingus prop plane, whose stewardess, another Patricia, patted her corn-coloured hair each time she entered the cockpit carrying juice cups. The pilot and co-pilot took turns calling her up on the intercom, in green and lilting voices—like Joyce's, I imagined, flying Ireland's nets—though not quite the kind of voices to inspire airborne confidence over a tossing Irish Sea.

8

Minding the Gap

FIVE YEARS LATER, almost to the day of my returning to Vancouver, something unforeseen would happen to change my voice forever. I would lose it in the hope of regaining it from muteness.

Meanwhile, I continued to travel intermittently and to work on other books, including a memoir of my old friend with Parkinson's who died the following year. As ever, I wanted to understand how listening to other voices might lead me to some pre-Babel oasis of oral harmony. I continued to believe that in setting out to find this place, the real success was not in finding it but in continuing to imagine it as central to my life. Wherever I went, trespassing into Third World hospitals in quest of damaged voices and their treatment, usually while on journeys to monitor projects for Canada India Village Aid in different Indian states, I deepened my understanding of where such an exotic place of voice might be.

Paradoxically, I was increasingly struck by how there was no *far* any more when it came to voices. Even hearing voices in so-called exotic places, including glasshouses, I discovered my wonder at them grew in ratio to how I was able to absorb them imaginatively, domestically. Later that year, for example, I came to think of the Palm House in Toronto's Allan Gardens, where I found myself opening the first copy of my novel *Popular Anatomy* to rehearse a reading for its launch that evening, as the first home of its voices. I

found that after each journey the inner one lasted longer, went
farther, became indelible in a way the surface trip never did. The
business of writing it up needed to render any journey as if I had
made it up. The fiction writer's presumption of genre was perhaps
not as egocentric as it seemed. In my novel, I'd been trying to
understand what fiction might be in the context of more than one
context, voice, world. The wonder inherent in this multiplicity
had become my obsession.

Listening for the exotic at home and the domestic abroad had
probably infused me since I began to write fiction. This was what
fiction was, it seemed to me, the narrative voice unsettling the
familiar by talking a foreign language in my own tongue. Finding
that tongue, not unlike finding my voice, had taken years. I was
still listening for it, had not yet found it, possibly never would. Yet
what mattered was the journey of freeing oneself to tell a story
about something as familiar (and foreign) as the human voice.

A movement disorder seemed to confirm a disordered person's
desire to be a traveller, even at home. That summer I fell into the
temptation, after returning from abroad, of wanting to make narratives of even the shortest odysseys. In September, for instance,
on the last weekend of summer, I launched a leaky dinghy into the
sea and rowed out to where the forested mountain behind our
cabin on Bowen Island had yet to cast its late-afternoon shadow. A
voyage of no more than fifty yards.

Listening through headphones to voices united in love, I cast a
buzz bomb with my son's fishing rod. I caught a salmon trout and
reeled it into the boat. An eagle glided by. The peaking Lions
grew golden in a westering sun. Above these coastal mountains,
surging voices bathed me under the cerulean sky.

> *Tristan du, ich Isolde, nicht mehr Tristan!*
> *Du Isolde, Tristan ich, nicht mehr Isolde!*

I caught a small flounder and kept it too. My wife, reading on the
porch, waved down to where I moved my mooching wand over

the sea. The white-painted hull of the shallow dinghy gleamed. The silver coho drifted back and forth in an inch of bright, salty water. Currents carried me toward shore and I would row back out into sunshine, a wake gurgling, my brown arms pulling the varnished oars. I felt heroic, Birgit Nilsson enveloping me by now in the Liebestod, her swelling voice on a flooding sea.

At 6 p.m. I rowed back into shadow and landed on the rocky shore. Stepping out, I was close to emotional wreckage. I had circumnavigated the world. So transporting an instrument was this human voice that my homecoming felt as cathartic as my return from abroad earlier that year. I removed earphones and oarlocks. I dipped my catch into the sea.

Earlier that year, in April, after correcting page proofs, I had travelled to Texas to learn more about my disorder. A spring or two later I went to California for another gathering of people with spasmodic dysphonia. Knowing that SD was now a neurological and not a psychological disease, we were willing to come out of our closets for these regional and national conferences, particularly with Botox lubricating a way to fluent interaction. Indeed, the National Spasmodic Dysphonia Association had not existed before Botox, the notion of such a public community of closet dwellers impracticable.

In Dallas and San Diego, I watched us gather like rare birds, thrilled to open up in a hothouse environment devoted to nurturing talk about our (usually) poison-assisted voices. There were so few of us at large we could, for weekends such as these, imagine ourselves a significant flock within the confines of a small hotel. We were alert to the tweeting sounds of fellow-sufferers, to their anxieties evolved sometimes over many years of self-exile, to the warm feelings of a community charged up by organized gab sessions, by the latest reports of medical hope and genetic research into our dystonia, by the inescapable feeling that we were indeed rare and even lucky birds.

This was the chance to spread our wings, socialize freely as we never used to, gossip happily of our woes, establish pecking orders of long-suffering or unselfconsciousness, and of medical knowledge about our species—about unilateral versus bilateral injections, mouse units per injection, elevated intraglottic and subglottic pressures (these last if you were a professional in the field—then only if pressed), and whether Botox would affect our perms.

Rarely, it seemed, was *voice* discussed at these gatherings. When it was, in support-group sessions devoted to renewing self-esteem and sharing medical autobiographies, it took on the understandable timbre of social agony overcome by the sustaining salvation of toxin, or some other temporary amelioration. I listened and heard encapsulated stories of the kind encouraged on my travels: lives threatened by the lack of integrity caused by fractured voices. Yet the drama of jobs lost and relationships threatened left us little time for indulging a sense of wonder at voice itself.

Our wonder was absorbed by white chatter in the heady light of these hotels in the Sunbelt. It was taken for granted, first of all, by the mellifluous medical doctors at the top of the SD pecking order, striving to maintain position or else to reacquire it, speaking to the pilgrims who had gathered to learn the latest about dystonia as a genetic disorder, and about outmoded or maybe bizarre new surgeries as alternatives to injections. Even speech therapists, no longer the answer they seemed a decade earlier, dealt in the technicalities of voice production but never its poetry.

I was sitting in the coffee shop at the Marriott Quorum Hotel in a turnpike ghetto somewhere outside Dallas, thinking it would be good sometime to invite an Oliver Sacks or a Patsy Rodenburg, a Jonathan Miller or a John Updike, to address such a gathering on the wonder of voice and its capacity to render us whole. To remind us that taking our voices for granted—which, astonishingly, some of us were in danger of doing in our new-found confidence— was exactly what people did who were *un*affected by quirky basal ganglia, and that we should be the ones in whom resided a narrative (*the* narrative) for what made us different from other animals.

I could see I was losing my bird analogy. I reached for a napkin. *Do you want your real voice back again?*

I began to scribble down the kind of politically incorrect answer Hugo Williams, an English poet who once wrote an ironic poem called "When I Grow Up" about wanting to become a senile, smelly old man, might have read aloud to this particular convention if he had SD. I sensed what we needed to find wasn't so much a Famous Spokesperson, as a character as reiterative and one-note as Yossarian or Mr. Micawber.

Do You Want Your Real Voice Back Again?

... No, I want to miss it when I speak. I want to poke a finger in my ear to encourage this one. I want to tug an earlobe and make myself sound cracked. I want to croak like a deaf mute. I want to choke when the waiter asks me to order food. I want to pinch my nostrils and blow echoes out my ears like smoke.

In court I want to sound strangled before the judge. I want to sound like the perpetrator. I want the jury to write me off as a passive-aggressor. I want to break down when I know I'm in the right. I want to pay the price of perjury.

My children I want to imitate my spasms. I want them to hear sentences as they should be spoken, with lots of air between words. I want them to grow up with an ear for discord, so when they study music they'll remember what it was like to have a fireside squawk with dear old Dad. When I address the take-out box at McDonald's, I want my son to ask when I had my last "venom" shot.

When I get to be an opera singer, I want my glottal attacks to command critical attention. I want to ride glissandos like a bucking bronco on coke. I want my arpeggios to sound like clothespegs strung out on a rusty, sagging line.

F   u   rtherm   ore ...

As a real estate agent, why not, I want to greet prospective clients with full-blown spasms. I never want to return their calls about offers to purchase. I want to waver on any promise made to them. I want them to decide I am unreliable, nervous, untrustworthy.

As an architect, I want clients to pay the withdrawal penalty on a house they feel will collapse if they let me build it.

When I become an actor, God willing, I want to forget my next line over and over, because of the pressure I fe   el to s   peak this o   ne, no   w, w   ithout cr   oa   king. . . .

Even a notable victim, such as PBS broadcaster Diane Rehm, who would attract Ted Koppel's interest four years later in an interview on *Nightline*, was no guarantee the weird complexity of SD would ever boost it to the familiar, if untreatable rank of stuttering. Interestingly, hers had been a voice found charming by (stutterer) John Updike, in the persona of his fictional novelist Henry Bech, in *Bech at Bay*: "She had fascinatingly blued hair and a crystalline, beckoning voice—as if from another room she were calling some sorority girls to dinner—and in this particular chain of interviewers put Bech least on the defensive." This told me more than *Nightline* had about the voice she (not to mention Updike) had lost. Perspective was somehow needed to enlarge our fall from vocal grace, from oral beauty, which among ourselves we might silently remember as equivalent to the loss of childhood.

At these conferences I ran into friends met in earlier travels and made new ones. Over a luncheon banquet in Dallas, I talked to a psychologist from San Antonio who'd suffered from SD since she was twenty-four and hadn't been diagnosed for another thirty years. She was once committed to a mental institution for three months and had undergone electric-shock treatment (even as an educated psychologist she had believed in her own madness). Now in her late fifties, this trim blonde spoke with a high but fluent voice. What had "changed her life" was the now discredited RLN surgery, which she had let the confident, charismatic Dr. Dedo perform on her recurrent laryngeal nerve. She and another woman present had undergone this recidivist surgery, and they tended to have high voices, she admitted, difficult to project, having agreed to give up one vocal cord to incision in the interest of liberating the other. But she never regretted her choice.

On my other side was Norma Parker. She had studied voice at university years ago, taught voice, sung oratorios, and supported opera and all circles choral. We talked about Joan Sutherland. "She isn't just a technician," Norma emphasized, "but a coloratura. Focus, focus, focus." Norma was passionate about the singing voice, having lost her own to dystonia years earlier. Norma's hair was raven in colour and she wore a green, big-shouldered dress as though ready to stand in for Sutherland in a pantomime production of *La Traviata*.

At such conferences I encountered airline pilots with laryngeal dystonia, flight attendants, ministers of the gospel, ecstatic old ladies, band singers, office workers, actors, schoolteachers, lawyers, medical students, housewives and no blacks. It was as if our disease possessed a not-so-hidden colour barrier, governed by the amount of medical care available to uninsured sufferers who also needed to be diagnosed correctly in the first place. I listened in break-out sessions ("Pushing the Boundaries" was one) to a new political assertiveness among people determined not to be defined any longer by other people's smug and facile conclusions about our "stress levels," "fragile nerves," "depressions" and "nervous break-downs." Whether or not we chose to smooth out our voices with toxin, we all had the "right" to be the selves we thought we had lost, or never been. We might be excused, inside our collective trysts, for feeling our tiny number amounted to a movement.

I made a point of seeking out the two youngest delegates in Dallas, to see how far a politics of voice had entered their own thinking. Were these young women any less mortified than the rest of us by simple spasms?

Tall and thin, New Yorker Jackie Leamy had begun to speak spasmodically eleven years ago, at fourteen. "It was really mild," she told me. "There wasn't anything major about it. Then crack-ing started. A grabbing. I just thought it was something in my mind. Something I needed to stop doing." When the strain and anxiety of trying to talk grew she kept self-doubts private. She forced herself to speak in front of theatre and drama classes, a humiliating memory. It was as if she had been pleading for help, only to encounter a conspiracy of silence and mutual embarrassment. By graduation year her stress had become intolerable.

To listen to her now you would have thought she had simply outgrown her adolescent voice. She spoke quickly, laughed easily, appeared delighted to be meeting sympathetic strangers—one of whom, a grad-school anaesthetist from North Carolina, was having trouble projecting his own voice in operating rooms. He and Jackie had grown close over the weekend and planned to see each other again in New York.

At college, although attracted to courses in education, Jackie had found herself avoiding classes in which she would have to speak, and this affected her grades. "I wanted to be a teacher, but there was no way." She actually diagnosed her own vocal disease while researching a course paper. "'This is me, me, me!' I said." But realizing she couldn't be cured only caused her to delay any professional diagnosis for another two years. She was about to graduate in sociology.

"There was like a crack in every word. You had to almost look at my mouth, to see what I was saying." Oddly, an otolaryngologist thought she sounded fine. A speech pathologist with a better ear told her about Botox. "I was like, Wow. This great cloud started to lift." Two neurologists and four months later, she received her first shot. It failed to take. The doctor refused to inject her for another four months. So she put her job interviews on hold until after summer, following a second needle in August.

Then, said Jackie, "I never shut up. It was just a whisper voice. I loved it. It was kind of this miracle thing." Having suffered as a vocal cripple for ten years, she was reborn a self-seeking philanthropist. "Every three months, I give myself the gift of a voice again. This is my gift and I'm thrilled I can give it to myself."

Tired of being hotel-bound, the two of us willingly shuttled down the highway to Arcadia, a vast multi-storeyed shopping mall roofed in glass. Instead of finding tropical vegetation at its heart, however, we discovered, down a long, store-lined gallery, small children just being released onto a full-sized ice rink.

"I never realized how much everything relies on your voice. Everybody thought I had nothing to say, no mind of my own. It was so frustrating. I've got my own mind and my own thoughts! It really opened my eyes. I really had a connection with people who couldn't speak. People would judge me. And if I disagreed, it was a real battle."

Jackie needed a voice for her new job. She was a live-in counsellor of autistic, retarded youth at a Wildwood group home in New York State. She found it ironic to be teaching them social skills, such as talking on the phone, when she herself had had so much trouble doing the same thing when *she* was fourteen. "Sometimes my voice will still crack."

This didn't matter now. "I've got to the point where I'm not going to let it hold me back. I never got to the point where I ever developed things *I* wanted to do. I mean, I don't even know who I was. College years were the worst years of my life. My parents now want me to go to grad school. Would I really be able to do it, if I were to become a teacher?" Not that she couldn't do it, added Jackie. "I don't care any more if my voice cracks now and then."

The other young delegate was twenty-seven-year-old Kathy Lachenauer, from California. I talked to her as the conference buzzed around us in the corridors. Similarly slim and fast-talking, but straight-haired and blond where Jackie was dark and permed, Kathy had also acted in high school. "Your main actress has a cracky voice," was the critique she received at a drama competition. She, too, kept self-doubts private. Her parents expected a perfect daughter, and perfection was more or less what she presumed she offered them (though her "cracky" voice embarrassed them). She was valedictorian of her graduating class, youngest-ever editor of the college paper at Stanford, and youngest reporter hired to write for the Pulitzer-winning newspaper, the *Sacramento Bee*.

Kathy had been working as a reporter, often on the telephone, when her voice began to deteriorate. "What's the matter with you?" The answer to this question took her longer to find than the answers she usually sought as a journalist. She expected a quick fix. One GP told her nodules. An ENT then diagnosed spasmodic dysphonia, the complexity of which upset her. "How would I cope as a reporter with this chronic problem?"

Her mother paid for a trip to another ENT, in Chicago, who satisfied the family by telling her she did *not* have SD and to consult a speech therapist. Which may have pleased her mother, but it didn't help Kathy, who stopped seeing the therapist in Sacramento after three months. In distress, she quit her job and joined her boyfriend in Berkeley.

Kathy now worked for a non-profit charity in San Francisco, devoted to helping pregnant and addicted girls. Not unlike Jackie, perhaps, she had chosen a job in which her fall from "perfection" was in a sense mirrored in the problems of the young people she assisted. But reaching this current stage had forced her back through medical hoops to the original diagnosis of her disease. Over the last year, in finding relief for her voice in drug treatment, she had become a kind of addict herself. "Botox has made a big difference to my life." Yet while it allowed her to make fundraising phone calls during the six smoothest weeks between injections, it also caused her withdrawal frustration when *she* knew she needed an injection, only to be told she sounded all right and to wait for the following clinic. "Man. Who wants to listen to a cracky voice, asking them for money?"

A cure, of course, was what the Voice Doctor to the Stars was offering delegates at the conference in San Diego a couple of years later. I recognized him, one morning at the Bristol Court Hotel, passing out advertisements for his cure among breakfast tables. Pointedly, I refused his envelope. "Thank you very much," he said, impossible to offend. He bowed like Uriah Heep, dipping smoothly on to the next table, this grinning fellow who billed himself "A Speech Pathology Corporation." I remembered him, suavely forbearing from dropping Names I Would Recognize, on my visit to him not far from Beverly Hills, ten years earlier. He believed spasmodic dysphonia was not neurological in origin but rather the result of vocal abuse. It could be cured by visiting his West Los Angeles office, often, for expensive therapy, with its gimmicky machines.

Dr. Voice would not have recognized a former patient like me. I had escaped his office after only a session and a half, lighter in wallet but wiser to the corporate game. But not all patients had been as fortunate. I learned that in one of the breakout sessions, later that day, where he was aggressively and rudely promoting his self-satisfied heresy, one exasperated delegate had finally accused him of bilking a member of her SD support group back in Texas out of forty thousand dollars, with misleading promises and extravagant fees over umpteen sessions of no vocal improvement. None.

"Well," replied Dr. Voice, unperturbed, "we all make mistakes."

He would have become a comical figure in San Diego had he not inspired the rancour he did. Evidently, he attended these conferences on SD to hustle business and to disparage the medical speakers. At the plenary session, I found myself sitting behind him. He was scribbling notes and leaning over often to chuckle in the ear of his female companion. When an attractive young latecomer sat down in a vacant chair on his other side, he automatically passed her one of his envelopes.

"Just read that," he told her, grinning. "Just read that."

He eyed her, beaming, as she glanced at his letter. Meanwhile, an aging bejewelled woman had sat down beside me, passing forward to him what looked like a cheque. Soon she was handing him little notes, which he would read like a surreptitious schoolboy, signalling her his pleasure by making a perfect circle of his thumb and forefinger. I watched his well-shod foot jiggling in anticipation of the afternoon's breakout sessions.

I arrived late to one of these called "Personal Stories." There he was, commanding the portable mike, performing as I remembered him in his office. He had a woman standing beside him, saying "*Hm. Hm.*" Then he said, "No. Put your hand on my stomach. Feel that? What happens when I count? . . . Feel that?

Now, what happens to yours, when you count?" Dr. Voice had a pleasant tone. He wore expensive spectacles and his bald head looked becomingly tan. He was used to public appearances and to relating how he taught the Stars to shine vocally. A cure for SD? No problem—that is, if you came to him for as many years, I supposed, as it took starlight to reach earth.

In this modest circle of ours, he was denounced suddenly by a woman who accused him of being "a quack." For once perturbed, Dr. Voice replied, "Be careful. That's libellous." He was warning her, as though he were used to litigious threats. "Don't talk to me what's libellous," she answered in a smooth voice. "I'm a lawyer." A murmur of approval ran through the suite. This woman now turned to the rest of us. "I didn't come here to listen to this outsider. I thought we were here to share stories, not to be preyed upon. I don't feel comfortable with this outsider in the room. I'm not going to say anything more unless he leaves."

Dr. Voice sat down and clammed up—though not, I noticed, without slyly attempting to ingratiate himself with the ex-actress and mother he found seated beside him in the circle. A Speech Pathology Corporation who might just as well have called himself A Fox in the Hen House.

I was invited to dinner that evening with several delegates, including Dot Sowerby and her husband Dick, a tall languid Carolinian who did not have a speaking disorder but rather a fetching drawl. He informed me that Dr. Voice, in spite of his rough ride, had still managed to attract four prospective clients from among the delegates. Not a bad investment of time and chutzpah, thought Dick, for a day's drive down from LA.

I had discovered I liked San Diego, remembering only a dirty motel from an overnight stay many years earlier on a trip to Mexico. A friend and I had more or less failed, earlier that evening, to talk our way into the hearts of two college-bound girls in LA, who wanted to know if we had frat houses in British Columbia. These girls claimed they could hear the British accent in our voices, evidently a sound in our favour, if not quite pleasing enough to entice them away from the twangy beer-can tones calling out to them as they drove us down frat row at UCLA. They dropped us back in Westwood, the neighbourhood where I would reside half a lifetime later, during my visit-and-a-half to Dr. Voice.

The birds in Balboa Park were happy glasshouse guests, except here in the open-sided Botanical Building the glass was missing, and tropical and sub-tropical plants shared the same warm air as gum trees and birds in the sage-smelling canyons beyond. The dry landscape and blue sky, the ocean air and urban architecture, brought back Perth. In these years, much brought back much, especially these birds—and the Yeats image I loved, "set upon a golden bough to sing / To lords and ladies of Byzantium / Of what is past, or passing, or to come." Their voices eased for me the transitions between what I heard and what I remembered, by being both places at once, including inside the glasshouse of my head.

A pursuit of the human voice seemed to gather me increasingly into an artifice of time, governed by the myth of Babel and a perishable, but infinitely cherishable present. It gave me, if nothing else, a domestic perspective. The past and the future sounded to me, at the present age of fifty, in harmony. And I was aware this would not last.

As with any writer of dependable voice, some of my public performances went over better than others (I seemed to come off better reading in festival cornfields, for example, than city nightclubs). The euphoric thing to me, of course, was I went over at all. It still felt like a miracle that I could speak on command, without a tight, broken voice. My recurrent fear was that sooner or later the Botox bubble would burst—not in a fireworksy way, but in some deflating spasm to erode confidence in the poisoned elixir that not so long ago had brought me back to life. When one remembered the Elysian results possible, it was corrosive to think of making do with less. At such times, I didn't want to recall that my chronically afflicted voice could not be cured. Or that I needed to plan ahead, like some booked-up operatic baritone, not to ensure my calendar was free (it usually was) but to make sure my larynx was.

I sometimes wondered if the singing-masters of my soul, to finish off the Yeats analogy, weren't opera singers. I could imagine no more ideal sages of the human voice, and no less artificial ones, than the operatic. Their existence in the eternal moment was everything. They were everything I myself might have aspired to, given the gift of a healthy voice and the luck to train it into gold. But unlike gold, no voice lasted. The wonder of it resided in its transient, bird-like passage into other seasons, other places, into age and silence.

When I returned to Vancouver from San Diego, I heard the diva Jessye Norman say in a CBC interview how comforting it would be if she could pack away her voice after every performance like an instrument in its case. She included her lungs in this, to remove them from her body and place them in cotton, in order to ensure the same fresh sound her next time out. I wondered again if the habit opera singers had of referring to their voices as "instruments"—somehow at a distance from them in performance, and invariably a surprise and a wonder to their owners when singing well—wasn't really a wish to make durable as wood or metal what was susceptible as muscle and tissue. The human voice was more like Heraclitus's river, I thought, a stream from which you could never tap the same sound twice.

In vocal wonder, paradoxically, lurked fear. Both were endemic to the art of performance. A woman I met in Vancouver told me, "I loved singing. My voice was huge. Operatic. Maybe I was afraid of it, the power of it, and I tried to cover it up by putting a lid on it." She was trying to account for its decline. While still in her twenties, Margaret Glavin found her voice starting to crack. "With singing lessons, I thought maybe I had learned some bad techniques. I had a powerful voice, and I always thought there was a connection between developing spasmodic dysphonia and having to put a lid on the power of my voice."

Most of us who had developed the disorder felt, at one time or other, the fault lay in ourselves for having somehow tampered with our brakes. But Margaret still refused to accept the neurological critique of dystonia, and was exploring alternative, holistic therapies to keep her disability within the "normal" range of understanding it.

Psychological explanations were always the first to appear and the last to go in discussing vocal production. They collaborated seductively with knowable character and operatic narrative. The circuitry of motor neurons had little apparent relevance, and even less drama, except in medical papers. I myself was interested that same year, as I polished the title novella for a collection of stories, *Telling My Love Lies*, in exploring the voice of an operatic narrator, a schooled baritone confronting his past on a farm for discarded tires. His coming out of the closet gay, of course, was originally intended as a metaphor for my coming out of the spastic closet, before I had ever heard of chemical transmitters.

(I sometimes wondered if my nostalgia for the trained voice could be traced back to remembered accounts of my soprano mother, an adolescent in the late thirties, at adjudicated vocal competitions in now vanished Vancouver venues such as the Empress Theatre and Georgia Auditorium. The later effect of her steady voice in church choirs could only have divided me further from my shameful wobble as an adolescent at the same age.)

Early the following year, before this collection appeared, my gay novelist-friend Sinclair Ross died in his nursing home. I liked to think he might have cared for the "swing" of this novella, with its operatic allusions and underlying threat of disease. The last time I saw him conscious, he had lost his own fading voice to incipient pneumonia. He could not speak a distinguishable word. As I pushed his wheelchair, I was remembering our visit just the week before, when his voice was lucid and calm, and we'd had one of our best and most wide-ranging conversations. At other times he was less lucid, but it always seemed important to listen to what he was saying, whether or not I understood him. This seemed the honour one paid to friends, dying or otherwise, this attention to their voices.

I was aware of another irony that day. For I was on my way to a Vancouver New Music performance on Granville Island, where an internationally known vocalist named Richard Armstrong was performing what had been reported as a short, remarkable history of the human voice. *The Muscle of the Soul*, said the program, was "An astonishing vocal journey to places known and unknown." Hung very loosely on a kind of seven-ages-of-man structure, it showed off Armstrong's stunning vocal virtuosity in a moving, witty anthology of sounds, from the mewling baby and a primitive ceremonial chant, to Prospero and Frank Sinatra, via open-throttled motorcycles and a shrill head pitch, which resembled keening wind on a winter plain.

I had hoped to report back on this vocal journey to my friend, but he lost consciousness that night and died five days later. Stricken with Parkinson's, he was a man who had loved above all other voices Jussi Björling's, having heard it not only on his favourite radio program, *Saturday Afternoon at the Opera*, but in person at the Met. A self-taught pianist, as a novelist he had brought to the page an acute ear for the human voice. I sometimes thought of his own voice, when healthy, as not unlike a description in his third novel, *Whir of Gold*—"He spoke with a slight French accent that gave his voice a precision, small and careful, exactly like that of a moustache." (But you had to substitute "prairie" for "French.") In his famous first novel, *As for Me and My House*, a Canadian classic, I'd always admired his brief summation of one minor character, with her "voice like a teaspoon tinkling in a china cup."

And so it was that Ross's quiet voice, having grown quieter in the last dozen years to the point of muteness, had mirrored his declining body. He no longer possessed the power to speak up and go on. I was still sad I had not been able to participate eight years earlier on CBC radio, in a proposed tribute on his eightieth birthday, because I knew my own voice would have failed on air. The shame of this lingered now, even as I spoke with fresh Botox in my larynx, at the memorial service in his nursing home.

A week later I flew to Bombay.

Waiting to return to Bombay Hospital, one hot afternoon, I watched TV soaps in a small fan-cranked room across the street in the West End Hotel. I was amazed at the endless Hindu maidens singing their quixotic hearts out to befuddled men. These suitors seemed neither to understand nor appreciate the overgroomed charms on show, against the virginal backdrop of a palm-and-paddy countryside, more alive than the men to these lip-synched, torso-twitching songs.

I liked the wavery Indian voice in Hindi songs. Perhaps this was because it made an art of the kind of adolescent voice that once humiliated me, and which I couldn't have imagined seductive in any variation short of silence. Ignorant of all Indian languages, I judged local voices purely by sounds. A couple of weeks later, in Colombo, I thought the Sinhalese voice in Sri Lanka even softer than the Malayalam voice in Kerala. How did speech therapists cope in this part of the world, with a score of separate languages and hundreds of dialects? Did speech therapists exist in India?

In Bombay, I located an office the size of a cupboard at Bombay Hospital, where a male secretary was matching referral slips to each one-hundred rupee note he had collected from voice patients earlier that afternoon. The irony was I could barely hear him over the din of the hospital.

I found the diminutive "Miss" Jyotsna D. Nadkarni in the tiny audiology lab across the passageway. She was dressed in a sari and wore her hair tightly wrapped. This was one of four clinics she attended every week in Bombay, and she had been coming to this hospital for twenty years. Besides English, she spoke three other languages fluently, and Arabic less fluently. I found her English to be quick, bold and somewhat singular, as she told me of the range of therapies she offered patients recovering from vocal nodules, throat cancer, stroke.

For a stroke victim whose language she might not speak, she would "let him have his vernacular," using an interpreter in helping him reacquire the meaning of words, and then speech itself. She also dealt with "effeminate" voices. "I find optimum pitch level and turn it into a male voice." There was no question of tolerating this kind of voice in a young man. She taught a conventional range of relaxation, breathing and vocal techniques, to teachers, singers, stage actors. She was partial to the stage.

"I love music. Acting on stage. Reading, speech, whatnot. Any form of communicating. I was a dancer, when I was small. Stage performances . . . I give these now for the hospital. They are the things that interest me." She organized skits and musical celebrations at the hospital for patients and staff. And had no reluctance in telling people, "what is the matter with their voice." A singing doctor, for example, "had a lot of tremors" and Miss Jyotsna, in diagnosing this woman, taped her and told her to go home and listen. "Now she's singing on the radio."

Her extrovert nature was outspoken. For a child brought to her for "misarticulation," she told me, "I'm sorry to tell the father *he* has the misarticulation . . . that is the reason your child is talking that way. And when I tell him, he can then see, yes, he may have caused it."

I asked how she treated stuttering.

She believed this was "often a mental problem in childhood," since it lacked apparent organic causes. She related the case history of a child who, "reacting in a bothered way" to teasing from other children, had started to stutter after his parents had left him in a crèche. When she discovered this, she told the father, who removed the child from the crèche and was very grateful.

I assumed there must have been some improvement.

Miss Jyotsna, besides generously talking to me, was also testing a young man for hearing loss, having attached earphones to his head, asking him to raise and lower his arms as she turned the volume slowly up and down on her machine. He resembled a man conducting the andante movement of Mahler's Fifth. Or else one of the large-winged kites in lazy flight over Bombay.

For adults as well as children, whom she particularly loved, Miss Jyotsna believed in psychology. Her prototypical case was male. "I try to give him hypnotherapy, to rectify his personality traits, if he's having confidence problems, for example, or if he's having impatience. I have a personality chart and ask the patient to go through the chart, to pick out his own characteristics. I think counselling is more important. Then therapy."

I was naturally interested in whether she had treated any cases of spasmodic dysphonia. "Spastic dysphonia is a very tedious disorder. They talk like this . . ." And here she mimicked spasmodic speech. She had treated ten or fifteen cases, not very successfully. "I personally feel psychiatric therapy is best. There are mental tensions in the home environment. But I have a lot of dropouts. I don't know why. There is a special injection—Teflon or something." Evidently unavailable in India.

I did not hold Miss Jyotsna's aggressive psychological counselling against her, as I sensed she truly loved the speaking voice, and that her sometimes crude approach arose not out of stubbornness but ignorance.

She was open to self-improvement. She had been to Temple University for a month six years earlier, to study the effect of "tumour on the brain." At the same time she'd toured parts of Ontario, including Toronto and Niagara Falls. Yet foreign places were not what held her, any more than foreign neurological theories. The local held her. When we walked out of the hospital together, she raised her umbrella against the tropical sun that always gave her headaches. No paddy and palm for this singer. "It may be dirty and hot," she said attractively, standing on the curb, "but it's mine." Bombay, she meant, where she was born, and to which she had confidently and unselfishly dedicated her career.

One person's neighbourhood, of course, was another's exotic quarter. I had once tried to familiarize myself with Bombay by buying a Raleigh and riding it coolly out of town. My intention had been to cycle south to the tip of the sub-continent, on my way back to Kerala. In the unfamiliar heat of the Western Ghats, on a bicycle apparently made in India and not England, I failed spectacularly. My machine began to fall apart. So did my energy. Lazier now in middle age, I took taxis and took in streets as if they were mine. Little surprised me in India any more, least of all its apparent chaos in these back streets of smoking fires and vegetable peels, pots and prostitutes, animal carts and mirror factories. A city like Bombay or Calcutta was so overwhelmingly local it ceased to be exotic. Vancouver, on the other hand, not least because of its natural beauty, had become for me the most exotic city in the world. It was Ulysses' nostalgia, I think, that eventually turned him from a tourist into a traveller.

I was on my way back to Kerala for a third visit, this time to monitor a women's employment project that CIVA was sponsoring on the rural outskirts of Trivandrum. Twenty-three years earlier, I'd ended up in a Dutch colonial palace for six weeks, on an island between Ernakulum and Fort Cochin. There, while nominally still a student in London, I was absorbing voices around me for a novella I did not begin for another decade. Every day, I had listened to disappointed voices of men working Chinese fishing nets along the coconut-fringed backwaters of the Malabar Coast, and to irrepressible babble from children ferrying home from school on swarming launches.

Eventually, in making a minor character of a talking crow, I'd tried to domesticate the exotic tendency of my main character, an actress from Canada, to "lapse out" in a kind of degenerate, broken-up time and space. These gaps in consciousness, not unlike my own gaps in speech, needed to be anchored in a familiar if slightly askew world. I had remembered "the crow that talked" to us as children, from an elm tree, every morning we lined up to troop inside primary school. The squawk, the rasp, the broken speech became familiar enough for us to believe we could actually make out words. "Troop in! You pack of goodies!" When I developed my own spasmodic caw, I often thought back to this aggressive, iconoclastic crow who "talked" to us outside Immaculate Conception School. In time, the fierce blackness allied itself with my vocal disillusions.

A crippling, yet transcendent light still governed Kerala outside of monsoon season. Tropical vegetation, mainly palm trees, softened the intensity of population in this most literate of states. I wrapped up my business at Mitraniketan, a rural development centre, by listening all day to ingratiating, fuzzy-voiced managers instructing me on vocational training in smithing, horticulture and computers, and where the proposal to train fifty women over three months in the art of weaving palmyra palm leaves into placemats and baskets, to supplement their incomes, struck me as worth our support. But listening, and hardly talking myself, was draining.

So were three days in the heat of the Mascot Hotel, watching kites circle overhead. Then I flew to Sri Lanka on an armed-guard Air Lanka flight, across the Gulf of Mannar. We arrived just as the victorious national cricket team was expected from Lahore, having the night before won the world championship by defeating Australia. A national holiday had been declared. I rode the twenty miles into Colombo ahead of the cricketers, along a highway and through towns festooned with banners and clogged with soldiers, families, buses and schoolchildren waiting to mob their heroes. I slipped through in a scooter taxi.

On this trip back to Southeast Asia, and the one that would follow two years later, it embarrassed me how easily I could smuggle myself into hospitals thick with waiting patients. "Patient" was the operative word, so used were poor people in the Third World to waiting for any medical treatment. A Westerner, on the other hand, interested in talking to Westernized doctors, was usually invited to the front of a line and into offices or surgeries, given tea, and generally indulged amid underlings, pathetic stares from those in line, and pressing messages to your host that he was late for a lecture elsewhere in the hospital.

In Colombo, where I had last been twenty-six years earlier, I visited the General Hospital and was suitably appalled by the desperate, seedy atmosphere of too many people seeking too few services. I was asked to fill out a slip at the admittance desk, as if I was a patient inquiring about speech therapy, which of course I was. A barefoot man then led me to another wing of this stifling, one-floor hospital of underperforming fans and overflowing corridors. Outside room 48, devoted to ear-nose-and-throat cases, dozens of patients waited on benches.

Several policemen emerged with a beautiful young man, dressed in fresh white shorts and a singlet, a large bandage across his throat. They had bound his wrists with a leather thong. Someone had cut his throat. A Tamil Tiger prisoner of war, I assumed, as mute as a knife. Someone had been trying to make him talk, or maybe he had tried to silence himself to make sure he wouldn't. A month earlier, the massive truck bomb that destroyed the business district downtown had exploded like a colliding comet. Identifying suspects in your midst who might be responsible for this, and other sectarian crimes, began it seemed with the voice, listening to whether it spoke Sinhalese or Tamil. The policemen were leading him out to try again, possibly. Or maybe they were taking him to a speech therapist, to help recover oral evidence of his guilt. An accent, a language, a confession.

The line-up went through the door, right up to the doctor's desk, where three nurses were consulting fat file folders, and dealing with petitioners like me. The nurse who spoke English said if I wanted to interview someone about "voice problems and treatment" to try Neurology. This department was in a large, modern-looking building, across from the blood bank down the road.

I found it on the fifth floor, along a dark corridor full of sorry-looking patients on pushcart beds, including a child who was awaiting a brain scan from industrial-looking machinery I glimpsed through an open door. Still, this was a prosperous building compared to the other. Standing outside the office of the head neurosurgeon, where patients awaited him on benches, I was summoned immediately inside by a servant. Three secretaries scrambled around Dr. Colvin Samarasinghe, who was signing letters they slipped under his pen, at the same time as he was speaking on the phone, all the while surveying the monitor on his large desk showing him who was waiting in the corridor outside. He gestured for me to sit down, in the three rows of chairs where he usually addressed students.

A large bespectacled man, with wide-combed hair and a pleasant manner, he had received part of his training in London. Inside his chaotic whirl and world, we chatted about dystonia and its treatment by botulinum toxin, of which Dr. Samarasinghe had only vaguely heard but about which he seemed genuinely interested in learning more. Then, because he dealt not at all with speech, he placed a call through to the chief physiotherapist, summoning him immediately into my presence.

Donald Wadanamby, an equally hospitable man in his mid-forties, invited me to his clinic down the corridor, where more patients were waiting. We sat amidst the drab machinery of his profession, talking about his rehab work with patients recovering from traffic accidents, brain surgery, paralytic aneurysms, war.

"Can you understand me?" he asked thoughtfully, in a heavy accent difficult to follow. He spoke four languages, he said, by way of apologizing for his English. He too had trained in the UK, on the Colombo Plan. Any voice work carried out by Mr. Wadanamby, very little, arose from the trauma of bomb blasts.

"These stress victims will say, 'We open our mouth only to eat and drink.'" In other words, not to speak. Unfortunately, with only two speech therapists in the entire country, speech therapy wasn't a priority. But he promised to find their phone numbers, and we retreated farther down the corridor, where a smiling assistant in a blue sari offered us tea. Then back to the clinic again, where I watched him treat one of his waiting patients, a young girl hoping to recover from last year's surgery to remove a brain tumour. She was unable to smile, or move any muscles on the left side of her face.

She said nothing, merely lay down for the treatment she was resigned to, and arranged a pillow across her stomach. The therapist attached electrodes to her face, in an attempt to surprise the paralyzed muscles in her chin, cheek and forehead with a shock. Mr. Wadanamby hoped to reactivate these muscles in order to regrow nerve ends, thus preventing her need of a second operation. The girl's left eyelid, when she shut it, only half closed, and I watched the eyeball roll involuntarily up and disappear, until only the white showed like the side of peeled, hardboiled egg. The odds on this mute girl's avoiding a second operation did not strike me as good.

It seemed ironic that while she lay here, hoping to regrow nerve ends to trigger facial muscles, I was standing alongside her with Botox in my tank, hoping to *avoid* the regrowth of nerve ends in the laryngeal muscles of my neck (indeed, to keep them in a paralyzed state for as long as possible). Were we both deluding ourselves?

The numbing effects of the war had reduced the number of guests at the decaying Galle Face Hotel to a few stragglers. The lobby was as empty as a museum under curfew. Any arriving taxi or vehicle was examined underneath for bombs, as though for bad molars, the sentry staff manipulating mirrors on long poles like unemployed dentists. The hotel's mustardy paint was blistered, the waiters old, the salt-water swimming pool from the last century, or shortly thereafter, deserted every day. I loved this palmy seediness. I beheld its addenda: fermentative sunsets over the sea, lightning-threaded skies during power blackouts after dark. I would try to avoid the day's worst heat by morning walks along Galle Face Park into the city. It was a little like paying a visit to no man's land.

I stared down an entire city block destroyed the previous month by a gigantic bomb: eighty-six civilians killed, fourteen hundred injured. It was eerie, roped off; soldiers stood futilely at guard over the dead heart of Colombo's financial district. Colonial façades of once busy banks had crumpled. There were missing buildings. Structures as high as twenty stories now stood as blackened shells. Lofty windows in the nearby Trade Towers were covered in plywood. No voices on the pavement, no life. Later that year, sixty-three people would lose their lives when two bombs went off in a train. Since 1983, forty-three thousand people had died in this civil war.

"We never had a problem with them, and then suddenly they wanted their own state." This was how Mr. Wadanamby had put it to me about the Tamil minority. Though he spoke Tamil, Mr. Wadanamby was not sympathetic to Tamil politics. His voice seemed to echo the sentiments of the Sinhalese majority. Even if an outsider couldn't understand the eternal, institutional piety of this majority, he shared its shock and horror at the war.

At the Grand Oriental Hotel, overlooking the harbour, I was late again for the buffet lunch. It didn't matter. Most of the few diners had left, though one or two waiters remained in silent attendance over the coffined remains of curried chicken and saffron rice. I was slouched at my table, gazing down over the wharfed freighters, attenuated tea sheds, and brilliant yellow cranes punctuating mile-long piers. The sun was splashing tile-roofed houses to the east, a mosque, the cupola of a cathedral. I sat wondering what to write on a card to a missing friend. And noticed, five or six tables away, a gaunt old man staring out to sea, his bony white head propped up in his palms. He was teetering over a teacup in its saucer, emaciated and dying, perhaps from a virulent strain of cancer.

I returned to my card, when I abruptly overheard the voice of a somewhat younger man, unmistakably English, trained to speak from the diaphragm and to enunciate clearly. It was a strong, public-school voice, possibly that of a plantation owner, who might well have lived most of his transplanted life in the valleys around Badulla. He was talking about the war, but not the present war. I looked up and was astonished to discover this voice belonged to the wasted man staring out to sea. He was talking to his Japanese companion, at the other end of the tablecloth, a man in a chauffeur's cap.

It was not a voice that matched at all the old man's frailty. In time and space, it seemed years behind his advanced age and decrepit physique. It possessed a still discernible muscularity of tone, and an apparently effortless projection. Clearly, here was a man who had learned long ago how to maintain his vocal instrument, and the air he now deployed to use it seemed all that was keeping him alive. He needed to use his voice to stay alive. And it was allowing him to fill in, with spoken rhythms, the perspective he appeared to be viewing across the ocean. There was solace and curiosity in its music.

I thought of my old friend who had died, just three weeks earlier. I thought of the woman I was trying to address in a distant city. If I suddenly felt tearful, it was because the value of life had suddenly emerged in a voice near its end. Its arc resembled a rainbow in time. An hour later, I wouldn't even recall what words he had spoken, about the war or the Japanese. It was *how* he had spoken them, with vigour and inextinguishable fortitude.

I was often struck by how you could seldom tell the age of a stranger on the radio or telephone by their voice alone. A voice did not seem to age at the same rate as the body. Disease could affect it, but years of aging much less so, as if its sound was less physically determined than mentally shaped.

My theory about aging was that we seldom felt our age, because nature's way of preserving us from the eventual despair of mortality was to set the clock of our brains ten, twenty, or more years back. Asked how old we feel, we will almost never answer our present age. That evening, listening to a not-so-young German woman over dinner, speaking fervently of her past work in Rwanda for the WFO, and now on her way to Kandy to apply for a job, I decided you were the age your *voice* sounded. She sounded young. The age of a voice was closer to the age of the mind than to the body.

After a while, the Englishman struggled up from his table at the Grand Oriental, and toiled to attach a backpack to his shoulders. He was still tall, if stooping badly. The other man, presumably his driver, picked up a suitcase, and together they slowly made their way to the lift. They had been stopping here at the hotel. I had no idea if this white-haired gentleman had ever owned a plantation, was finally leaving his outpost of empire to enter a nursing home in Devon, or was simply returning on one last journey to Ceylon, before he took up residence and died in a bungalow in Bandarawela.

I mentioned this old man, two days later, to the woman who had introduced speech therapy into Sri Lanka. We were sitting in the outside bar of my hotel, drinking lime juice on a torrid afternoon, the palms combed too infrequently by breeze. My interest in voice had encouraged in her a desire to share her world of vocal experience, extending back to childhood. She had loved singing as a child, winning prizes in school. She had taken voice training at age thirteen. She . . . I noticed a middle-aged Sri Lankan man, wearing a chunky wooden necklace, pretending to read his newspaper at a table behind us, and eavesdropping.

Shiranee Joseph-de Saram appeared not to notice him. She was used to attention. A beautiful, saried woman, she told me she had gone to London in 1968, intending to study either design or speech therapy. Voice won out. Thirteen years later, she returned home and started working as a volunteer in the hospital system, setting up speech therapy clinics in Colombo, and at the general hospital in Kandy.

I found her voice calm and gracious. It resembled the way she picked up and put down her frosted glass. In 1988, she had persuaded Save the Children (UK) and the Colombo Rotary Club to help finance her clinics, and to give her a salary. Four years later, after seeing over four thousand patients, the clinics lost their funding when the Department of Health proved delinquent in taking them over. With so many patients on file, and nowhere for them to be treated now, Shiranee had opened up her ancestral home in Thimbirigasyaya Road.

Here, since 1993, she and three assistants, along with volunteers, treated at no charge mainly poor children from all over the country. The only income at her Rehabilitation Centre for the Communication Impaired (RCCI) came from grateful families and private well-wishers. Any personal income appeared to derive from her part-time hospital practice, where she treated better-off patients from the middle class.

Shiranee's dedication to treating voice was obviously motivated as much by philanthropy and compassion as by professionalism and love. Her life seemed consumed by treating voices, listening to voices, raising awareness. In her unassuming way, she was mapping the vocal disorders of an underdeveloped nation, setting out to treat them in an indigenous manner.

This model was rather different from western models of speech therapy. Hers was a socializing clinic. In treating damaged voices, she dealt with deprivations such as malnutrition and isolation. Family involvement remained central to her holistic approach. Treating children, especially those from low-income families, gave her most satisfaction. This treatment included low-cost wooden toys and toilet-training. She mentioned that 70 percent of her patients were children and adolescents.

"It's loud and busy in one room, and I wonder how we get the results we do."

Her centre treated stammering, cleft lip, palate problems and hearing-impaired voices. Also brain-damaged voices owing to stroke, autism, dyslexia, Down's syndrome, cerebral palsy. Her ambitious program for RCCI meant training seminars and workshops for parents, teachers and new therapists. Eventually, she hoped to establish a diploma course, as well as regional voice centres.

In the heat, Shiranee delicately pressed her moist upper lip with a napkin. I gestured to the greying waiter, dressed in red epaulettes and soiled trousers, for another round of lime juices. The eavesdropping man behind us remembered to turn his page.

I asked about her work with war victims. She said civilians, very young soldiers and children suffering from trauma would all develop stammers and need to be resensitized to sound. They required exercises for relaxation and voice production. Yesterday, for example, they'd had seventeen young soldiers at the clinic. From time to time she would also visit the military hospital, where in 1990 she had persuaded authorities to start up a voice treatment program. "A lot of them are stammerers. Sometimes, it is hysterical dysphonia."

She picked up her fresh glass. "There are also malingerers."

After an hour's conversation, Shiranee glanced at her watch and asked if I had a few extra minutes to meet her husband. I heard the newspaper behind us rustle. Her husband, it seemed, was just finishing up an orchestral rehearsal of an upcoming production of *Il Trovatore*, in a church across from the Oberoi. He was artistic director of the recently established Opera Lanka, as well as conductor of the Lanka Philharmonic Orchestra. I decided this must have been the man I spoke to briefly by phone a day earlier, who sounded a little skeptical of my intentions towards his wife.

She drove us over to the church, but the rehearsal was finished. She wondered if I could come home to meet him.

Along the way, through treed streets in the late afternoon heat, passed occasionally by soldiers in trucks, Shiranee talked of her love for opera. It was as if her holistic approach to voice needed to include the artistic as well as therapeutic. Until recently she'd sung in her husband's opera chorus, and she still designed costumes and sets for his productions. This year, she told me, besides *Il Trovatore* in April, Rohan had scheduled *Madama Butterfly* for November. In between, he was to conduct four different programs of grand opera highlights, concert style. No wonder his wife had no time left, while designing sets and administering vocally to the nation, to continue in his chorus. Some of her patients, incidentally, included singers who had misused their voices. And, peering cautiously both ways at intersections, giving way to military vehicles, Shiranee spoke of the difference between Eastern and Western singers from her unique perspective.

The Asian singer, with her emphasis on a head voice, sounded more internal and private, specializing in smaller audiences. Yet she could damage vocal resonators by singing too high. The Western singer projected more, breathing from the diaphragm, though she might attempt to sing roles too early—off a recording, say—without realizing the need to develop her vocal muscles, systematically, so as not to misuse her throat.

Shiranee taught relaxation, breath control.

Her value to a husband dedicated to music was manifest. Besides helping him with opera sets and voices, she was also building him a quiet underground music room in her ancestral home.

We pulled up in front of their temporary, rented house in Kirula Road, where a servant woman opened the steel gate at our honk. Inside, yapped at by a short unpleasant dog resembling an empty Tibetan purse, I met a beautiful thirteen-year-old Lolita in shorts. She was responsible for the abstract painting on the wall, having inherited a love of art from her mother. I learned later she was the offspring of Shiranee's earlier marriage. This second marriage was her husband's second, too.

Rohan Joseph-de Saram descended to greet us then, a rotund man of bluff but distinguished demeanour, and for the next hour we sat chatting and drinking tea while Shiranee quietly deferred. The sound of his voice, a kind of international marmalade that reminded me a little of the Canadian opera director Irving Guttman's, spread easily through this room decorated brightly with pictures and handsome printed cloths. He wanted to talk of Canadian musicians, such as Jon Vickers and Glenn Gould, as well as Canadian hockey players he recalled from his fifteen years of living in New York City.

Rohan, I learned later from last year's *La Traviata* program, had left his native Sri Lanka as a teenager to pursue piano studies in New York, before apprenticing as a conductor and making his Carnegie Hall debut with Bruckner's Third Symphony, at twenty-six. Debuts followed at Lincoln and Kennedy Centers, and in South America where he conducted Mahler's Fifth in 1982. As music director of New York's American Philharmonic Orchestra, he had conducted many singers, including Birgit Nilsson in her Lincoln Center farewell concert. He had specialized in Verdi, Bruckner, Mahler. His recording debut, six years ago with the London Philharmonic, had been of Prokofiev.

He soon warmed to talk of the singing voice. Although he invited American, Australian and European principals to Colombo and Delhi, where he was also artistic director to Opera India, his familiarity with up-and-coming voices was no longer so current. I mentioned the Canadian tenor Richard Margison, whom I'd heard for the first time in a recent Vancouver Opera production of *La*

Bohème. Margison had lately debuted in *Madama Butterfly* under Domingo's direction at the Met. Rohan, because of his friendship with a local Canadian diplomat in Colombo, *had* heard of another Canadian tenor, Ben Heppner. But not the wonderful mezzo, Judith Forst.

He had a special fondness for voices of the past. Today's voices lacked . . . whatever they apparently did among those who knew. Rohan insisted on playing me a recording of a Puccini aria, by a tenor he refused to name, but which he said put all the famous singers since this one to shame, as none should have sung it after him. I wondered if he was testing me. To my layman's ear, this voice lacked the power I was used to hearing in Domingo, say, whose recording of the same aria I had at home. But then I wondered if I'd forgotten how difficult it was to compare recorded voices, especially from different generations. By way of commenting, I mentioned the voice sounded a bit like Roberto Allanya's, though not as brilliant, which I'd heard on a flight to Hong Kong on this same trip. Rohan's tenor turned out to be a singer from the fifties, whose name I was ignorant of, and Rohan went on to wax enthusiastic about his musicality and phrasing.

In the end, my host had given up on New York as a younger person's town, resplendent with music, sure, but "a place that makes you cynical and sarcastic." Still, he enjoyed reminiscing about how, at midnight on Broadway, waiting for reviews of his concerts to appear in the *New York Times*, he had been solicited by gay men. I glanced at Shiranee, who must have heard these New York stories often, but you would not have guessed it by her attentiveness.

When she drove me back to the Galle Face, in the dark, the sun having fallen early in the tropics, she talked of London and friends there she sometimes missed. Her mother here had Parkinson's. A certain sadness in Shiranee's voice, which I was unable to divorce from her country's, lingered. She said she tried to take as her model the best of the West and the best of the East. From anyone else, it might have sounded trite.

I could not recall meeting another person in my travels who seemed to possess a firmer sense of self, through her selfless dedication to others. Not surprising, it came out in her voice, full of composure, which I would remember as the most cosmopolitan voice in my voice gallery. In English, and I was sure in Sinhalese, it possessed the integrity of her conviction that the human voice could cure, be cured, endure. It made someone like me a more complete person listening to her.

This journey to Sri Lanka brought me closer to vocal wholeness than I could remember coming as a traveller. I got carried away. When I went to visit our foster daughter outside Badulla, something happened in these mountains to give my voice a cathartic sense of well-being. I thought later this illusory feeling must have begun in the fatal humidity under my foster daughter's iron roof, after she had welcomed me shyly in her white school tunic and red tie, bending ceremonially to the ground to offer betel nut. Chewing the leaves, I began to babble in the heat.

To come this far from Colombo I had arisen sleepless before dawn and listened to George drive me up a highway full of uniformed school children and near collisions, a highway giving way to mist-filled fields and sharper hills. George was my Brylcreemed driver, in gold-frame glasses and butter-coloured slacks, whose voice had a molasses-like mix of vowels, making his English an indistinct undertaking and for me a frequently incomprehensible one. For him, the civil war was entirely about Tamils, financed by rich Tamils living abroad, especially in Canada, who were prolonging the terror.

We had reached the high cooler air of Kandy, full of lakeside magnolias in blossom, before entering wilder mountains, where occasional treehouses had been erected for harried rice farmers fleeing rogue elephants. George would get out at checkpoints to yak with soldiers guarding hydroelectric dams. Nearer Badulla, silent men and women toiled with hammers to crush rocks for use in widening the narrow road.

Widening was what the mountainous track above Badulla needed, a treacherous thirteen-kilometre stretch I travelled in a 4WD driven by a Plan International worker, to Renuka's house, located in a mountain valley across another range. We twisted up for half an hour, then turned off to plunge down a rutted lane until forced to climb out against a hillside and continue by foot another kilometre or two, along a steep path through sultry jungle.

Renuka's mother had prepared a feast of fruits and pastries. I sat conversing with siblings and neighbours through a laconic interpreter, and felt we were communicating more through eyes than voices. We might just as well have been discussing lipstick as homework, ratatouille as pomegranates. I was the foster father, come from an unimaginable distance. The real father, I learned, had rigged up this lightbulb over the dining table, where electricity had yet to arrive. He travelled home on weekends from a distant job with the electricity board. The heat felt homicidal.

Before saying goodbye, I helped Renuka plant and water a pair of orange trees in their garden, to commemorate our meeting.

That was my surface, chatterbox visit. Underneath, something else was going on. It was as if I had been galvanized by a connection between looking and breathing. This was now manifest in my voice. Seemingly, I could speak for the first time in my life, with an effortless linkage of voice and breath, floating and resonant, the result of having had the courage to look into Renuka's face *and to really see it*. This had carried over into other faces.

I was singing.

This was absurd. I was fagged in the heat, nearly prostrate. I could barely believe I wasn't hopped up on some narcotic plant. The betel nut? Yet it felt as if by looking at and absorbing the face of this daughter, whose voice I couldn't even understand, I was seeing what I was hearing and hearing what I was seeing. I had entered an opera, inside this country of operatic settings, this doomed earring on the ear of India. But I was getting carried away.

I was thinking fondly of myself as an operatic character, the baritone Giorgo perhaps, singing in *La Traviata* longingly of home.

Renuka, too, was a character on this stage of home, which Lorraine and I had apparently helped to roof, and I felt whole in a way I never had before, as if in having gained a daughter to go along with a son, I was now complete and breathing as fully as I ever would. My voice "out there" sounded so beautiful I wanted to cry. The fiction was preposterous. I was Gauguin, who had come alone to the South Seas and discovered here, in the murmur of voices *he* hadn't understood either, his art. This art—his "opera without libretto"—I was standing inside of and singing out.

Cathartic stuff. For as Renuka and I swam back up the path, escorted by a chorus of village children, I also discovered a vast glasshouse without glass, ablaze this afternoon with wild flowers. Lianas, banana palms, birdsong . . . It was as though my search through the world's glasshouses had come down to this natural one under a tea plantation in the mountains of Badulla, where my voice had taken root like an orchid nurtured by our un-surtitled conversation and stage-struck gazings. I was breathing more deeply than I had in the most intoxicating glasshouse at Kew.

I supposed I had found Babylon. Renuka probably felt she had found a sugar daddy, in spite of my broken rubber sandal, smiling as I hobbled along the forest path to the spring—to the Toyota, I mean, getting carried away by the strange comfort afforded by my profession. For under my arm, as a gift from her, I was carrying her uncle's wooden carving of a bare-breasted maiden from Sigirya: coincidentally the subject of my first published travel story, a quarter century before, set on a hot day in the centre of Ceylon, that very image I now recalled comparing in my narrative to Gauguin's *Breasts with Red Flowers*.

I felt a circle closing in my oral education.

That evening, walking at dusk on the outskirts of Badulla, and greeting strangers in the smoke-tinged air of supper fires, stars and planets popping out, the electrified chanting of monks sounding *o-m-m-m-m* across paddy fields from their hillside monastery,

I examined the truth of what I was hearing and seeing, and it still came up operatic. No cracked voice, no diminishment of vision. I was looking as I had never looked, at faces, at people. I was a very whole guy. The wonders of travel were not fully appreciated, I thought, by the vocally undereducated.

It struck me I might still be drunk on betel nut.

The following morning, when I arose from under my mosquito netting in the Dunhinda Falls Inn, and opened my mouth at breakfast with George, I half expected what had befallen me in Perth, at another motel. Instead, my voice continued operatic, in tune with the world. I grandly asked George to take me back to Colombo via the long coastal loop, tunnelling out of Badulla through high carob trees, past terraced paddies and little sawmills, climbing further into the waterfalling mountains, through tea plantations with clouds of pickers spreading saris like wings, before we descended south to salt flats and Hambantota, then along the muggy sea through Matara and Galle, in our air-conditioned van, toward cheesy Mt. Lavinia as darkness fell like a tragic curtain.

A fortified police station along the way had hung a sign outside. Central Voice Squad. I had misread "Vice" and wondered if my perfect vocal instrument weren't about to come under investigation for imposture. It was the old feeling of coming down from transient Botox bliss. Soon, without assistance, I would begin to waver and crack again, as if I had spasmodic dysphonia. Condemned to spoil the opera, by opening my mouth to sing.

The sign that I misread reminded me later of Rohan Joseph-de Saram's closing line, under "Production Credits," for his last opera— a kind of generic warning appended to every program: "The production of Grand Opera is indeed so complex and so VAST that oversights can and will happen."

So it was, in real life too, with the production of voice.

On the night I left the country, I read in the newspaper that I was going to miss the finals of the Seventh All Island Best Speaker Contest, the Bartleet Challenge Trophy to be presented by the Colombo Toastmasters Club at the Kings Court of the Trans Asia

Hotel, where the principal guest that year would be the president of the Board of Control for Cricket in Sri Lanka.

There were so many kinds of opera I had never imagined.

────────────

At Christmas that year, back across the Pacific, my family was given the use of an apartment in Maui, and I remember listening to the careless voices of the rich at shuffleboard, across the barbered lawns and barbecues of Napili Bay, wondering like Scott Fitzgerald how they differed from mine. Maybe not from mine, as I was sounding on the skids just then, but different from someone without SD. So I was surprised when I overheard a CEO type at the steak grill, sundowner in hand, sounding somewhat spasmodic: "Trouble – is – now – I – have – to – talk – like – this – for – it – to – recognize – my – voice – and – not – mishear – what – I – am – saying." Turned out he was lamenting the demise of his shorthand secretary, and the current gaps in his voice-recognition software.

Money talked, I supposed, a different language. I had read the year before of speech pathologists encountering patients with severe glottal attacks from talking to their computers. Evidently, having to dictate for extended periods in the same pitch and inflection caused swelling, hoarseness, even a loss of voice. Which probably explained why the computer industry would soon manage to overcome its discrete speech and program the smoother variety. NaturallySpeaking, VoiceXpress, Now You're Talking, ViaVoice, would all require only a consistent and fluent voice to train each to its particular owner (as if Pozzo, say, to Lucky), His Master's Voice.

I smugly supposed I could have made a case for impoverished voices of the wealthy, as opposed to the rich ones in Renuka's village, and I would have been just as misleading about both. Opera traded in clichés such as these. So did the palaver about operas, where the imagined wealth of past voices always outperformed the stock exchange of current ones—not least because of those singers' old-fashioned ways of patience, sounder training, and a general integrity divorced from the temptations of modern jet-setting, including poor humidity at altitude. The myth of Eden, where the principals sang intoxicatingly, in meticulously cultivated settings lit by genius, was alive and well.

One of my dreams in Maui, which for anyone else would have been the well-known flying dream propelled by atavistic wings, included *vocal* wings, a sweet soaring vibrato (instead of flapping arms) keeping me gloriously aloft. The doves in the morning, when I awoke, had never sounded so bathetic. What I lost by waking wasn't just vocal soaring, but a way of hearing myself as I might have been, had I not since fallen irrecoverably from the clear voice of childhood. I seemed never to have partaken of the opera of life. Poor me. I was Butterfly's silent child, wandering the world and sounding for a voice. This was my own evolutionary myth of human anatomy—not extinct wings, but vanished vocal folds.

Down here, by the tropical ocean that winter, my voice was once more in decline from its artificial means of well-being. It was drying up. The recurrent need to keep my Botox level up, keep it from dipping like some good kind of cholesterol after an intermittent binge, was tiresome. Talking one night to a friendly couple from New York, I sounded strained and effortful, against the tumbling, phosphorescent surf. I slipped off up the beach, feeling I had let them down. Having attempted to sound relaxed and forthcoming, to cover up the effort of this, I had ended up talking *too much*. Had forgotten to listen. Had forgotten to *look them in the face*.

Camel-like, I needed another visit to the artificial oasis for a refill. Whereas for most people, the Hawaiian tropics were just what the doctor ordered, for me they remained less than restorative. The voice barked, the caravan moved on. I seemed to have acquired a taste for the tropics of glasshouses instead. No longer "within" myself, I was straining paradoxically to keep the circumference of my voice from shrinking further inward. Or, to put it another way, the range of my useable voice was narrowing as the potential gap in individual words widened.

This gap was the spasm.

My metaphorical interest in the spasm peaked a year later in London, after hearing a voice from the past. As the most cosmopolitan city in the world, London, with its three hundred spoken languages ranging from Abe to Zulu, was still surprisingly susceptible to the voice of the English nanny. Lorraine and I were sitting in the tube at Waterloo, going home early from a banal new play at the Lyttleton, when a bossy, repetitive voice, familiar from years earlier, claimed our attention: "Mind the gap . . . Mind the gap . . . Mind the gap . . ." This, of course, was the ubiquitous recorded voice of subterranean travel in London, reminding us of the narrow but dangerous space between car and platform. I seemed to hear this worn-out idiom as if for the first time.

For me, it took on a bizarre undertone to do with the recurrent gap in my speech. It was like listening to an old-fashioned elocution mistress, training her student not to stumble over spasms. "Social catastrophe lurks in your gap!" Her taped voice would probably run on for as long as trains ran under London. Across the aisle from us, an Indian mother and her daughter had finally begun to giggle at the sound of this voice, and we too started and couldn't stop for the rest of our stay in London. "Mind the gap," we would pompously mimic to ourselves. I now had a *title* for my dystonia opera-slash-ballet, dreamt up in London two years earlier, and destined never to be composed.

I was on my way to Calcutta.

When I got there I made a point of riding the new metro, listening for a voice commanding me to mind the gap, yet hearing none unless it was the polite Bengali announcement I couldn't understand at Rabindra Sadan station. Once the train started up—an attenuated parade of cars to fit the long, pillared stations clogged with people—travellers had to yell to be heard over the track-clattering racket and furiously spinning fans. It was too loud for most voices, even those without a movement disorder. Which didn't stop the mother opposite from calling elaborately to her daughter, who was reading a chemistry textbook in the seat beside her, something I imagined to do with minding her *p*'s and *q*'s once they reached persnickety relatives in Tollygunge. The kind of vocal gap I would discover in Calcutta, however, had less to do with class and more with my own fictional past.

Just as onerous as minding my gap was watching out for the "hole." Some months before, needing my public voice as much as ever in five years, I had come close to becoming a mime when an air-filled, pitchless voice refused to settle down. I rediscovered the difference between a gap, or spasm—from Botox drying up—and a hole, or air sound, as a result of too much recently injected. Gapping resulted when the vocal folds clenched and couldn't open; holing happened when they couldn't close because of paralysis.

Even if too much poison was injected for a quick, ideal recovery, new nerve endings would eventually sprout to deepen your voice. Unfortunately, if the release of acetylcholine at the motor end plates was delayed too long, this could occasionally take weeks. A planned period of recovery might continue into the period when you'd scheduled to have a smooth voice. This was what happened to me. The fine art of timing had contributed nothing but residual breathiness.

This happened a year after the publication of my novel, when it was chosen for a national award. I had nightmares before flying to Toronto, to read from the novel and make a speech. My voice, like Swiss cheese, had gaping holes in it, no bite in its vowels and little resonance. Surrounded with cocktail chatter that evening, I might as well have had aphasia. I drank bottles of lubricating water, and struggled with a defective microphone in St. Lawrence Hall. I was pathetically grateful for any microphone. I was even more grateful when people stopped talking and listened.

CBC radio followed up in a brief interview. Unlike other authors my age, who had done many such interviews, this was my first with CBC, the network that ten years earlier had cancelled after someone heard me read at the International Festival of Authors. It seemed miraculous I got through the interview, a milestone having nothing to do with literary accomplishment and everything to do with not falling apart on air. Sitting in this boxy little studio reminded me of my attempt, years earlier, to record a demo tape for blind students. Ashamed of my inability to read a page without sounding strangled, I'd wiped the tape before it could be auditioned, and sadly walked out.

The most satisfying event on this Toronto trip was the chance to visit again with an old student of mine, who had since become a speech pathologist. We met at my hotel one afternoon and talked about her career, just as I had talked to other pathologists about theirs. She kindly expressed surprise at learning of my covering up in front of classes, including the two she was in. With no suspicion of my enervating ruses, she remembered only an occasional broken word.

She also remembered how an unbearable shyness had prevented her from speaking at all in those classes herself, compensating for a timorous voice with her fluency as an essayist.

Helen Smith then told me how, for nine years of her life, she had been "electively mute." (I thought of Flaubert, who hadn't spoken at all before the age of seven.) Her "obsessive-compulsive shyness" had evidently crippled her first try at university, although I recalled an A student. She dropped out and became a travel agent. When this job lost its appeal, voice therapy still rated low on her list of career options. She'd returned to college with enhanced confidence and completed a degree in English literature. This she followed up with a degree in speech language pathology, specializing in young children. Never having babysat a single child, Helen was now working successfully with stuttering schoolchildren. I was struck by her poise and pleasantly measured voice.

She caused me to wonder again exactly why I had given up teaching. I could remember the pleasure in discovering a good essayist such as Helen in class. I could remember the pleasure in sharing my passion for literature with students who were wide open to the imagination. Despite the effort of keeping the spasms out of my speech, of the strain and unpredictable nature of my voice, I felt paradoxically relaxed with students. I could make them laugh. I could enthuse them about writing. In submitting my resignation, I regretted that I would no longer have an influence over the ones who could be persuaded to believe the literary imagination could transform their lives. Save for two bad terms, I had thought of myself as a sound and even popular teacher. I supposed I might have gone on teaching had the effort of doing so been less, and had I not always dreamed of writing full time. The voice in my head had finally needed to come out more than the voice in my throat.

The other Helen I knew in voice, Helen Sjardin, had come to Vancouver earlier that spring as part of a world sabbatical, taking her to McGill to study bilingualism and stroke, before returning to Perth via Europe. In the Fish House in Stanley Park we ate oysters, which she and her husband used to grow in Tasmania, and talked about the dystonia voice. Five years later, when an article appeared in *Nature* on voice recognition, from the Neurological Institute at McGill, I wondered whether this was the sort of thing she had gone to Montreal to pursue.

Robert Zatorre's lab had evidently discovered, through brain imaging, a particular fissure of the temporal lobe that was activated by the human voice and by no other sound. If this area of the brain was deficient or damaged, as after a stroke, the listener could no longer tell whether he was hearing a man's voice or a woman's, a sad voice or a happy one. Moreover, the listener's own voice might still function perfectly. This condition, known as "phonoagnosia," seemed not unlike a condition called "prosopagnosia," in which a stroke victim no longer recognized faces (famously studied by Oliver Sacks in *The Man Who Mistook His Wife for a Hat*). The latter condition was the visual equivalent of the aural one, in which voices weren't recognized. The area in the temporal lobe activated by voices—"Quite close, it turns out, to the region that recognizes faces" (as one researcher put it)—was what astounded me.

Naturally, I remembered looking Renuka in the face and really seeing her, then seeing others, that day in Sri Lanka when my voice seemed to have achieved its most natural sound. There now seemed to exist scientific support for my intuition. It was as if the sound of my voice, when it was working best, allowed me not just to listen well but to see faces I was otherwise unable to see. This was human recognition at its deepest level.

The more I meditated on this, the more it seemed happiness and unhappiness arose from the voice. In possession of a healthy voice, which allowed you to look into people's faces and actually see them, you were infectious with happiness. You made others happy. You might even, speaking beyond yourself, give them back their own voices. This was stretching it. Yet I thought of Butterfly's mute child wandering the world searching for his dead mother's voice. Of increasing interest to me now was this unwritten Puccini opera of the peripatetic mute.

I was coming to think of the Beautiful Voice as one I would trust to sound more or less on top of things in perpetuity. I was beginning, in other words, to regard it as mythical. If only I could hold on to such a voice. My own voice was in constant movement, declining subtly day by day. You knew it had run out when, at Ecco Il Pane, the bakery on Broadway, the salesgirl you asked for a b a   guette didn't understand you any more.

The longer view of things was on my mind when I travelled back to India again, to meet up and journey with my fellow directors of CIVA. We were visiting one of our projects, in the village of Sitla, located in the foothills of the Himalayas, where we could sit in the mornings and watch a panorama of snow-capped peaks in the Tibetan distance. At night, when the moon shone down on a sea of cloud below us, I could still see these gleaming peaks of Shangri-La. I knew there were leopards in the surrounding forest. I knew the New Zealander Allan Sealy was living somewhere underneath us in Dehra Dun, his Indian home away from home.

Relaxing to the long view was akin to relaxing to the scents of India deeply breathed. Both served to remind me of how often I forgot to look, forgot to breathe. Both served to remind me how much of my life I lived without perspective, without wonder. For most people, to breathe correctly was to speak with a healthy voice. It was to live. I could live too when mine was healthily injected. But I lost perspective in losing confidence in my voice. I needed to cling like a dying man—like that dying man, overlooking the sea in Colombo—to my wonder occasioned by such vistas. I knew my voice should have been working better than it was.

On our last day here, visiting the site of a proposed hospital, on a ridge between watersheds, I stood transfixed on a hillside in the falling light, as the sound of tinkling voices washed up on the breeze from descending terraces in the valley below, along with the scent of woodsmoke from kitchen fires. These voices were connecting us to centuries of unchanged rural domesticity. They made me feel younger than my age. It was for such moments I felt operatic arias were composed, to celebrate imperishable beauty. *Vissi d'arte.* I was mute. I thought of Yeats's silent Asians, carved in lapis lazuli, pausing on their mountain slope to listen to the melodies of old civilizations.

There were many other voices here we listened to in our visits to schools and health clinics. The clear, vigorous voices of small children reciting, the murmuring voices of bright-saried women sitting on patios. The contending voices of puppet shows. How to describe the untrammelled power of these voices, their direct connection of breath to sound, impulse to expression? Speaking voices, singing voices, in the local Hindi dialect of Kumaan, punctuated by the ubiquitous silences of heat-filled oak forests we walked through to reach these villages.

In the state of Rajasthan, on the same trip, in the arid country-side that must have once belonged to the bottom of an ocean, before all the trees were cut down, I remember sitting on a village hilltop listening to the melodious voice of a tall young woman in a gold-threaded sari, telling us in her dialect of Mewar how far the village women had come in finding their place "on the carpet." This was the metaphor she used for their being allowed "to speak up," to use their voices along with the men's, at public meetings such as this one.

Earlier, I had been gazing out to a reforested hill in the distance, across little goat herds and the occasional date palm, listening to the men speak. Then the voice of this woman lifted me from my slouch, causing me to look deep into her unveiled face, to hear words I didn't understand but whose meanings I could imagine easily, even without translation. She seemed to have gathered in the perspective of the commanding view, allowing it to produce in her a voice of independent *celebration*.

I thought of Daisy's "low, thrilling" contralto in *The Great Gatsby*, "the kind of voice," wrote Fitzgerald, "that the ear follows up and down as if each speech is an arrangement of notes that will never be played again." This impoverished desert of Rajasthan was the farthest thing in the world from opulent Long Island in the Jazz Age. *Except for this voice.* You heard—no, saw—how rich and poor people could be united over time and across space through the voice of an anonymous village woman and the imaginary voice of a famous cosmopolitan character in American fiction.

Voice was, if not everything, then a way of managing the world.

Was I straining, to make this connection? We were, after all, in this aid organization to bridge, in any way we could, the inequity between East and West. The hot afternoon sun was baking my head, and we had been up before dawn for the long drive over rutted roads to drought-stricken villages and simple dams. I was exhausted from listening to voices. I noticed how I was not hearing them well these days, as an increasing loss of fluency interfered with my ability to listen. The odd hobbled camel in the desert had reminded me of the Botox oasis I needed to revisit soon.

But then this woman's voice had reconnected me to the world, reaffirming my desire to see what I heard and hear what I saw. At such times, the human voice was remedial.

Even in dance. In Delhi, at the International Centre one evening, I had gone to a Bharatnatyam dance recital by Anita Dhar Kaul and been struck by how her movements seemed a perfect bodily extension of the voice. The voice belonged to a male singer, sitting on the floor with his legs folded. He sang the stories of the dancing maiden's approaches to Lord Shiva, tapping his small finger cymbals, accompanied by a drummer and flautist. The dancer's red-footed jumps, choreographed twirls, and her stalking gestures with red-painted fingernails were frequently thrilling to the audience.

His voice and her body looked and sounded inextricably one. No more could you separate these than you could Yeats's dancer from the dance. I was seeing what I heard and hearing what I saw, as though finally discovering the modus operandi for my dystonia opera, *Minding the Gap*.

In Delhi, incidentally, I happened to read in the *Sunday Pioneer* how "a voice stress analyser" had exposed the lie of a man in California, who claimed to have had his penis cut off by a woman named Brenda, when in fact no such woman existed. He had done it himself. As a male with SD, my immediate thought was how could *I* have undergone such vocal analysis and not failed miserably: although, in this particular case, I supposed pass or fail would have amounted to pretty much the same thing.

It made me wonder what growing up with the voice of a castrato was like in the eighteenth century, when the testes of boys were removed to keep their soprano voices from changing. A week earlier, in Calcutta, I'd wandered into St. John's Church (built in 1787), surrounded by an overgrown acre or two of brambles and headstones, where a mixed children's choir was rehearsing hymns and Christmas carols. Earnest, slightly off-key, they sounded Eastern, as though their ear for Western choral harmonies had been affected by a Bengali tradition of solo song. A tall, bespectacled Anglo-Indian, eighteen or twenty, had interrupted his tightly gestured conducting to scold the children in a baritone voice.

As the singing resumed, I was reading stone inscriptions in the walls and floor commemorating imperial lives of British civil servants, dead at inordinately young ages of disease, accident and heartbreak. The choir's Christian voices seemed increasingly poignant, by their isolation and immateriality, in a country far from home at Christmas. This choral tradition had been going on for over two hundred years.

In the wide echoing nave, a piercing voice, which I assumed belonged to one of the older girls, suddenly soared spookily above the others. Sitting down in a pew to listen, I couldn't quite see which girl might be singing out. None of the girls, or boys, appeared to possess the vocal power required for such a sound. I concluded it was coming from the conductor, his back to me, singing the treble part himself, in the strenuous hope of recharging his choir. In a piercing falsetto, he sounded like a castrato.

This strangely beautiful voice rang in my ears. The speech pathologists I had interviewed in India and Sri Lanka on my earlier trip, Jyotsna Nadkarni and Shiranee Joseph-de Saram, had both mentioned treating puberphonia among adolescent boys, whose voices, subject to involuntary breaks, hadn't evened out and still suffered from a high pitch unacceptable to families and potential employers. I learned it took a minimum of six months to turn one of these perfectly natural voices into "a male voice."

It occurred to me, listening to this conductor, that among boys with treble voices in ancient European churches like St. John's, our Western tradition was somewhat more sympathetic of hanging on to childhood. Butterflies, I thought, on stone. Boys in India had traditionally been expected to grow up faster, because death at earlier ages was expected.

Outside in the rank graveyard, in a kind of time-warp surrounded by apartment buildings from a later century, more testimonials to the British dead adorned mausoleums and obelisks, from the city's founder to those who perished in the black hole of Calcutta. On the following Sunday, I made a point of walking to the English cemetery in South Park Street, an eighteenth-century oasis of two or three acres given over to outlandish pagodas and tombs, intended to undercut mortality with their stonework—especially, I supposed, when the Hindus all round were burning up their loved ones on pyres.

Here, as I listened to the high-pitched voices of young boys playing cricket among the headstones, there drifted in the inextinguishable smell of India—of cow paddies, garbage, engines, pyres—the smell of burning. This most domestic and familiar of smells was also the most exotic and mortal. I had known it myself in another way since my childhood, when wood furnaces had heated houses and people burned autumn leaves in the street. From the latter, a pall of pungent smoke would hang over my city for a month.

I now decided this smell of burning was the olfactory equivalent of the treble voice. Both seemed, in their own way, a memento mori: in the attractive key of death, as Mahler kept discovering in his Fifth and Ninth, in those evocative treble horns by way of Anton Bruckner.

In Calcutta, I had found in one of its desperate, dirty hospitals a memento mori I did not need. A twitching, half-naked young man, lying on the floor of the neurology ward, resembled someone with generalized dystonia. I couldn't decide if he had crawled in off the street, or was a patient temporarily mislaid by the staircase for lack of beds.

Another young man soon accosted me, saying I would have to leave the hospital without a permission slip. I explained my mission. "Speech therapy? You want to meet someone?" He then led me through confusing corridors to the ENT ward, where I was rapidly introduced to several people, including Dr. L.M. Ghosh, a surgeon who resembled a cross between V.S. Naipaul and the TV detective Columbo, if one could also imagine an older man with still-dark wavy hair, who spoke four languages, stuttered only in

Bengali when he got tired or emotional, and who wore a good, sand-coloured cardigan to lectures he'd probably given here at the Medical College Hospital since 1962, the year he had qualified as an ENT. I liked him immediately: his fortitude in the face of underfunding, his generosity to strangers midst expectations of his presence elsewhere, his deference to colleagues regardless of his own accomplishments: qualities rare among Western healers.

His specialty seemed to be deaf and mute children, and he extracted from the glass case in the dingy, windowless room a cheaply copied chapter he had contributed to a book on pediatrics. He gave it to me. Perhaps he hoped I could bring a bit of publicity to the lamentable lack of government money available to speech therapy.

I inquired about his treatment of voices.

These he told me ran the gamut from deaf children to stutterers and stroke victims. How did he treat stuttering? "Do you know pranayam?" he asked. This was a Hindu breathing exercise, alternating between nostrils. As the fan spun low overhead, he demonstrated with his finger. It had helped cure his own stutter. "Once I stumbled over every other word. Now cured," he insisted. I wondered. His jerky, rambling English was difficult to understand, and I thought of how my own speech became partly incomprehensible when I tried to cover up spasms. I asked if he ever treated spasmodic dysphonia. He knew the disorder, but confessed, "We are helpless here."

Outside, College Street was full of toilet-fixture shops, sleeping dogs, incense clouds, broken sidewalks, urinating men, a large bathing tank and diving tower, and about nine hundred tin-roofed book stalls full of antiquated textbooks and paperbacks smelling badly of mildew. When I sought refuge in the soiled foyer of the library at Calcutta University, the sign instructed me to please speak in a LOW VOICE. It was hard to think of why I might wish to lift it above a monotone within such dingy walls.

At my hotel that evening, I talked over dinner to a young English couple on their way back to medical school in London, after a six-week practicum in Kandy. When I mentioned Dr.

Ghosh's belief in the importance of singing and drama in speech therapy, they smiled at each other, revealing that they'd first met during a production of *Guys and Dolls* at St. Mary's College, London. Talk about the palaver of opera. James had directed and Caroline had sung.

The Fairlawn Hotel in Sutter Street had been written up as "funky," and it was certainly full of mismatched junk and cosmopolitan, transient voices. I would sit writing in the palmy courtyard, glancing up to catch a fluttering crow slowly propelling itself atop the blade of an otherwise powerless fan. I waited for it to address me knowingly from its perch. "Think you are aiding the poor, my friend? Just as well dump sand in the Hooghly. I am hearing your spasms." This once grand house dated from the Raj, and the furniture in the drawing room upstairs, deep of cushion and roseate in mutation, had not been dusted since. Water pressure had declined with the plumbing's sclerosis.

I wondered to what degree, when the name of your hotel was an illusion, the hotel itself was an illusion? (Just like this talking crow, recognizable to me from my earlier novella with a fabulously refurbished Calcutta.) There was no lawn, fair or otherwise, this side of the vast and chewed-up Maidan off Chowringhee Road, yet the name persisted like some worn-out idiom without association.

India had this effect of dissociating your assumptions, while seldom challenging its own. What difference did charity make? I could barely speak the language of development. I wondered if this came from knowing my voice sounded like a guilty conscience, whereas in reality I myself felt no such thing. Maybe I just didn't believe in its vocabulary of "ecological components" and "bottom-up sustainability." I went on minding my gap over dinner with two women whose Australian NGO was doing relief work in Bangladesh.

Later, in Rajasthan, I fantasized about glasshouses in the desert. Not even Udaipur, with its architectural history of palaces on hilltops and palaces in the middle of lakes, boasted any glass buildings I could locate, while the outlying villages, where we travelled to visit projects in hills and desert, were too poor to construct, let alone indulge such unreal structures. In addition to anicuts (small dams) and women's health centres, I would have liked CIVA to subsidize a glasshouse. The kind of relief I knew anything about seemed mainly to arise, in my own case, from fiction and artifice.

We returned from the desert in darkness. Stars and planets had appeared, and the air through the dust smelled sweet and rural. I peed in the dust, listening to the Milky Way. How could a mere speaking voice convey the relief of such experience? I saved my compromised voice, next morning, for an overheated account of our driver hitting a pedestrian crossing the road. The anonymous pedestrian had not only survived, but quickly disappeared into the night. As had a roadside fox, its rust-coloured coat grazed by our headlights, before it too vanished. I didn't mention the fox. I would have had to mention the crow, earlier in Calcutta, as part of the same fable about losing one's voice.

One day, I took a scooter taxi to the General Hospital in Udaipur, a pigeon-infested structure even more in demand than the one in Calcutta. The corridors smelled latrinal. The orthopaedic ward and its surgery looked indescribably soiled. Voice and speech therapy were nowhere to be found. The muscular and short-cropped ENT resident who greeted me, behind a curtain in his busy clinic, had trained at medical school in Jaipur, where he hoped to return in order to complete a two-year "super specialty" in neck surgery.

I got the impression from Omendra Ratnu that poor voices in Rajasthan did not necessarily stand a better chance of receiving treatment at a public hospital if an emergency was involved. Granted, he had recently tended right away to a woman whose vocal cords wouldn't open, who couldn't breathe, upon whom he'd performed an emergency tracheotomy. But as for young female patients with "hysterical aphonia" arising from an accident or physical abuse (via husbands perhaps), he told me he could only console and counsel them.

He knew little about people without any voice. These he rec-ommended sending to a local school for the deaf—which, three years later, turned out to be the place I would remember him sending me.

———

Dr. Ratnu seemed not unlike the kind of young, intelligent residents I often met from elsewhere at the Pacific Voice Clinic in Vancouver. Among other techniques, they came to learn how to administer botulinum toxin to patients with spasmodic dysphonia, from head and neck surgeon Murray Morrison. The art of injecting the larynx, even for a physician as experienced as Morrison, remained an imperfect one of delicate procedure hampered by variables in each affected voice.

One went on trying to manage these variables with less letdown after each injection. Grateful as you were for bull's-eyes scored, when you seemed to know right away the toxin had reached its target—and equally resigned to its misses, when the poison enigmatically failed—either way you expected to be back again in hospital before long. A sense of failure was unavoidable. You heard about the discovery of genetic markers in dystonia research. And awaited the advent of nerve cell therapy, with all the expectation of a repeat lottery loser foreseeing his fate.

The fantasy of a cure, or at least a permanent treatment for chronic laryngeal dystonia, abided. Every other year, I would bring to my otolaryngologist, a man of lively curiosity, a notice of some new surgical technique reported elsewhere for this or that vocal disorder, including mine. One year, after the Pacific Regional Conference of the NSDA in San Diego, I brought him back my laconic account of a paper given by the UCLA surgeon Gerald Berke, who had pioneered a new experimental surgery for SD, by cutting into the larynxes of dogs and paralyzing their barks. Then rerouting the laryngeal nerves and eventually returning these barks, or rather voices, to their owners.

It was supposed to be an advance on the RLN surgery pioneered by Herbert Dedo, who had first demonstrated the neurological linkage of the larynx. The recovery of a permanent voice now seemed possible, if unlikely. Berke, whom Morrison knew from professional conferences, was reluctant to proselytize his surgery, making the point of telling us that anyone who was getting good results from Botox shouldn't consider it. I had already heard from a prosperous-looking evangelist, at the breakfast table that morning, what *he* knew about Berke's surgery. Evidently, the good doctor slit your throat from ear to ear and you lost your voice for five months. It didn't sound tempting. The cost was prohibitive. Few patients had had it. No results had been published.

Over two years later, knowing of my interest in the surgery, Dr. Morrison mailed me a copy of the results Berke had just published in *Ann Otol Rhinol Laryngol.* Not incidentally, it included a couple of bloody photos revealing an incisioned neck, to illustrate the involved surgical technique for treating adductor spasmodic dysphonia. Knowledge of the intralaryngeal anatomy had evidently grown since Dedo's work. Twenty-one patients had had the surgery, and been tracked over three years.

Their recovery of normal voices, with no need of further treatment, was a result of having the adductor branch of their recurrent laryngeal nerve, to the thyroarytenoid and lateral cricoarytenoid muscles, selectively and bilaterally severed. It sounded serpentine. This nerve was then reinnervated bilaterally, with a branch of the ansa cervicalis nerve.

I understood all this as reinnervating the laryngeal muscles with a swallowing nerve, unaffected by dystonia, so as to allow normal movement of the vocal cords without spasms. But it took six months or more for a voice to recover fully. It took six hours just to perform. I came to think of the procedure as persnickety, open-neck surgery involving two surgeons and an anaesthesiologist, who were required to cut your neck and reroute the brain's wiring in hope of deceiving it. Just so you could lose your voice entirely, in the vain hope of becoming a smooth-talking dude.

I began dreaming of travel to Los Angeles again.

Then I learned how much it would cost.

I got on with minding my gap.

I got on with my oral education. I learned how unfinished it was, upon discovering that what people most wanted to hear, when scandal broke, was the only thing they still hadn't heard: "that woman's voice." Headline: "The Last Lewinsky Mystery: What Does She Sound Like?" Sub-headline: "Secretly recorded tapes to be released." It was as if Monica Lewinsky did not exist, except as a pornographic fantasy fuelled by rumour, until we heard her voice. And in a way, this was true. She required a voice to dispel (or perhaps improve) the fantasy. We read a found poem, culled from newspaper reports, describing it in phrases like, "Rapid-fire ramblings, more Buffy than Bacall . . . An average American."

Predictably, all curiosity quickly faded when Monica began to speak (and speak) in an uninteresting, not very well produced voice.

Public voices, in particular a singer's voice, were fair game. When soprano Kathleen Battle sang at a sold-out Carnegie Hall, one Sunday afternoon in the last year of the millennium, Anthony Tommasini wrote in the *New York Times*: "But for those who remember what an exquisite artist she was not so long ago and who are dismayed by her current state, Ms. Battle's singing has become a caricature of cutesy-pie mugging, coo-coo phrasing and breathy delivery. The recital was a strange and sad event."

When Frank Sinatra died, the obituaries praised his dramatic ability to inhabit every line he sang. They lauded his phrasing, range, intonation, control. For good reason had he been known and recognized through much of the century, in North America and Europe, as "the Voice." Even that other vocal synecdoche, the Three Tenors, had paid him tribute in their tawdry stadium concert in LA. His voice was unique and crossed boundaries. I listened to it again on record, pleased by its sheer effortlessness, not unlike a good speaking voice, full of natural expression married to feelings conveyed without any wind-up or rhetorical crutch. Without any "singerese." It seemed a sincere voice.

One thought of change as the millennium approached. Change was in the air. It seemed somehow in keeping with the times that I should resolve never to return for another injection of botulinum toxin. I could not believe what I had done.

It happened like this.

I was back at the voice clinic for my twentieth-something injection, when Dr. Morrison made a suggestion. "I've asked Berke to fly up one weekend, to give a demonstration of his selective denervation-reinneveration surgery. Would you like to have it done?" Because another patient had been more ingenious than me, asking him about the possibility of signing medicare forms to cover the cost of this leading-edge surgery in LA, Murray Morrison had decided to learn the technique himself, after talking to his American colleague at a recent American conference of laryngologists.

Unfortunately, Gerald Berke's flying visit to Vancouver that autumn allowed him time to perform only a single operation. So I was scheduled for the following year, as the Canadian laryngologist's inaugural patient. I waited seven months from the last injection, which itself had been less successful than the previous, and my voice gradually reacquired the spasms and prevarications known from its earlier life. A resurgence of the transmitter acetylcholine made nerve ends as spasmodic and capricious as they had ever been. Normal stress made them worse. It felt depressing to have fallen back into an abyss I had crawled out of seven years earlier. No longer above the gap, I was the gap. Mr. Crow and I met regularly for debriefings. The good thing was I retained the knowledge of my condition, something I had not owned in the gap spanning seven and twenty-seven years before that.

This knowledge was something to hold on to now, as the saving toxin leached out of my larynx in preparation for surgery. My vocal nerves fired away like undisciplined soldiers of fortune, as though reconnoitring the plan to cut them out in this laryngeal civil war. The pleasure of speaking in a light, fluent voice had disappeared. Sometimes I made a fool of myself on the phone, or when ordering food. "Egg McM u ffin," mimicked my embarrassed son. I enjoyed going to the dentist for a root canal, only because when I spoke to the florist after this operation I had an excuse for sounding like I'd just had a root canal. I could no longer think of speaking in public.

In these recidivist months, leading toward loss of voice and expected muteness, I experienced anxiety and self-doubt. The simple business of changing pitch was now fraught with entanglement. A monotone was never far away, verbal manifestation of a flattened spirit. I never knew when I would sound like chopped liver and begin to babble in compensation—which merely got me deeper into the chopped liver.

When the neurologist diagnosed early-stage ataxia in my wife, a neurological disorder that she discovered ran in her family, I wondered about its impact over time on her sense of balance as well as on her voice. Her chronic cough had worsened, yet her speech remained precise and unslurred. In a way, the idea for this memoir had arrived the morning after the night she lost her memory of what had happened during her one and only seizure. Since then, small gaps in her memory had slowly widened, so I was aware in meditating on voice, how I might also be filling in forgotten memories over our years together before and since.

This perspective began to lift me out of despondency. Like Mrs. Moore, in Forster's *A Passage to India*, Lorraine helped me to understand how everyone failed, but that there were many kinds of failure. I had a responsibility to others, including those who had shared with me stories of their voices. I was going to have a new voice, and I was going to remember everything about waking up mute, and coming back to voice a second time in less than a decade. I looked forward to speaking at my parents' sixtieth wedding anniversary, after botching their fortieth, and then avoiding their fiftieth. I looked forward to spreading joy like Lazarus.

I had been amused to read in his paper, published in *Ann Otol Rhinol Laryngol*, Berke's suggestion that because his new operation was "somewhat difficult to perform, it should be first attempted in cadaver larynges." I quietly considered myself Murray Morrison's cadaver (and that of his microsurgeon, Scott Durham, who would introduce new nerve ends to one another in my neck and suture them), as we had a pre-op chat, and I tried not to look concerned over what he might have forgotten in the intervening months since observing Berke's dissection. Lazarus indeed. *I* was going to remember everything.

The surgery was then delayed another month.

Before I woke up from it in hospital, throat sore after hours of sawing and soldering, I had time to dream an entire night's desert journey, searching for an oasis. Some fusion of inner and outer selves—of I and "I" one supposed—was whimsically achieved in this dream, and yet my memory remained a stubborn blank on what had actually *happened* during my anaesthetized trip to a glasshouse. In the following days, *sotto voce*, my imagination did most of the talking.*

"You talking to me?" said the mirror. "You talking to *me*?"

I was expecting to come back to full voice, yet what guarantee had I that my speaking muscles had not been permanently desiccated, rendered as effective as a dummy's? Before surgery, I had promised to speak that fall at the Festival Theatre in Stratford, Ontario. Into the mirror I now mouthed titles for follow-up papers in *Ann Otol Rhinol*: "Stratford Indulges Charlie McCarthy Type after Berke's Work Proves Premature"; "Mime Visits Stratford and Bombs at Reading." I had agreed to attend this conference of writers without knowing whether my voice would be back by then from its underworld journey, let alone prove useable on a public stage. (It did, so to speak, it was.) Shame and fear still hovered like a crow over the prospect of speech. It was as if, before I could come back to life, I needed to go through the valley of the shadow and be reinstructed in the wonder of speaking at all.

Easter Week seemed a suitable one for beginning anew, not least because of the pear tree in blossom, tulips, lilacs and wisteria.

---

*Indeed, it was busy reconstituting the voice patient's dream of finding his oasis, arising from his snooze through surgery, harmonious with his notion of Babylon. I later wrote a story, "The Anniversary," in which numerous wandering voices gather in tribute to Puccini one starry desert night inside a glasshouse in Rajasthan. *Una bella notte* . . .

Feeling full of optimism for the future, but more or less voiceless in the present, was a little like writing a book, a period in which silent striving was precedent and talking about it undesirable. I was used to living in my imagination. Writing fiction was not a dissimilar submergence into silence, waiting for a new voice to emerge.

I listened for it. Days, into weeks, into months. Eventually, if the regeneration went well, I could expect to recover a strong voice and even shout the following winter at my son's basketball games. I could remember what it was like, every few weeks, not to need a voice clinic. I could return, a willing volunteer, to CIVA. I could slowly, over the coming year, in recovering inflection but probably not a falsetto or much of a singing range, understand how different might be a permanent from an impermanent voice, and how this could lead to unfamiliar courage. To a vivacious future of regret for a history of missed opportunities there wouldn't be time in the world to make up. I could become part of the world again, in a way that seemed to me anything but common.

When I visited the deaf and mute school for poor tribal children, on the outskirts of Udaipur, I had no expectation of my later denervated voice. I did not expect to find Babylon here—the lushness of voice I was still listening to recover from some mythic time, before the Tower of Babel—and I did not. Instead, I came to understand in quite a domestic way—it was brought home to me, shall we say—what it meant not to have a voice, as if I had never really comprehended such a loss. Certainly not among children of families who spoke some of the world's oldest dialects.

Mr. Paliwal, a young man with kind eyes and a small moustache, presided over the school wrapped in a plain cotton shawl. It was impossible on one level not to equate the "voicelessness" of his pupils with their tribal status as Bhils and Minas, from the impoverished hills and desert of Rajasthan. Poor himself, he had spent a year in Bombay in speech therapy training. Here in Udaipur, he and his staff now taught a "total communication method" to over a hundred deaf children, each of whom spent eleven years in residence. Mr. Paliwal tested their hearing every six months, in a little soundproof room on the ground floor, where vocational classrooms enclosed a courtyard.

There was usually no change in their deafness. Not that the children minded. Hearing meant nothing to them. Voices meant nothing to them. Voicelessness was no more cause for regret than not being blond. Some of these children were capable of piping sounds, even grunts, as I learned when two boys came in to see Mr. Paliwal for help in arithmetic. He asked them, for my benefit, to make any sound they could. Not that they heard these themselves. Their spoken communication remained visual. They needed to see what they heard, by hearing what they read in sign, lips and faces.

It occurred to me, in watching their vigorous exchanges, the deaf enjoyed a more dramatic sense of voice than the hearing did. They put more body into language, possibly more soul. Their kind of voices seemed to encourage them to breathe deeper, see farther. My empathy with deaf-mutes was specious at best.

Upstairs, Mr. Paliwal showed me the long dormitory of sixty or seventy beds for the boys who boarded. Girls came only during the day. Today, a holiday, the boarders were playing football energetically on the flat roof outside. The sun was hot, even in December. Some of the boys wore maroon sweaters, as part of their uniform, and all wore frazzled shorts. Their subdued vocal noises amounted to involuntary notes of exertion, like sweat beads. As they crowded round us, I was tempted to mistake their silent curiosity for impeccable manners.

When one younger boy could no longer contain his excitement, demanding by rapid sign to know where I came from, Mr. Paliwal extracted a ballpoint pen from the boy's shirt pocket and printed on his palm. The others bent forward to read it. Instead of writing "Canada," Mr. Paliwal had slowly penned "Toronto"—in English—which immediately elicited a wide rabid signing, naturally annoying to a traveller from Vancouver. Then I recalled that

Toronto had recently hosted the test match between India and Pakistan. These children had probably watched it on satellite TV. Recent violence in Calcutta over international cricket meant only a neutral city that relished ice hockey could have ensured a peaceful outcome to a bitter sporting rivalry in Asia.

Scooter-taxiing back to the walled city of Udaipur, to visit the City Palace high above, from where I gazed out to arid hills once prowling with tigers, I thought about the soundness of these deaf children. They were not cursed by the kind of after-Babel abashment I felt. By exploiting their voicelessness, they were making themselves whole. Unlike parents and tribal ancestors who had helped Rajput rulers fight invading Mughals, these deaf boys were literate, numerate, and in training to be carpenters and artisans. This meant more to them than having a voice. Having voices, they would probably never have trained for anything, or even gone to school. Deafness had given them a community and, surprisingly, a future.

My voicelessness after surgery was nothing like theirs. They knew how to make their way in the world without a voice. They did not accept vocal failure, because they did not understand language in the same way I did. Without a voice, I had no language to overcome my state of distraction. Deaf since birth—most of them— they lived in a parallel world unvisited by the myth of Babel.

As a boy their age I had run fast. I could remember a priest saying, as we donned cassocks before mass one May morning, that on school sports day he'd heard I had run as fast as "greased lightning." Like all operatic idioms heard for the first time, especially inside our local convent of Gothic arches, this one sounded surprisingly apt. I could remember my pleasure in having its greasiness applied to me.

I never suspected Father Riffle of just wanting me to get a wiggle on, another idiom familiar from my mother, since it was not yet 6 a.m. and I was tired, slow-moving. I was probably still dreaming of trying to inveigle my way past the flailing arms of older boys. These were boys who had told me afterward I ran with splayed feet that looked like Charlie Chaplin's. I had taken consolation in the reality, even in my slow-motion dream, that they must have been running behind me in order to make the observation.

I never dreamed that forty-five years later, after the surgery to fix up vocal cords moving as awkwardly as my feet once had, I would also end up sounding like Charlie Chaplin. There were so many kinds of muteness. Indeed, I'd already found myself in an odd but pregnant alliance with Harpo Marx, during a matinee performance up the street at the Dunbar Theatre of *A Night at the Opera*. I had decided to take up the harp.

I already sang like an angel.

Acknowledgements

Although not every story I heard in the diaspora could be included here, I am grateful to all my fellow travellers for helping to shape this memoir—for convincing me there was a memoir. Their hospitality was as unstinting as their voices. This is their story too.

For sharing additional written information I wish to thank Marie Allison, David Barton, Faye Bergosi, Ivy Black, Dr. L.M. Ghosh, Shiranee Joseph-de Saram, Alwyn Knight, the late Ann Laidlaw, Shirley Linton, Robyn Mundy, Monique Riessen, Helen Sjardin, Cynthia Turner and Renata Whurr.

I am also indebted to the physicians and pathologists who patiently answered my questions about treating voice disorders in Adelaide, Auckland, Bombay, Calcutta, Cape Town, Colombo, Dallas, Dublin, Johannesburg, London, Perth, San Diego, Sydney, Toronto, Udaipur and Vancouver.

A book of abiding inspiration along the way was John Hix's *The Glasshouse*.

I would like to express my gratitude to Dr. Trevor Hurwitz at Vancouver Hospital (UBC); and to Patsy Rodenburg at the National Theatre in London.

Much appreciation is owed to the volunteer board members past and present of the National Association of Spasmodic Dysphonia (www.dysphonia.org). This branch of the Dystonia

Foundation supports research into the causes and treatment of laryngeal dystonia, and helps to raise awareness of the disorder through conferences, newsletters and an on-line bulletin board. Charitable donations to NASD may be sent c/o One East Wacker Drive, Suite 2430, Chicago, Il. 60601, USA. (Some of this book's royalties have been donated to NASD.)

I am also grateful to the Dystonia Society (UK).

For his faith, a special thanks to Patrick Crean at Thomas Allen Publishers; and to Katja Pantzar. For their peerless work I am especially grateful to editors Michael Holmes and Doris Cowan.

No expression of gratitude is adequate to acknowledge my deep appreciation of the gifted otolaryngologist Dr. Murray Morrison at Vancouver Hospital, who, for a number of years, gave me a functional voice through injections of botulinum toxin; before he (and otolaryngologist Dr. Scott Durham), following several hours of surgery, gave me back my life.

Finally, for allowing me to share her story while patiently enduring mine, a garden of the rarest orchids for Lorraine Fraser.